Comimals
of ES

"People see this as animal communication. We see it as people communication."

—Gulliver the llama

"I get to meet lots of people and watch them learn about the peacefulness of animals."

—Topaz the horse

"I really love workshops the best because people love to talk and listen to me. I will help you find your way around. I'm very busy though trying to be the head cat around this place. It is really a great place with lots of love."

—Jasmine the cat

"Come in for a visit. I love company and I love to share some of the wisdom that I have learned."

—Amber the donkey

"This is a cool place to hang out. We ducks are given a place of honor. But they make us move from the driveway. Great people here. You could come, too! We have lots of room for people, but no more room for ducks."

—Onyx the duck

"I found a great home here. Lots to do. Lots to see. I look forward to meeting EVERYONE!"

—Snowball the poodle

"I have asked to stay here and retire. I have my own room with my other dog friend Monica and am treated like the princess I am."

—Rosie the shepherd mix

"I love to have visitors. I tell great jokes and am pretty handsome."

—Taffy the cat

If Only They Could Talk

Talk

The

Miracles *of*
Spring Farm

Bonnie Jones Reynolds *and*
Dawn E. Hayman

POCKET BOOKS

NEW YORK   LONDON   TORONTO   SYDNEY

POCKET BOOKS, a division of Simon & Schuster, Inc.
1230 Avenue of the Americas, New York, NY 10020

ISBN-13: 978-0-7434-6486-4
ISBN-10:   0-7434-6486-9

This Pocket Books trade paperback edition September 2005

10 9 8 7 6 5 4 3 2 1

POCKET and colophon are registered trademarks of Simon & Schuster, Inc.

For information regarding special discounts for bulk purchases,
please contact Simon & Schuster Special Sales at 1-800-456-6798
or business@simonandschuster.com

Designed by Jaime Putorti

Manufactured in the United States of America

To Three Mothers:

Willa Dean Newcomb Jones
(Deanie)

Jacqueline Hayman
(Jackie)

Bertl Unkel
(Mu)

We couldn't have done it without them.

Contents

A Note from the Authors:
On Talking with Animals—
and Listening Back

It is said that a journey of a thousand miles starts with the first step.

Yet so often it seems to us that our steps take us nowhere. Frequently, they seem aimless, accidental, ill advised—even stupid.

Yet, like droplets descending from the angel realm into a rain barrel—plopping here, then there, sometimes in profusion, at other times with scarcity—the seeming lack of purpose finally produces a full barrel, a cohesive collection of liquid that is a purpose in and of itself, which gives life to thirsty passersby, a collection that eventually overflows, keeps refilling and overflowing yet again, giving life even to the green things that surround it.

Neither Dawn nor I, Bonnie, had journeys in mind when we took our first steps in this life nor as we each faltered, stumbled, and rambled along differing paths in the years that followed. Goals were sometimes achieved, yes, but, immediately upon being achieved, those goals lost importance. There were other places to wander, more meanders to investigate. It all seemed pointless—a chaos rather than a cohesion.

Even when we chanced to meet one day and decided to investigate a path together, we didn't sense any journey.

Then one day here at Spring Farm we found ourselves with a full barrel. Indeed, we realized that we were the barrel and the fullness therein, the sky above and the earth below, the ones who drank and the drink that was given.

For here at Spring Farm, that place of so many springs, we learned that *all is one.*

We discovered that all of creation communicates with itself— each atom, each molecule, each rock, tree, and living thing talks with all others.

We found ourselves talking with our animals—and listening as they talked back.

Passersby came to drink from the vessel that we had become— bottomless, ever filling, forever overflowing.

All those steps that had seemed pointless, foolish, were now seen to be the endless particles that had created an ever-expanding whole.

Yet we're unfinished here at Spring Farm. We're in a state of eternal becoming.

We are all the journeys. We are all those who journey. There is no destination. For we are all already there.

If Only They Could Talk

I

The Halloween Inferno

To my dying day I'll relive the moment in that Halloween night of 1993 when Dawn burst into the bedroom where I was sleeping.

"Bonnie! The barn's on fire!"

In Spring Farm parlance the "arena" and the attached "stable" were the places where we kept our horses. "The barn" was home. Everything.

I pulled on sneakers and, in my nightgown, ran behind Dawn out the back door of my mother's house into the darkness and fog and fourteen inches of wet, heavy snow that had fallen in a freak snowstorm that night. Flames were dancing behind the windows of the kitchen in the barn.

"Call the fire department!" I cried to Dawn and began running through the snow as best I could.

"Let's see how bad it is first," she said, running beside me.

Surely it was already so far out of control that we couldn't put it out by ourselves.

Yet as we plowed toward the barn, I wondered wildly about the quickest source of water.

Snow! We might be able to throw snow on the fire.

We knew that if we opened the eight-by-eight-foot overhead door that was the entrance to the barn, we'd be feeding oxygen to the fire. We knew it could flash over and engulf us. But some of the small animals of the Spring Farm CARES sanctuary were in there. There were twenty-eight of them throughout the barn.

The door was warm to the touch, not hot. We threw it up.

Two of the dogs were right inside, in the spots where they always slept. Cookie, a miniature German Shepherd crippled in the back legs, snapped to attention and pulled herself out into the snow. Spangles, a black Labrador cross, seemed drugged. We dragged him out. None of the others could be seen. Or heard.

Any thought of extinguishing the fire was gone. We were looking at a wall of smoke—black, ugly, hot, and noxious. In that smoke was an inferno in what had been the kitchen. There was no hope of saving possessions or structure.

But please God. The animals.

The evening had begun as usual. We finished our chores in the stable at 7:30. Remarking on the sudden heavy snow and sodden mist, we went to the barn—the old Spring Farm cow barn, converted into home, Spring Farm CARES offices, small animal and conference facility, thrift shop, library, and workshop. There we fed and walked dogs and topped off water bowls and cat food dishes. We'd recently turned the old granary in the second-floor haymow into an office, where Dawn could conduct her animal communication consultations in peace. There we covered the parakeets Babcock, Chartreuse, and Dove for the night and left the cats George Bump Bump, Peaches, Blackie, and Cauliflower curled in favorite spots. In the main nave of the haymow, the cats Tessie and Thistle were crunching on their kibble. In our second-floor apartment, connected by a spiral staircase to the first-floor bathroom, a dog named Keisha and ten cats—Marsha Mellow, Archibald Peabody III, Pazazz Purr, Sidney, Sylvanna, Timothy Tyler Butts, Rikki, Julie, Otto Sharie, and Heidi—were settling into their preferred spots, as were the animals on the first floor, in the large open area that was our office, kitchen, and meeting room—the dogs Buddy, Zoe, Daffy, Spangles, and Cookie, and the cats Oliver Augustus Perrier, Queenie, and Pink Flower. Never thinking that it might be for the last time, we bade our friends "Sweet dreams" and went to the house for supper and TV with Mother.

With us, in his carrier, was a six-week-old kitten named Georgie Belinda. I nearly left him in the barn that night. He'd begun sleeping right through, never crying for a bottle. But at the last I couldn't leave him. "I'll keep him with me for just one more night."

My eighty-six-year-old mother hadn't been feeling up to snuff of late, so I'd been sleeping in the house with her. We'd usually all sit late watching TV, but that night I turned in early. Dawn habitually watched the first fifteen minutes of the eleven o'clock news, then went out to the apartment to sleep. She'd check on the horses in the arena, then enter the barn through the haymow door, entering the apartment by the door from the haymow. She'd be asleep within minutes, blanketed by Keisha and the cats.

Had she followed her usual routine, she'd have died in the fire, overcome by smoke.

For we know when the fire started. The electric clock in the stable stopped at 11:35, the moment the power surge entered the downstairs of the barn, frying our electrical entrance and setting the refrigerator on fire.

But both Dawn and Mother fell asleep watching the news. Dawn woke at 11:45 and started for the barn. Once out the back door she stopped, staring at the kitchen window of the barn. Had we left a light on in there?

The light began to dance.

She ran to my bedroom.

"Bonnie! The barn's on fire!"

It's all a blur, really. Comfortable in our beds, we've all often wondered, "What would I save first in a fire?"

We learned that night that smoke, even before fire, will make your decisions for you.

Desperately, with Cookie and Spangles out, we called into the smoke for the other three dogs and the cats. No response.

We ran to the bathroom windows just beside that door, smashed them, and began calling there. The cats Archie and Rikki sometimes slept in that bathroom, and maybe some of the others would come down the stairs from the apartment above.

If anything, however, the smoke in the bathroom was worse than in the main office. Only silence answered.

"Call the fire department!" I cried again. Dawn sped off while I ran back to the main door.

Then I heard a meow. I dived into the smoke and snagged Pink Flower—our shyest cat, yet there she was, letting me grab her. Quickly I stashed her and the two dogs in Mother's car, then ran to the back of the barn and up the barn bridge to the haymow door, hoping to save the animals in Dawn's office, in the haymow, perhaps even some from the apartment.

But as I opened the door, fire from the kitchen below exploded through the floor and shot up the wall opposite where I stood. A wave of heat seared over me. It was impossible to reach the apartment door just in front of that sudden wall of flames and smoke. Surely, though, I could reach Dawn's office and save the cats in there. That door was only twelve feet away.

Just twelve lousy feet.

I couldn't make it. I had to back out.

Writing this, I conjure the scene in memory and say, "You could have done it, Bonnie, you could have saved them."

But nothing is ever as bad in memory. There in the heat and smoke, unable to see, unable to breathe, not knowing if or when the fire would flash over and engulf or trap me, there was no going forward.

I propped the door open, hoping that at least Tessie and Thistle would escape and ran back down to the front door. By now Andy Magyar, who lived upstairs in Mother's house, was there with a flashlight. And we heard a dog crying in the smoke. I got down on my belly and crawled into the blackness, calling out, groping toward the sound. Twelve, fifteen, twenty feet. From the cry it was either Zoe or Daffy. So close, right there in the smoke ahead of me. But my flailing arms couldn't connect with a body. And I couldn't breathe. I should get out. Immediately. Or I wouldn't get out at all.

I got out. Leaving my friend still there, crying, lost and confused in the smoke, was the hardest thing that I ever had to do. But shock is a blessing, insulating from pain, and certainly all of us were running on pure shock at that point. Still calling, Andy and I propped the main door open and prayed.

Dawn was back, moving her truck away from the building and calling out that firemen were on their way. Realizing that I was still in my nightgown, I raced to the house for clothes.

Mother was waiting inside the kitchen door, looking, I remember with a stab of guilt, bewildered and alone.

"Is it bad?" she said.

"It's gone, Mother. We can't save a thing."

I wish I'd stopped, taken her into my arms. But I had no arms to give at that moment, I was on autopilot. I raced to the bedroom, got on slacks and a sweater and ran back out.

"Bonnie!" cried Dawn. "Thank God! Where were you?"

"Getting clothes on."

"I thought you'd gone back into the barn to try to save animals. I thought you were in there!"

Several volunteer firemen, including our neighbor Alan Lloyd, had arrived. One of them, tall and authoritative, took me by the shoulders to be sure I was paying attention.

"*Is* there anyone in there?" he demanded.

"Yes!" I cried. "All our animals." And I started telling him how many and where.

He sort of shook me and said, "Do you know where the main electrical breaker is? Go and throw it. We need all power off."

Dawn ran with me, back to the house. We found a flashlight. Dawn went down into the cellar and threw the breaker while I turned on the burners of Mother's gas stove. Leaving her with the stove and flashlight for light, we ran back to the barn.

The tall fireman, who turned out to be the fire chief, was waiting.

"How many horses are in your stable?"

Dawn and I stared at him stupidly. "About twenty-five," I said. Then the light dawned.

"They're in danger, too?"

The fire chief laid heavy hands on both of our shoulders and said, in tones calculated to pierce the smoke in our brains, "They've got to be evacuated. *Now.* Not out this way"—he gestured at the arena door, so close to the barn bridge—"all of them out the *other side* of the stable. *They've got to go away from the fire.*"

It was a blessing, really. We didn't have to stand there and watch our dear old barn burn. We didn't have to watch as flames reached our trapped friends.

Yet as we plowed through the snow to the arena, I was thinking that he was crazy. Why drive the horses out? Surely the fire couldn't get to them where they were.

Shows you how well you think at a time like that. The west wall of the arena was just a dozen feet from the burning barn.

One step into the arena brought me to my senses.

"My God," said Dawn. "I can't believe the smoke in here already."

"That alone could kill them."

"Oh, Bonnie! How are we going to do this?"

We felt almost more frantic about driving the horses out into the night than we'd been about the fire. Sure, I'd been careful to plan a fire route when constructing the stable and fences. We had only to drive the animals quartered in the arena and in the stable proper out the back door, along a fenced runway about thirty feet wide, and into either of two pastures. The smallest, of about three acres, was the domain of the mares Deeteza, Scherry, Tina, and Dulcie. All the rest would have to be driven into the back, eighteen-acre pasture. Many of them had never been in that pasture or even out the back door, accustomed to being led to paddocks on the barn side. Many of them had never met, so there were sure to be fights and injuries. Plus which we had three colts who'd not yet been castrated and several mares who were infamous for producing instant heats. There went our antibreeding policy. On top of it all, there were two Shetland pony mothers with five-month-old foals, one foal 90 percent blind, plus a crippled Shetland pony, a foundered horse, and two goats. The ducks and barn cats we assumed would make their own escapes. Accomplishing this exodus would be difficult even in daylight. In total darkness it seemed impossible.

"Let's get Deeteza's bunch locked out into their pasture," I said.

We felt our way through the blackened arena, down the aisle of the stable proper and out into the run-in shed occupied by the four mares. They went like lambs down the runway into their pasture— Deeteza told us afterward that they had been very scared, but they had known they could help best by cooperating. We then kicked snow aside and managed to get Deeteza's gate closed and the gate to the big pasture yanked open.

Ominously, as we worked, we began to see better. A faint red glow began to illuminate the night. We refused to think about why.

I returned to the arena to drive horses out the back door, leaving

Dawn to get them through the gate and make sure they stayed in the pasture. Calculations were split second as I stumbled through the darkness. Who to loose first?

The arena is 60 by 120 feet; it had originally been intended for riding, but, as Spring Farm CARES had gathered needy horses, it had been given over to stalls. At the east end, away from the fire, were nine horses. Along the outer wall were our goats, Roo and Rosebud.

At the west end, against the wall nearest the fire, were the most vulnerable horses. Chubby, our Quarter Horse founder case, ambulatory but only just. God only knew what this would do to her. Then there were crippled Sugar and the other four Shetland ponies, Missy and her baby, Mr. Bubbles, and Dream with her blind baby, Corri. Closest to the fire, those special cases should be evacuated first. But handicapped, slow, and vulnerable as they were—Lord, the snow was half as tall as those pony babies!—they might be trampled, injured, even killed when the other horses went charging out.

The others must go first so that the handicapped could exit safely. Actually, if need be, the handicapped *could* be taken out the front way.

Then everything became academic. Suddenly I was not alone in the dark. Firemen and neighbors with flashlights began to appear, the beams darting crazily. I had no chance to give instructions, they were shouting and yelling, people with no horse savvy at all, loosing horses right and left, slapping at them, trying to drive them out the back door.

Of course the horses panicked and ran in every direction except the desired one. The arena became a bedlam of men shouting and of horses racing round and round in terror. While what had begun in darkness grew brighter as the barn became totally involved.

All the while Dawn was out there alone, not only trying to drive the horses into the pasture as they came out of the stable but trying to *keep* them there. Many turned and ran right back in, so that just as the people driving them out would get one or two horses started down the aisle of the main stable to the outer door and safety, some horse would come rushing back in with all the finesse of a runaway freight train.

In deference to the horses being driven out, I should describe the gauntlet through which they had to pass. The main stable was in darkness. At the end of what was in effect a black tunnel, about fifty-five feet away, outside the run-in shed, was soft light, a reflection from the flames of the burning barn. So that ahead of the horses was an abyss and then dim light, while behind them was a lot more light, from flashlights and the burning barn, and frantic, shouting men. But horses are accustomed to frantic, shouting men, and ahead lay the great unknown. Most went down the aisle only because they ended up with a phalanx of frantic, shouting men behind them. But horse people know what horses who do not care to go down the aisle can do to a phalanx of frantic, shouting men behind them. So three cheers for our horses, who sometimes acted more reasonably than us humans.

One in particular was a Thoroughbred named Lady, the self-appointed leader of the Thoroughbred herd that used the large pasture. Lady was the first out, but then she turned and stood at the gate beside Dawn. As horses ran out, were driven into the pasture by Dawn but then either ran back into the stable or remained milling around just beyond the gate, threatening to run back in, Lady grew agitated.

"This is no good. Those men aren't getting them out fast enough. I should go back in and help them."

"No!" Dawn told her frantically. "If you want to help, make the others stay in the pasture once I get them in there."

Just then two of Lady's herd mates, the dependable Four Bales and her daughter Lamoka Bo, came galloping up the chute from the stable.

"Let's take them out!" Dawn heard Lady call to them.

All Dawn knows is that from that point on no horses remained milling around the gate, threatening to run back in. Lady and her crew were "taking them out"!

And they kept them out. Minutes passed, and no more horses emerged from the stable. Had it caught on fire? Dawn ran back to the arena to see what was going on, encountering a horse running hysterically hither and yon, being chased by volunteers. The horse ran up to Dawn.

She pointed toward the stable aisle and said, "Go out there! *Now!*"

And the horse ran out.

Dawn saw the volunteers exchanging glances. The community was rife with stories about the crazy women at Spring Farm who believed they could talk with animals. They'd just seen that craziness in action.

Satisfied that the arena was not on fire, Dawn followed the horse back out to her post at the gate.

Meanwhile I was doing my best just to breathe. I hadn't realized how much smoke I'd inhaled when I'd crawled into the barn. My lungs felt ready to explode. My mouth was so dry that when I tried to speak nothing came out. I had little to do with the exodus of the sound horses from the arena; there were volunteers enough for that. Instead I worked with the cripples and ponies.

The foals had never been away from their mothers' sides. As we dismantled their pipe corral enclosures, foals and mothers panicked in the confusion and became separated. The nearly blind Corri ran off, screaming. I and two others chased him from one end of the arena to the other as he crashed into this, then that, falling, scrambling up, running headlong into something else, breaking free each time we caught him and tried to comfort him, screaming ever more pitifully for Dream, who was herself running about lost in the confusion, calling for him. I could hear a like performance from Missy and Mr. Bubbles. All this with thousand-pound, terrified horses running right along with us. You could only do what you had to do and hope to hell that you came out in one piece.

Suddenly one of the men chasing after Corri with me called out, "He's trying to follow flashlight beams!"

Of course! I realized. Light was the only thing he could see and cling to. I snatched the man's flashlight and made a dive for Corri, getting him around the chest and the rump with the flashlight in the hand around the chest, its beam pointing forward. I then walked Corri forward.

And he was suddenly calm, "safe" in my encircling arms, with something that he could see traveling in front of him. In this fashion I walked him down the long dark aisle of the stable abyss, praying that no horses would come running out or back in.

Lord, the snow *was* half as tall as he was.

Dream was still screaming for him back in the arena, but we marched on, out to where Dawn waited. I abandoned Corri to her and ran back in. Others were just managing to herd Dream, Missy, and Mr. Bubbles out after him. But we worried about Corri all night. The last time Dawn saw him, he was falling down a hill, out of her sight.

By the time I returned, volunteers had removed the stock gates from around Sugar and Chubby. They were both very calm. The burning barn was now casting so much light that I could see them well. I went to Chubby first.

"You have to go out, girl."

Clearly I heard "I can't do it. Just let me stay here and die."

Unsaid but strongly received by me was the thought "I'm not worth it. Don't bother."

I got angry.

"You are *not* going to give up *now.* You and Dawn and I have worked for a year and a half to grow your new hooves. You *are* worth it."

I spanked her hard on the behind, got her moving, and consigned her to the many waiting hands.

"She's terribly crippled. Take her very, very gently over the cement."

To Dawn's utter amazement, when they got her out to the pasture she literally galloped off to join the others!

So much for being ready to die.

Sugar gave no trouble when asked to ski forward on her deformed front feet. She was a serene, undemanding little thing, and her calm comforted me. Again I consigned her to volunteers and cautioned them to take her gently. Dawn had her put into the small pasture with Deeteza's bunch, friends all, where she wasn't in danger of being trampled.

By now volunteers were working to get the horses out of the main stable—the three young stallions, Tutti, TLC, and Meloudee, a partially blind gelding named Cody, and a high-strung filly named Breezie. I left them to it and ran to the wing that we call the nursery, to loose Topaz, Amber, and Mariah through a separate door into their own yard, where I then opened a gate into the alley leading to the big pasture.

Just then, however, TLC, the first young stallion, burst out of the main stable, acting like a complete airhead (as young studs of whatever species often do). He first tried to go back into the stable, then rushed into the nursery yard and into the nursery itself. Topaz, Amber, and Mariah followed, all four of them squeezing into one of the nursery's stalls. I yelled for help, and we finally got them out into the pasture.

In the main stable I found half a dozen men trying to coax the very last horse, the young stallion Meloudee, out of his stall. He wouldn't budge. Nor would he let the men get hold of his halter. I was able to go in and talk to him quietly, take hold of the halter, and get a chain lead onto him, but he still wouldn't budge.

He was going to have to. The smoke was getting really bad. Three strong men got in front, one pulling on the lead, one on each side of the halter, with a reckless Andy Magyar behind him, slapping and pushing as the others pulled, till Meloudee fairly exploded out into the aisle. He then allowed himself to be led out to the alleyway and driven into the pasture.

Relieved, we closed the gate.

There were only the goats now, Roo and Rosebud. They gave almost more trouble than the horses. Determined not to go out into the snow, they kept breaking away and running back to their stall. We finally just shut the stable door and left them bleating pitifully in the run-in shed.

Alan Lloyd and others had begun moving items stored in the grandstand on the wall closest to the fire away from that wall.

"We're moving anything flammable," he told us. "The wall could spontaneously combust."

Horrified, we pitched in.

"You don't seriously think *this* building will catch on fire," I said.

"We hope not. We're keeping it cooled down with hoses."

Even so, at the end, the steel siding was glowing cherry red, and we later found that the interior beams had been singed.

Finally—the animals out, the grandstand cleared—there was nothing for us to do except look at the sight from which we had, until that point, been spared. We went to the arena door and looked at the barn.

It was just at that point that someone shouted, "Get back! The roof's gonna go!"

The barn had been waiting for us. For one instant it was all still there, the magnificent cathedral roof, every upright, beam, and brace etched in brilliant red. Then it collapsed, an inferno of flame and sound that sent a million sparks climbing toward Heaven itself.

I bent and scooped up some clean snow, ate it, scooped up more. My lungs were on fire along with the barn, but snow couldn't cool their fire, nor quench the dryness of my mouth.

We kept watching, silent. Only at one point Dawn turned and laid her forehead against my shoulder.

"Oh Bonnie," she said. Which said it all.

But then, after we'd watched for many more minutes, she said, "You're going to think I'm crazy, but I'm getting a peaceful feeling. It's all okay somehow. They're all right."

She meant, of course, our animal friends, being consumed there in the flames.

"Yes. Of course they are." We'd talked with enough dead animals to know that. "Have you gotten anything from any of them?"

Dawn shook her head. "I'm not up to trying yet."

"Same here." I, whose specialty, by force of circumstance, had become taking messages from just-departed animals.

Overhearing us, a fireman said, "I'm sure they didn't suffer. They probably never even woke up. They were all dead of smoke inhalation before the fire got to them."

Dawn and I exchanged glances. All except one—the one who'd been crying.

I saw my brother-in-law, Bob Miller, then, arms folded, leaning against my scorched van. I ambled over and stood beside him. Bob, too, had memories of the barn. He'd kept heifers there for several years after my father had gone out of farming.

"I wonder if Harwood is watching this. I wonder what he thinks" was all he said, referring to my deceased father.

"He's probably very sad. I'm sure that Grampa's here."

Francis Jones, he who'd built this barn, who'd made Spring Farm an internationally known name with his champion Holsteins back in the first decades of the twentieth century—who'd lost two previous barns to fire—Grampa Jones, who, for years, had been one of our benign "haunts."

Nan Labrecque, from next door, came to me, put her arms around me and started to cry.

"It's all right," I heard myself saying. "We all create our own realities, and everything happens for a reason. Dawn and I just have to decide what the reason for this one is."

Only then did I begin looking at faces—at some of the people who'd come to help, even to put their bodies on the line. The Labrecques, my nephews Scott and Bobby from across the road, and our neighbors Jay Burmaster and Tom Willis from farther on up the road—while my sister Peggy and niece Helen, I was told, had taken Mother across the road to Helen's during the worst of it.

Bits and pieces of information were floating around. How the Clinton Fire Department, three miles away, had already been out on calls, for two different cars that had hit light posts, when our call came in. How the county roads hadn't been plowed yet and there were tree limbs down across some of them, how they'd had to try two different routes before they could get to us. How the Paris Hill Fire Department, two miles away, might even have been in time to save the structure, but the firefighters had driven right past us in the fog, continuing for a couple of miles before turning around. How one of the fire trucks had caught on fire, so that as the firemen were trying to put out our fire they were also putting out their own. How, in the middle of the whole mess, an eighteen-wheeler coming down Route 12 had lost its brakes and barreled right through the fire department's roadblock at Burmaster Road, half a mile away. "Eighteen-wheeler runaway and he's coming at you!" was all the warning that the men in two fire trucks parked on the road had had. How, in desperation, they had driven up onto our lawn, one of them becoming hopelessly stuck. How a rookie fireman had fallen off the barn bridge into the fire and nearly been killed. Or how the sides of the barn had heaved in and out as the fire, like an asphyxiating monster, had gasped for oxygen until it burst the sides, got a big breath . . . and the barn was totally engulfed in flames.

Dawn and I realized that we were very cold. And wet. We went to the house to warm up and stayed there. There was nothing we could do. And we didn't want to watch anymore.

It was twelve-thirty. Had only forty-five minutes elapsed? How quickly one can lose it all.

We'd been told we could turn the electricity back on, but there wasn't any. Another car had hit a light pole somewhere, and the entire neighborhood was without power.

Andy got Spangles, Cookie, and Pink Flower out of Mother's car and brought them into the warmth of the laundry room; then he went across the street to get Mother. The animals seemed okay—confused, but okay. Same with Mother—at least so we thought at the time.

Pink Flower's was the amazing rescue. She'd been born in the bathroom of the barn and named Janice, after Dawn's sister. But as "Janice" grew, we noticed salmon-pink markings around her mouth, like little pink flowers. And she'd repeatedly pull pink flowers out of a vase of artificial flowers that I kept on my desk. Naturally she became Pink Flower.

"Pinkie," Dawn asked her that night, "how did you get to the north end of the barn?"

For Pinkie always slept on a windowsill at the south end.

A strange little smile touched Dawn's lips as she listened to the cat and repeated what she'd said.

"She was sleeping in her regular place. She woke up and saw the fire and heard you calling. She started to come to you, but the fire was too hot. Then a man with strong, kind hands picked her up and set her down in front of you."

"Grampa Jones," I breathed. "I told Bob he'd be there. Does she know about Queenie or Perrier?"

Just maybe they'd gotten out the front door when we weren't looking, for both of them slept near that door.

Dawn was silent, listening to Pinkie again.

"She doesn't know about Perrier, but she says Queenie got out. She saw her fly out the door. Like a bird."

"Oh."

"Her soul," Dawn murmured.

It was comforting to know that the souls of our friends had taken flight, that one soul had even been spotted as it left, and that Grampa had been there in that terrible fire with them.

And we needed comfort now. Dawn told me that the dog who'd been crying, who I'd crawled into the smoke trying to save, had continued to cry.

"I'm sure it was Zoe," she said.

Yes. Buddy and Daffy slept too near the kitchen. The smoke would have gotten them right away. But Zoe slept at the south end, near Pink Flower.

"I started to run around to that end," said Dawn.

Suddenly she could hardly get the words out.

"I was going to smash the plate-glass window and try to get her to come to me. But then Alan arrived, and the fire chief, and then we had to turn off the electricity and empty the stable—"

Our poor screwed-up Zoe, a basket case to begin with, running and screaming, experiencing all the horror.

We stopped talking about it. Some memories haunt you for life. This would be one of them.

Andy and Mother raided their closets and gave us dry clothes. Then we four sat down at the kitchen table. We sat there for the rest of the night. I can't remember what we talked about. What-ifs. If-onlys. I-should-haves. But mostly we worried about the animals out in the snow and cold of the pastures. Mostly Sugar, Chubby, the ponies, and their foals. And the stallions. Had there been fights? Injuries? Deaths?

By three in the morning the smoke had lessened to the point where we thought Sugar might be able to go into the run-in shed with the goats. Andy went out, ascertained that indeed the run-in shed was relatively clear of smoke, and put Sugar in there.

Poor Sugar. She told us afterward that, abruptly expelled into the snow with no shelter, she thought her dream had ended, that she was back in the hell from which we'd rescued her two years earlier. Then, safely in the run-in shed, she'd come to her senses and begun to worry about Dawn and me. She'd thought we had no place to live now. But she and the goats had gotten on well. So the three of them had decided that the goats could live with Sugar and Chubby in their enclosure and Dawn and I could have the goats' stall.

Without Mother's house to go to, we'd have taken them up on the offer.

At 4:30 the fire chief came in.

"We're ready to pull out. Watch for flare-ups. Call us if anything substantial develops. Now—what kind of insurance did you have on the place?"

I was ashamed to admit it. Oh, if only!

"None. We didn't have the money to renew it."

I saw a flicker of surprise.

"Gee, that's rough. Well, so it won't have to be inspected." He laughed awkwardly. "And there's no question of arson for insurance."

"Arson?"

We hadn't thought of such a thing.

Dawn and I looked at each other. There was resentment against us in the community. Not so much in our own little neighborhood of Chuckery Corners but throughout a greater community, taking in many towns and many square miles. It all got back to us one way or another, the gossip, the vicious and envious comments. Though I'd been raised on Spring Farm and my family had been on the place since the 1820s, I was regarded as an outsider, a traitor even, by some people who wouldn't forgive me for having left after high school and lived away for twenty-eight years. Adding to the resentment were my supposed riches—"millions," according to the gossip. While Dawn and I were jointly derided as kooks and crazies.

Mainly though, we'd come to realize, our real sin was that we were women, who lived together on the same property, who'd created something worthwhile together, and who might even be making a go of it.

But no, I put the thought aside. "No one would do such a terrible thing. We could see through the kitchen window and when we opened the door. The fire was in the area of the refrigerator at first."

"Yeah," said the chief. "A garden-variety electrical fire. An accident."

And he made the decision not to ring the ruins with yellow tape to keep the scene from being disturbed until it could be inspected.

It was a decision over which I would cry bloody tears in days to come.

First light found us in the pasture, lugging bales of hay and anxiously taking inventory.

Meloudee had jumped a fence and broken it partly down. He was in the small pasture with his grandmother Deeteza's bunch, one thoroughly neutralized stallion, for Deeteza was keeping him firmly in his place, threatening to kick his lights out whenever he approached any of them.

Tutti was trying to work up the nerve to jump the busted fence. Luckily the way to his heart was through his stomach. Hay diverted his attention long enough for us to repair the break.

Lt. Columbo had a minor cut over his eye.

Chubby actually seemed to be enjoying herself. A vet later pointed out that the deep fresh snow had both numbed the pain in her feet and kept them clean.

The other horses had separated themselves into small, congenial herds.

And all the ponies were safe. Snug as bugs. For our third young stallion, TLC, had appointed himself their lord and nanny. He'd driven his four-pony herd into one of the two run-in shelters and stood like a Gorgon in its doorway, forestalling the inclinations of other horses to enter.

Everyone was okay. It was a miracle.

And we still had Spangles. And Cookie. And Pink Flower.

And ourselves.

So a new day began. A night of horror that would never be over . . . was over. Feeling like Baby-New-Years in diapers, with sashes across our chests, stripped of the past, Dawn and I—and Spring Farm CARES—faced a new beginning.

2

Chuckery Corners: You Can Go Home Again

Since buying the farm from my parents after their retirement from farming in 1971, I'd dreamt of someday turning the barn into a home for myself. It seemed a ridiculous dream. Our hamlet of Chuckery Corners, outside Clinton in Upstate New York, was a far cry from the life I'd lived and was living, in New York City and then in Hollywood. Fat chance that I'd ever move back home.

But in 1978 I got a divorce. In 1980 my father became an invalid. And in December 1982 I moved back home to help Mother care for him, arriving with a moving-vanload of antiques and furniture; my Australian Cattle Dog, Mr. Fraser; Daffy, a Dachshund mix; Foxie, who looked like a cross between an Eskimo dog and a red fox; and Bonniecat Endore, a namesake inherited from a deceased friend.

In the spring of 1984 I began remodeling the barn. Carpenters blanketed the outside walls with Styrofoam insulation, laid another course of clapboards over that, and painted the boards the original barn red, so that it looked exactly as it had looked to begin with. Windows were repaired and doubled, with identical small-paned outer windows for insulation from winter cold. The eight-by-eight-foot door at the south end, that had opened to the barnyard, was replaced with a combination of plate glass and French doors, while the eight-by-eight-foot door on the north end, nearest the house, was left au naturel. As all of this progressed, I began cleaning the interior.

"You'll never get the smell of the cows out of the place," said Daddy.

"Just watch me."

Mother pitched in to help with her usual gusto. Actually, getting the smell of fifty-three years of cows out of the barn was no trouble. A couple of weeks of airing after cleaning was all that it took. The difficulty was in getting fifty-three years of hay seeds out of the hay-mow. Hayseeds! What tenacious, furtive little beasts.

Once the ground floor—the cow barn proper—was aired out, I installed "gutter-to-gutter" carpeting, a deep, rich red, laid onto a plywood floor over the old concrete center aisle and gutters. Only that center portion was carpeted. The rest of the barn was left exactly as it had been while a milk barn—the concrete platforms for the cows, the stanchions that had held our girls in place, their mangers and water buckets, the piping for the milking machines—all stayed. Our old calf stall became the kitchen. The old milk house became the bathroom, equipped at first with the sauna that I'd brought from California, cold running water, and a chamber pot. I installed my antiques and my collection of Tiffany-type lamps, put my antique brass bed in the old horse stall, filled the concrete mangers with soil, installed grow lights, planted flowers, and moved in.

"But it still looks like a cow barn," said my sister, Peggy, with furrowed brow.

"Of course it does. If I'm going to live in a barn, I'm going to live in a barn."

Word got around to the neighbors, of course. They thought I was nuts. But I'd been supplying them with lively conversation for thirty years. I wasn't about to disappoint them now.

My "house" did have drawbacks. For one thing, there was no heat.

"You can't stay there in the winter," said my father.

"I'll use kerosene heaters."

"You'll freeze."

"I'll wear a snowsuit."

And to prove how serviceable my new house was, I threw a tree-trimming party at Christmastime 1984, with a ten-foot tree and seventy-five guests. All those whom I invited came, and many whom I hadn't. No one was going to miss the chance to see Bonnie's barn. They all gamely trimmed my tree while wearing coats and mufflers, with nary a complaint about the fact that they could see their breaths as they did so.

At about this time Dawn Hayman came into my life. I couldn't know that Dawn would be one of the most important events of that life. But then, at that point, I also didn't understand that angels were guarding and guiding Spring Farm and its future.

Those crazy, wonderful angels. They love a project. And Spring Farm, we've come to understand, is one of their ongoing favorites.

Dawn's father and stepmother, Dennis and Jackie, had rented Peggy and Bob's old house when *they* moved into *their* cow barn. (It's a sickness that runs in the family, you see. But Peg and Bob had turned their cow barn into a *real* house. Magnificent.)

Shortly after my return home, Peggy told me about her "real interesting" tenants.

"You'll like them. They're into all kinds of stuff that you'd know about."

Which was Peggy-ese for "They're as far out as you are."

I finally met the Haymans at Peg's New Year's Eve party in 1983, and we began socializing. They spoke often of Dawn, the older of Dennis's two daughters from his previous marriage. It seemed she had severe emotional problems. Since she was away for her junior year of college at Brockport and rarely home, I met her on only one occasion—a quiet, unassuming girl, small and pretty, with dark hair and brown eyes.

Then one night Jackie, who'd come over to take a sauna with me, began to express complete frustration with Dawn.

"I can't deal with her anymore! I just don't know what her problem is!"

I'll never know why I said it, but of course the angels put the words in my mouth.

"Why not let me give it a try? Let me talk with her next time she's home. Maybe I can help."

"Wonderful. Take her. She's yours. I give her to you."

And so I received the gift of Dawn Hayman.

Of course it wasn't that easy. According to Dawn, later that night she received a call from Jackie.

"From now on you don't talk to me about your problems. You're to talk to Bonnie Reynolds."

Bonnie Reynolds? Dawn had heard a lot about Peggy's celebrity sister, but she'd met me only that once. Now she was supposed to come to me for counseling?

She avoided the issue for months. Whenever she was home, at Jackie's urging, I'd call and suggest that we meet. She always found reasons to refuse. Finally, in January 1985, I called and simply said, "I'm taking you to dinner tonight. Be ready at six forty-five."

We arrived at Clinton's historic Alexander Hamilton Inn at seven and closed the joint at one.

We talked and talked and talked. I hadn't talked that way since my teenage years, with girlfriends sleeping over. But our conversation wasn't kid stuff. It centered largely on the books of Jane Roberts, especially *Seth Speaks*, and on the ramifications of what Seth had to say. Dawn and I had known each other for centuries, millennia; we were completely on each other's wavelength.

Little did we understand the groundwork being laid that night.

Somewhere during the evening I remembered to get down to business.

"So what are these huge problems of yours that Jackie can't abide?"

Dawn stared at me blankly. "I don't know," she said finally. "I guess I don't have any."

Some people spend a lifetime in psychoanalysis and never figure that out. After that night Dawn just stopped having problems. It threw her family into a tizzy for a while—families get set on one person having the problems, and they have to regroup when that person stops having them.

Now she used any excuse to come home on weekends and to make a beeline for Spring Farm. I hired her for some secretarial work, and when summer came she was my gardener, at Spring Farm from sunup to sundown.

I never was able to get rid of her again.

Thank God.

It was also during this period that I acquired my first horse.

Kazinka, the Bette Davis of Arab mares. I should have fastened my seat belt, it was going to be a bumpy ride.

Like most little girls, I'd wanted a horse. In 1945 when I was seven, and we moved from the village to take over Grampa Jones's farm, I started begging.

"No," said my father. "You can't have a horse."

"You had a horse when you were a little boy here on the farm."

"Polly was our carriage horse. I only got to ride her when she wasn't working."

"Please, Daddy."

"No. We've got no place for a horse. Besides, they're too expensive to keep."

I nagged for years. He stood firm.

And he was right. Horses are *very* expensive to keep.

It's not that I went looking for a horse. It's all my cousin Gail's fault. One day in 1984 she stopped in on her way home from work.

"Maria, a girl in our office, is selling a half-Arab mare. Wanna go partners with me?"

You see, Gail was another little girl who'd always wanted a horse.

We were born twenty-three days apart, and, from the time we were eight, we spent summers together, as Aunt Ethel and Uncle Warren shipped her up to the farm from whatever town they were living in at the moment. I was closer to Gail than to Peggy, who was six years older and already into boys, one in particular named Bob Miller.

Gail and I had the good fortune to participate in two different eras, with aunts and uncles whose farms were still in the nineteenth century. No electricity or telephones; there were outhouses, cooking on iron stoves, cold water from a hand pump at the sink, baths in a galvanized tub on Saturday nights, and horses, rather than tractors, to pull farm machinery.

Uncle Carl's farm was our favorite. As kids while visiting him, we'd climb up onto his work horses out in the pasture. Tom and Dick. We rechristened them Cherokee and Apache. Wildly we'd gallop them across the land, bareback, no reins, just clinging to their manes. We never stayed aboard very long.

That was the gist of my early riding career. Gail, however, took English riding lessons. During our teenage years, when visiting at her home in Connecticut, I got in a few lessons with her teacher as well, at least learning to post. But even though as an adult down in New

York City I did a fair bit of riding at a stable out on Long Island, I always looked upon Gail as the horsewoman. I even sort of idolized her. Gail jumped horses, which, to me, was incredibly glamorous. She even taught riding at summer camps during her college days.

Now she'd bought a farm out in the boondocks about half an hour from us and, with her surviving parent, Uncle Warren, moved up from Connecticut.

And obviously, the little girl who'd wanted a horse still lurked within.

"Gail, I've got no place for a horse."

Where had I heard that one before?

"We'll keep it at my place," said Gail.

An *Arab* mare. (Well, at least half-Arab.) During my horse-crazed girlhood, not only had I wanted a horse, I'd wanted an Arab. Black. This one was chestnut, but what the heck.

I was seized with a madness.

As Elizabeth Taylor said in *National Velvet*: "Horses!!!"

Kazinka turned out to be a twofer . . . five months pregnant. You have to have slept beside a mare for a month, then assisted her foal into the world, to understand how badly I got hooked.

Viva, as we called him, was born on the first day of spring, March 20, 1985. He was chestnut like Kazinka, not as pretty as she, as he was only one-quarter Arab, but I was totally smitten. Each day for months I drove the half hour to Gail's farm to care for the horses and teach Viva his manners. When we purchased Kazinka, I'd known precious little about horses of any age, but since then I'd been educating myself, poring through books, taking riding lessons three and four times a week, endlessly questioning anyone who professed to know anything at all about horses, investing untold dollars in tack and supplies.

My riding career in regard to Kazinka, however, had been an embarrassing flop. I rode her just once, several days after we purchased her.

But not before a telling conversation with Gail.

"You should be the first to ride her," I said.

"I don't feel like it. You ride her."

"No, you ride her. You're a better rider than I am."

"That was years ago. You ride her. I'll watch."

You don't argue with my cousin Gail. I climbed aboard and signaled Kazinka to proceed.

Nothing.

"I must be doing something wrong," I said.

Gail came over, took one side of the bridle, and led Kazinka forward. The minute she let go of the bridle, however, Kazinka stopped.

"Come on," she said, walking ahead and beckoning to the mare.

Kazinka followed, with all the enthusiasm of a pregnant snail.

Thus, with Gail leading, we made our way up to the quiet country road that passes her farm. By the time we got there, Kazinka was going along pretty well.

"I'll just ride her down to the neighbor's and then come back," I said.

Gail stepped aside. Kazinka stopped.

I applied strong leg pressure.

A little heel.

A little more heel.

Reluctantly Kazinka started forward.

We proceeded, stopping, starting, stopping, starting, for perhaps a hundred feet.

Then she stopped, and no amount of heel would move her.

Dale, the little boy from next door, approached on his bicycle.

"What's the matter?"

"She doesn't want to go anywhere," I said.

"She followed when I led her," said Gail, coming up beside us. "But I'll be damned if I'm going to lead her all the way down the road."

This was mortifying.

"Gail, I'm just not enough of a rider yet. You get on."

"I don't feel like it," said Gail.

"Let's see if she'll follow my bike," said Dale.

He swung around in front of us and started slowly forward.

Kazinka followed. With no stops. Like a five-year-old at a pony ride, I was transported along, Gail walking at our side.

"This is crazy," she said. "What the hell good is she if she has to be led?"

"Now that I think back . . ."

Kazinka had captured my heart the day we went to the seller's to meet her. She was standing with her head over the door of her stall when we entered. When I got close enough, she reached out, hooked her head and neck around behind my back, and hugged me to herself.

"She does that," laughed Maria. "If she likes you, she hugs you."

It would be months before we learned why Zinkadink, as I took to calling her, had so many quirks. She was a creature as rare among horses as peepers in January—one of living twins. The runt, she'd been bottle-fed, treated like a big dog, and allowed to follow people about. Kazinka wasn't really sure that she *was* a horse.

When invited to ride her that day at Maria's, Gail and I had an exchange that was to become familiar.

"You ride her first, Gail. You're the real rider."

"I don't feel like it. You ride her. I'll watch."

But what I was realizing now was that Maria and her boyfriend, Marty, had saddled up two other horses and *led* the way out into the field. Throughout the entire test drive, Kazinka and I had followed.

Plodding along down a country road behind a kid on a bicycle, it became clear that Kazinka had just one gear: follow.

Of course, when I turned her back toward the barn the five-year-old on a pony became Red Pollard on Seabiscuit.

"Well," huffed Gail as she caught up to us at the barn some minutes later. "We've got ourselves some riding horse, haven't we."

Kazinka was already unsaddled, receiving her rubdown. Not that she'd exerted herself enough to need one.

"Maybe it's for the best," I said.

We'd been told that it was perfectly safe to ride her right up to her last couple of months. The gestation of a horse is eleven months, but . . .

"Yeah," said Gail. "Maybe it's for the best."

Gail did mention our little problem to Maria the next day.

"Oh, yeah," said Maria cheerfully. "She doesn't like to go first, does she? It never bothered us because we always ride together."

We probably could have returned her. But Kazinka and her unborn foal were family now.

And, I assured myself, once she'd had her foal, once I'd become a better rider, I'd be able to teach her to lead. The foal itself couldn't be ridden until it was a two-year-old. Some books even advised waiting until a foal was three or four. So it would work out perfectly. I had plenty of time to get good.

We went into a holding pattern, during which time we began to understand the cost of feeding a horse. Especially a horse eating for two.

There were also veterinarians' bills. And farrier bills. As she wasn't to be ridden, we had her shoes pulled, but she still had to be trimmed every month or so.

Then there was the cost of the nursery.

Gail's barn was an old cow barn, without box stalls. Instead, it had a large loafing shed attached, okay for grown horses but not for a newborn foal. Kazinka was due on the first of March. The first of March can be brutal in Upstate New York.

Besides, another animal shared that run-in shed. Gina. A little red Beefalo.

Gina was a pet. She'd come with the farm when Gail bought it. And she'd been without the companionship of another animal for years. Oh, there was Lassie, an untouchable, schizophrenic Collie who'd also come with the farm. Lassie often hung out with Gina. But on the day that we unloaded Kazinka from the horse trailer and led her into the pasture, we understood just how lonely that poor little Beefalo had been.

Gina made the strangest sound at the sight of Kazinka—a sort of whimper, followed by grunts of such joy that Gail and I found tears springing to our eyes. Gina ran to Kazinka, talking to her. Kazinka arched her head upward in shock. She'd never seen such a creature. Gina kept talking. Kazinka tried to walk away. Gina followed, trying to nuzzle Kazinka. Kazinka was scandalized. We feared for a moment that she might kick the little cow.

But they finally settled on a living arrangement. Gina quite simply worshiped Kazinka. And Kazinka quite simply ignored Gina.

What would happen, though, when the foal was born? Kazinka might think that she had to defend it. Especially if Gina tried to adore the foal as well.

We needed to build a box stall in the barn, where mother and foal would be warm and separated from Gina.

"Well, I certainly can't afford to build a box stall," said Gail.

"I'll pay for it," said I.

Little did I know how very much I'd be paying to support horses in the years to come. All because of a quirky, half-Arab Zinkadink.

Of course, the whole point of having purchased Kazinka was to have a horse to ride. Obviously, that horse was not going to be Kazinka.

The solution was simple.

Her name was Sertina.

Another half-Arab. I bought her sight unseen several months after Viva's birth.

The moment that the back door of the trailer opened and I saw those huge dark Arab eyes in the gray, almost white, face, I was a goner—while Gina's cup was verily running over at the arrival of yet another horse to adore, and Viva was childishly excited by this new potential playmate. Tina, who a month before had lost her own foal in a difficult delivery, took to Viva immediately.

Kazinka's response was reserved. And there were shrewish glints in her eyes as she watched Viva shining up to Tina. She and Tina had been pasturemates—because I bought Tina from Charlotte, who'd owned Kazinka before selling her to a man who just months later sold her to Marty and Maria.

That information should have given me pause. But I didn't yet realize that some horses keep getting sold for good reasons.

Not that there was anything wrong with Tina.

"She's been my own riding horse," said Charlotte. "I really hate to sell her, but we've got too many horses."

Some would say that even one horse is too many horses.

"I've trained her to stand when she dumps you," Charlotte continued.

"Dumps me?"

"Well, see, I'm epileptic. If I have a seizure when I'm riding, I fall off. But Tina stands right there until I come to. She won't run away on you."

"But you dump yourself. It's not that *she* dumps *you*."

"Right. Just don't ride anyplace where there are bees. She doesn't like bees."

"But bees are almost everywhere in the summer."

"Yeah, I mean where there are lots of bees."

Which made Tina seem like a very sensible horse. No one cares to go where there are lots of bees.

Charlotte knew all about Kazinka's refusal to lead. It was then that we learned about her fillyhood as a bottle-raised twin.

"But she only acts that way on the trail. She's great in the show ring. My daughter won a whole bunch of ribbons barrel-racing her."

Hard to imagine the snaillike Kazinka barrel racing.

"Now that you have Tina for Kazinka to follow," Charlotte assured me, "you girls will have some great trail rides."

Eager to actually ride my own horse—an Arab, almost—I went to Gail's the next afternoon and saddled Tina.

No problem getting *this* horse to move forward.

Across from Dale's house a trail led back into the woods. We'd been given permission to ride there. It was a lovely afternoon . . . with the buzzin' of the bees in the cigarette trees . . .

Bees?

Tina had the thought at the exact same moment. She leaped sideways so quickly that I could only realize that I was no longer on her back but hanging in midair looking down, like one of those characters in a Roadrunner cartoon. Then—*splat!* I was on the ground.

I will say, though, that Charlotte hadn't lied to me. Tina stood. I could almost, as I lay there beneath her solicitous gaze, hear her thinking, "Just my luck. Another owner with epilepsy."

From that point on I contented myself with riding Tina up and down Gail's U-shaped driveway, a substantial working area about two-tenths of a mile long, where one could be relatively safe from bees and also provide Uncle Warren with a spectator sport. He'd bring a chair from the kitchen and sit watching. When home from work Gail would sit watching as well. Just watching.

For one day, when Viva was about five months old, she finally admitted, "I've lost my nerve. I'm afraid to ride. And now I know what a horse costs. I can't afford it, Bonnie. This whole thing was really stupid on my part."

At which point keeping the horses at Gail's seemed just as stupid.

Some would have said that just *keeping* the horses, *any*where, was even *more* stupid.

But I was hooked—and, I know now, guided by angels.

I began making arrangements to move the horses to Spring Farm.

Silently, in a womb somewhere in the mind of God, Spring Farm CARES was coming along very nicely, thank you.

3

Crazy Over Horses

"You're nuts," said my father. "Three horses? You're headed for the poorhouse. Where the hell are you going to put them?"

"In the garage."

"You can't keep horses in the garage!"

"Just watch me."

Mother had been making noises about erecting a new garage on the site of the old. The old one was an authentic antique that had begun life in Clinton about 1890 as a blacksmith shop. In 1912, it became Clinton's first filling station. In 1929, it was to be torn down, but Grampa Jones bought it and pulled it up to Spring Farm, where it was placed on the west side of our road, Paris Road. Grampa's idea was to set my newly married parents up in the filling station business. Years later, Paris Road would become busy New York State Route 12. In 1929, it was quiet and unpaved, a road on which a filling station was an idea whose time hadn't yet come. The advent of the Depression doubly doomed the business. The structure was moved to the east side of the road and set down behind the Spring Farm house to serve as its garage.

For years it housed only a car. Then, in the mid-1940s, Daddy broke out the front wall of the office portion and ripped out the floor to make a parking spot for his tractor, while Gail and I maintained a supersecret clubhouse in a windowless, three-by-five-foot woodshed attachment behind the building. Many clandestine hours we spent in our supersecret hideaway, doing supersecret things—for instance, learning how to light matches.

It wasn't particularly attractive, our faithful old garage, its only distinction being the flattened, rectangular pyramid that formed the roof. It was painted just once, in 1946, when the color of all the buildings was changed from cream to red with white trim. By 1985, the wooden parking bay doors were gone, and the building bulged and leaned here and there. But, as we say, "They don't make 'em like they used to." Mother got a pad on which to build a neat new garage while the old stalwart departed for a new career.

It was moved just over two hundred feet this time and placed on a newly prepared pad out in the hay field behind the barn, there to be converted into a stable for my horses.

The day that I took the horses away from Gail's farm, we left behind a little red Beefalo named Gina making sounds for all the world like sobs. I'm grateful that I didn't know at that point that telepathic communication with animals is possible.

Of course I *had* done a lot of talking with Gina in the days before Viva's birth. Not word talking or idea talking, but grunt talking. *Feelings* talking.

I'd set up camp in Gail's barn a week before Viva's expected arrival date of March 1. At night I slept on a pile of bales next to Kazinka's new stall, but during the day I sat in a lawn chaise out in the loafing shed with Kazinka, Gina, and Lassie, in the sun and sheltered from the wind. Some of the gazillion books I'd read on foaling warned that mares don't want people around when they give birth. Some will actually hold back the birth until people leave. My plan was to become so much a part of the herd that Kazinka wouldn't even think of me as a person.

Because I had to be there for the birth. The same books were filled with horror stories of all the things that could go wrong, resulting in the death of the foal or the mare or both.

And we feared that Kazinka might be carrying twins. Because she was huge, and twins certainly ran in her family.

My resolve to become part of the herd was rewarded. Kazinka basically ignored my presence during the day as she went about her business, lying down, getting up, pacing, mumbling to herself, snoozing in the sun, enduring frequent, massive twitches. At night her behavior in the stall was the same. Lie down, get up, turn around, mumble, lie down, get up, pace in circles, drain the water bucket, nip at my sleeping bag to make me get her a fresh pail, finish the hay, nip at me to make me get her a fresh chip.

So much for mares resenting the presence of humans. Kazinka was delighted to have a servant to fetch and carry.

March 1 came and went. Then twenty more days passed—a long time during which to become part of the herd. Even crazy Lassie became comfortable enough with my presence to stretch out and snooze near my chair.

But the thing I'll always remember, mistily, about those sunny days there in the shed is Gina. What a gentle soul she was. Shyly, in the first days of my watch, she edged closer and closer. And she'd question me.

"Chufff?" Okay to approach?

"Chufff," I would respond.

"Chufff chufff?"

"Chufff chufff chufff," I would assure her.

Until, after a week, she spent most of the days standing right in front of me, head lowered almost onto my book, asking to be scratched, our mutual vocabulary expanding to a musical range of grunts and emphatic groans. We understood each other perfectly.

At night Gina was also there, in the stall with Kazinka. Because, for all her ignoring of Gina, Kazinka had a fit when we attempted to close out her cow. The new plan was for Gina to stay with Kazinka, then be herded into the run-in shed just outside the stall during the actual event.

Nights beside the stall were rough, the temperature in the barn repeatedly dipping well below zero. Yet I treasure the memory of those cold nights as I treasure the memory of the sunny days. I hardly slept, listening to Kazinka's every sound, rising up and peering over the side of the stall each time she went down.

It's the sounds that warm my memories: Kazinka chomping her hay, guzzling her water, swishing the straw with her pacing, bed-shaking thumps as she laid her huge self down, her mumbles, sudden ominous silences when I knew she was hovering over me, poised to nip at my sleeping bag until I got up and, shivering terribly in the cold, fetched fresh hay or water.

Then there were Gina's sounds: her own chomping of hay, a grunt now and then, and, occasionally, a sudden forceful *splat* as she loosed one of her diarrheic bowel movements onto one of our clean new walls.

Chomp, thump, grunt, mumble, swish, slurp, splat.

Sweet memories. I'd never felt closer to what things are really all about.

The day the horses left Gail's farm is a memory almost unbearable to me now. Poor little Gina, running along the fence line as the trailer pulled away, calling out, sobbing. Yes, thank God I couldn't hear her in words, couldn't actually speak to her then. I couldn't have borne it.

We do things and then suffer for them. Why didn't I at least ask Gail if she'd part with her pet?

But then, I didn't have room for Gina. The two stalls into which

I'd divided the garage—the larger for Kazinka and Viva, the smaller for Tina—would hardly accommodate those three, especially as Viva grew. There was no shelter for Gina, a situation not proper even in the summer and unthinkable in the winter.

In the years that followed, whenever I had occasion to visit Gail, I'd go to the barn to see Gina, and we'd chufff and grunt to each other for a few minutes. Lassie was now with Gina constantly. At least, I consoled myself, Gina had *some* company during the years before she died. And I was probably making more of the situation than it deserved—anthropomorphizing.

Only when we discovered Dawn's long-denied talent of animal communication and actually began to communicate did I come to fully understand the cruel toll that loneliness takes on animals.

Mea maxima culpa, Gina, little love.

And chufff.

Tragedy struck soon after the horses arrived. Neophyte that I was, I decided one day that it was time to begin weaning Viva. So, leaving Kazinka locked in her stall, I let Viva run out into the pasture with Tina.

The green-eyed monsters that were Kazinka's eyes whenever Viva got too cozy with Tina flashed. The stalls were open to the air for the summer. Only four boards separated Kazinka from her son and the usurperess. She went through them as through kindling and galloped off, shrieking, to reclaim her child.

I thought that only the stall was damaged. There was no visible mark on Kazinka. Yet the next morning her chest was badly swollen, with the swelling traveling down her two front legs.

I called in Kit Blackmore, a nearby equine vet.

"Has she had a recent tetanus shot?" was the first thing he asked.

"Last fall."

"Thank goodness for that." He gave her a booster and looked

her over. "Well, I can't find it, but she got herself a puncture wound. Let's hope this is just a bad infection and not clostridium septicum."

"What's that?"

"A cousin to tetanus. It's in the soil wherever horses have lived."

"But there haven't been horses on this farm since . . . 1939, at least."

He shook his head.

"Doesn't matter. This stuff will sit around forever waiting to get into a puncture wound. And there's no vaccine for it. Tetanus is garden-variety, clostridium septicum is rare, not worth a drug company's time."

"Then if it is this clostridium stuff, how do we treat it?"

He took a breath.

"We don't. I don't know of a horse that's survived it."

I could have sworn that Kazinka gave him the same double take as did I.

"There *must* be a treatment!" I cried.

"A place like Cornell would be equipped to try to save her, but I'm not. Look, I'm going to treat her for massive infection. Let's hope that's all that it is."

"How soon will we know?"

"If the swelling responds to the antibiotics, then it's an infection and we might be in the clear."

Once more I set up a bed beside Kazinka's stall, in a lean-to shed that served as storage for feed and equipment. A series of two-by-fours separated that space from the stall, so I could watch her. It was a Saturday. Dawn was home from college. Together through that day and the next morning we watched Kazinka continue to swell up, till her chest was enormous and her front legs were like those of an elephant. She couldn't lower her head to eat or drink, so we served her from a tall table placed in the stall.

Viva we kept in the other stall with Tina, occasionally allowing him in with Kazinka to nurse. The situation was not particularly to her liking, but he was just on the other side of two-by-fours. She could reach over and touch him.

Dr. Blackmore returned after lunch on Sunday. By then the swelling was even moving back along under her breast, heading for her belly.

He shook his head. "I'm sorry."

"Okay. She's going to Cornell."

I couldn't afford it, but that was beside the point. We had Kazinka on a trailer within two hours. We faked her out to get her on, leading Viva right up to the ramp with her. I couldn't go with her myself. Dawn was returning to college that evening, and Mother wasn't physically or emotionally up to caring for both Viva and Tina. There wasn't even time for a sentimental good-bye, because Kazinka screamed and began to demolish the trailer the moment that she realized that Viva wasn't going.

"I gotta get rolling," said Jimmy Volo, the trucker. "Don't worry. She'll settle down once we're moving."

That quickly, my horse was gone. Viva was okay, he had his Aunt Tina, but I was in shock.

What if I never saw Kazinka again?

No! She wouldn't die. I wouldn't allow it. Besides, she was too ornery to die.

The vet who called from Cornell after examining Kazinka gave her a 5 percent chance of survival. And that was the good news.

"Actually—I'll have to research it, but to my knowledge Cornell has never had a horse survive clostridium septicum."

I called Charlotte. I lived two hours from Cornell; she was less than an hour away. Bless her heart, she and her daughter visited Kazinka almost every day. Years later, after some miracle recoveries of Spring Farm animals at Cornell, we came to understand that being visited by friends is as important to animals in hospital as it is to humans. Indeed, it has much to do with recovery rates.

Kazinka was carved up like a side of beef. They had literally to cut the diseased muscle and tissue off and out of her. Her entire front, from under the throatlatch, down the chest and front legs and back under her breast, became raw meat.

Yet each day, cautiously at first, then with growing excitement, her vets upped the estimates for her survival. Ten, fifteen, thirty, sixty-five percent . . .

Finally they were asking if they could do a paper on her. Once again Kazinka had become as rare as peepers in January. She'd survived clostridium septicum. After only about a month, she was discharged.

But I sent her home with Charlotte.

"Bonnie, she needs constant care, her wounds have to be hosed half a dozen times a day, kept superclean, and there are shots, oral medicines, all kinds of stuff. We know horses and we know Kazinka. Let us take care of her until she's out of the woods."

Paying Charlotte for Kazinka's care was spending yet more money than I could afford, but surely Kazinka was better off with people who knew what they were doing. After all, this whole thing had been caused by my ignorance.

I saw Kazinka only once during her convalescence. Close to two months after her removal to Charlotte's place, I got Dawn to horse-sit and drove up to see her.

Horse farms are always magnificent in movies, with white rail fences, rolling green pastures, and rich-looking buildings. In reality, the majority of horse people live in borderline poverty due to equine expenses. Charlotte's place was ramshackle, given over entirely to equipment, tack, and horses. The barn I was led into was a rabbit warren, cobbled together this way and that.

And there was Kazinka in a makeshift stall with a ceiling so low that the bare lightbulb in a ceiling fixture was just inches above the tips of her ears. All she would have to do was toss her head, and she'd smash that bulb and fixture and either electrocute herself or send sparks showering down onto her bedding. And since she was the Bette Davis of mares, she tended to do a lot of head tossing.

I was so shocked by the danger in that stall that it took me a moment to really look at Kazinka.

A lot of skin had already grown back, creeping inward from the edges of the wounds. One could still see, though, how much of her had been cut away.

"Hi, Zinkadink," I said gently as I entered the stall.

She might have been a mess, but she hadn't lost her spunk. Nor her memory. She gave me a long look. Then her eyes flashed. She whipped her butt around and let fly with both barrels, trying to kick me through the opposite wall.

"Kazinka!" cried Charlotte. "That's no way to treat your friend who's come to see you."

I heard everything that Kazinka said in reply. At the time I assumed it was my own guilty imagination.

"Friend? She tried to take my baby and give him to that witch, Tina. She sent me to that terrible place where they cut me up. And she didn't even come to see me. Friend? Just let me at her!"

I drove home chastened, talking to Kazinka in my head and getting answers.

"Forgive me, Kazinka. I was only trying to start the weaning process. And you'd have died if I hadn't sent you to Cornell. And I couldn't come to see you. It's a four-hour round trip, and then I'd have spent a couple of hours with you—it would have taken most of the day, and I couldn't leave the farm that long. Mother's still so nervous having you guys around, she sweats bullets if I leave for even an hour."

"Excuses, excuses. You could have come at least once."

"Okay. You're right. But Charlotte was coming almost every day, and I thought probably you like her more than me anyway."

"What makes you think that?"

"You've known her longer. And she loves you. Look how she came to bat for you."

"She sold me. You'll never sell me."

"How do you know? We were together less than a year."

"I know *you*. And it only takes a minute to know some things. Look, I like Charlotte a lot. I'm grateful to her. But bring me home as soon as you can."

Home. She called it home. She did have a home now. For life. So what if the whole conversation *had* been my imagination?

I made arrangements to bring her home ASAP.

Of course Viva was completely weaned by the time she returned and thicker than ever with Tina. Due to the need to keep Kazinka spotlessly clean, she had to live in her own stall. I put her into an end stall, Tina into another end stall, and Viva into the stall between them. Viva gave Kazinka a glad kiss hello, then went to horse around with Tina. The green-eyed monsters flashed, but Kazinka made no fuss.

Little did I know that she was simply biding her time. Years later she'd take suitable revenge on "that witch," Tina.

So why were there three stalls for three horses?

After Kazinka's accident the garage stalls had seemed amateurish and inadequate. Looking forward to the winter, I had realized that they just wouldn't do. So I put up a prefabricated package stable: five stalls and a feed/storage area.

Why five stalls with only three horses? Well . . . I like to be prepared.

The building went up in a thrice—thirty-two by thirty-two feet, yielding four ten-by-twelve-foot stalls and one twelve-by-twelve-foot stall. It was attached to the old garage; I'd had a door cut in the back of one of the garage stalls and a short connecting hall constructed, so that the old stalwart acquired yet another function, that of run-in shed between pasture and stable.

With the five indoor stalls, and two stalls still in the garage, one could have said that I had stalls for seven horses.

Not that I would ever have seven horses.

* * *

Nature abhors a vacuum, and so does Bonnie. Number four was the Haymans' horse, Buckwheat. I guess Dennis and Jackie figured that since Dawn was spending her every spare moment in my stable, their horse might as well live there, too.

Buckwheat was the John Wayne of horses.

"Ev'nin', little lady," I fancied he said as he was led in.

The two mares nearly swooned at the sight of him. What a splendid fellow! A buckskin of course, massive, sixteen hands, weighing at least twelve hundred pounds—probably Percheron crossed with Quarter Horse.

He'd been a school horse where Dennis had taken the family for riding lessons when Dawn was a child. Dawn, ever a reluctant rider, remembers moments of panic, even terror, during those lessons. Luckily she had never had to ride the behemoth Buckwheat. Dennis or Jackie rode him.

The family had dozens of "Buckwheat-isms." As, for instance, in that riding school the students moved along a track around stalls and storage in the center. One day toward the end of a lesson, the instructor was leading the family in a canter. And Buckwheat had about had it. As they cantered past a stack of hay bales, without missing a stride, Buckwheat reached over, snatched up a bale, and cantered on, carrying it in his teeth and trying to eat it at the same time.

"Pilgrim, there's times when a fella just has ta have some grub."

Then there was the day that, with Jackie aboard, Buckwheat took a spill, falling onto his side and potentially crushing Jackie's leg. But when people ran to help her, they found the gentlemanly Buckwheat holding himself arched upward, carefully protecting her leg.

Finally the school closed, selling its horses. Not young, and large, Buckwheat would likely go for meat. Dennis wouldn't hear of it. The Haymans had no place for a horse, but they had bought Buckwheat and, in the ensuing years, paid his board at this stable, then that. At the last stable he'd made himself *horsona non grata.* He took to throwing hay into his automatic waterer, clogging the drain and repeatedly flooding his stall. The owners of the stable wouldn't be unhappy to see him leave.

It was also getting hard for Dennis and Jackie to come up with the ever-rising boarding fees. So they made me a deal: they'd pay a token board, see to the mucking of his stall, provide his food, and be available to care for all the horses whenever I needed to go anywhere. No longer would I be in the position I'd been in when Kazinka was at Cornell.

Having Buckwheat at Spring Farm had a calming effect on everyone. The honcho had arrived. The mares regarded him with fluttering eyes, and Viva looked up to his great height and girth with "Wowgeewhiz!" admiration. Peace reigned, both in the stable and out in the pasture. Buckwheat had only to give them a look, and the mares would stop bickering or Viva would cease his childish teasing of this one or that.

A nice little herd. Four horses. And that would be all.

4

A Killer Horse and

a Ride from Coast to Coast

Bonnie, we're retiring Rocky Red. We've decided to give him to you."

February 1987. My friend Linda Becker was calling from Hollywood. Rocky Red was a racehorse belonging to her and her husband, Terry, "Chief" of *Voyage to the Bottom of the Sea* fame.

"Why are you retiring him?"

Terry was on an extension.

"Because he won't run," he said glumly. "We should never have gelded him."

Gosh. A racehorse. Next to Arabs, my girlhood imagination had been most infected by racehorses—*National Velvet, The Story of Seabiscuit* . . . Hollywood had done a number on me.

"All it will cost you," coaxed Terry, "is his shipping."

Terminally afflicted, I came up with $1,500 to bring Rocky Red from California.

There was great excitement the evening that he arrived. All the Haymans were there to greet him, and a sigh of pure delight went up as Rocky was unloaded.

Lord, he was gorgeous. Just under sixteen hands, chestnut, splendidly muscled, but spare in a lithe, athletic way. And so docile as we led him into the stable.

Buckwheat's greeting nicker was low and dignified. Another horse might have been intimidated by this potential rival for his throne, but remember John Wayne. Buckwheat had no need to quarrel with a pretty boy.

As for Kazinka and Tina, mares will be mares. Another word for "mare" could be "hussy." Their greetings were excited squeals.

While Viva, though gelded, commenced bucking around his stall, kicking the walls and hurling youthful challenges at the newcomer.

Rocky Red seemed hardly to know they were there.

We put him on cross ties and groomed and massaged him, to relax him after his long, tiring journey. An honest-to-goodness Thoroughbred racehorse at Spring Farm. Just like in the movies!

It would be a few years before I ceased viewing the world of horses through 1940s Hollywood-manufactured rose-colored glasses.

Yet if I hadn't viewed horses in that fashion, Spring Farm CARES would never have come into being, and thousands of animals would have been the poorer for it. I was as on a roller coaster, going very fast, with no time to think about anything. Looking back, it seems as though I often acted like an absolute fool.

But angels look after fools.

The morning after Rocky's arrival, Dawn and I led him to the outdoor arena . . .

Oh yes, I'd had a huge pad constructed on yet another part of the field behind the barn, 110 feet wide, 200 feet long. Seven years later, that outdoor arena would become the pad for the postfire small-animal facility of Spring Farm CARES. Looking back, I can see the progression, the secret steps toward the future.

But that morning neither Dawn nor I had a clue. All we knew was that we were taking our beautiful new Thoroughbred out for some exercise.

I leaped back as I unhooked the lead from his halter, for he took off bucking and kicking, enjoying his first freedom in days. Dawn and I laughed, cheering him on. I climbed up and sat on the top railing, leaning forward and clapping.

Finally Rocky turned and zeroed in on us. Then he galloped toward us. Not for a moment did I sense danger. He'd veer off before he got to the fence.

But he didn't. Instead he galloped right up to me. I saw his jaws opening only at the last moment.

His teeth closed on my shoulder. He shook me violently, pulling me off the fence. Then he galloped off again.

You have to have been savaged by the jaws of a horse to understand the power—and the pain.

Dawn, timid around horses to begin with, was in total shock. I wasn't far behind. Somehow I summoned the courage to call Rocky back to the gate, get a lead onto him, and return him to his stall.

Then I went to find a mirror. I stripped off my top and looked at myself.

Amazing. I was already a deep purple from my shoulder down through my trunk, front, and back. Before the black-and-blue had finished, it reached nearly to my toes.

Surely, though, this had just been a case of overexuberance. Surely Rocky hadn't meant to hurt me.

That evening when I went in to feed him he attacked me again, teeth bared, ready to kill.

Whoa!

We realized then that the docile creature who'd stepped off the trailer had been drugged. The drugs had worn off.

What had I gotten myself into?

I called Terry and Linda. They were stunned. The Rocky they knew wasn't vicious. And they were speaking truthfully. They loved Rocky and had sent him to me to be sure that he received a kind retirement. But they loved me, too, and would never have sent me a vicious horse.

We've realized since that owners often don't know about some of the things that are done to their racehorses. Rocky's behavior hadn't been normal. I had the feeling that he thought that was the way he was *supposed* to act, to gain our approval. He didn't know that he didn't have to race anymore, that he didn't have to seem mean and aggressive.

Terry put me in touch with the facility where Rocky had gone for R and R between races.

"You sure we're talking about the same horse?" asked the manager. "Rocky Red's one of the nicest horses I ever had here. I had a fourteen-year-old girl grooming him and taking him to the pool. He's a peach."

So Rocky could be sweet and gentle. Evidently though, in this new and threatening situation, he thought he'd better be tough.

I couldn't sell him. I wouldn't do that to either Rocky or a buyer. I was stuck with a "vicious" horse, and I had to find a way around it.

I forbade anyone but myself to enter his stall, and I got out a large, thick, sheepskin jacket that I'd bought while living in Australia. I also had a sheepskin helmet, with a visor that came down over the eyes and flaps that came down over the ears. Several hours a day we turned Rocky out into the outdoor arena, to get the piss and vinegar worked out of him, and also to get his stall mucked. The rest of the time he was in his stall and had to be managed in that stall. So, wearing my sheepskin armor—unbuttoned, so that I could slip out of it if necessary—I'd enter and calmly change his water, give him hay and grain, or do whatever else needed to be done.

And Rocky would attack, biting with all his strength. Usually on my arm.

Except, with inches of bulky sheepskin cushioning me, nothing happened. He couldn't get a purchase; his bites slid off.

While I would say calmly, "No bite, Rocky. No bite."

His confusion was pathetic to see. I was supposed to shout, hit at him, tell him that he was bad. Instead I just stood there. Where was the fun if I wouldn't react? Being Rocky Red, the lean, mean, racing machine, didn't seem to work anymore.

Deliverance arrived for both of us in the form of Linda Tellington-Jones and T.T.E.A.M., the acronym for the Tellington-Jones Equine Awareness Method. I'd been calling every "authority" that I could think of, seeking advice on how to deal with Rocky, when my riding teacher gave me a flyer regarding a two-day clinic to be given in nearby Cazenovia that very weekend, by a wonder woman from the West Coast.

I called the number on the flyer. The clinic was filled. I couldn't possibly get in.

"Then you're ready to read of my death in your newspaper," I told the girl. "You're ready to read that I was savaged to death by my horse. You'll take that responsibility."

I got in.

I spent the first day watching spellbound as the miracle named Linda Tellington-Jones turned problem horse after problem horse, some of them downright vicious, into relaxed, licking, and chewing pussycats. There was one technique in particular, working the mouth, that I felt sure would help Rocky.

A new world opened to me. A new way of dealing with horses, of *thinking* about horses.

And one could study with Linda, learn her techniques, even become a T.T.E.A.M. Practitioner and teach others to work miracles.

I arrived home on a cloud. Dawn had been horse-sitting.

"I've found out what we want to do when we grow up," I said.

Dawn turned pale.

"If it has anything to do with horses, forget *me*."

Poor Dawn. I dragged her kicking and screaming into her new life.

In 1986, by the skin of her teeth, she graduated from Brockport with a B.S. in social work. Not that she was a poor student. Indeed, she graduated magna cum laude.

But she burst into my barn one weekend near the end of her senior year in a terrible state.

"I'm quitting college."

My mouth dropped.

Her face was set, but her eyes looked wounded.

"The social work system is dishonest. I won't work in a dishonest system. I'm quitting."

Dawn, I was already beginning to understand, is one of the world's most ethical people. She's as true as the earth upon which we walk, as honest as the rising and setting sun. She'd selected social work as a career because she wanted to help people. If she was ready to turn her back on four years of dedication and sacrifice, always working at least two part-time jobs, it must be bad.

"I turned in my final report for my field placement," she said tersely. "My supervisor has instructed me to falsify it." Field placement is actual on-the-job work done by social work students in their senior year, actual work with actual clients in actual agencies. "If I don't do as he says, he'll fail me."

"What does he want you to falsify?"

Dawn described some of the clients to whom she'd been assigned.

"They're ready to go home. They can function as outpatients. He wants me to say that they need to stay."

"Why?"

"Agencies get paid for their inpatients. They keep them there so they'll keep getting paid for them. I'm quitting."

"Dawn, you're just weeks from graduation!"

"I can't change my report!"

We talked for hours. Desperately I looked for ways to make her stay, which boiled down to convincing an honest, superethical person to just once not be honest and superethical.

"You know," I finally said, suddenly realizing myself, "the social work system isn't the only sick system. Our public schools are funded per student. And municipalities get federal and state aid based on population."

"Yeah," said Dawn thoughtfully. "Legislative districts are based on population. Scientists do ridiculous studies to keep getting funded. Academics have to publish or lose their jobs."

"Right!" I sensed approaching victory. "Every organization that depends on government or corporate funding eventually turns dishonest in order to keep that funding. Back in the 1950s, my father's cousin became commandant of Fort Monmouth in New Jersey. The first budget he submitted was for twenty-five million dollars. It got kicked back. Higher-ups said it had to be at least fifty million, because that's what it had been the year before. So Dar went through catalogs, and ordered twenty-five million dollars' worth of stuff that he didn't need, and put it all in a warehouse. He did that every year till the warehouse was filled. Then he bought an old cargo ship, had the stuff loaded onto it, had it taken out into the Atlantic and sunk. And that's just *one* military installation! At 1950s prices. It's not just one system, Dawn. It's *all* of them. All systems are based on a flawed model."

I was sailing. Surely now I'd convinced her.

"Right. So the answer is to stay out of any system. I'm quitting."

Back to the old drawing board.

"Look, consider this. Maybe you can do more good from inside the system than from outside. Maybe you're the one who can change the system."

She shook her head.

"No. Any system will eventually corrupt anyone who enters. If I go into social work, someday I'll be that supervisor telling a student to falsify her report. I'd have to, to keep my job."

I threatened. I told her that I'd ban her from Spring Farm forever if she didn't get her degree. She didn't believe me. I finally pointed out that getting her degree didn't mean she'd actually have to be a social worker.

That line of reasoning got her attention. She finally agreed to return and to do what had to be done to graduate.

But that discussion, about staying outside any system, was one of the most important that the two of us ever had. That understanding would eventually protect all that is good in Spring Farm CARES.

Upon graduating, Dawn rented a little house, just up the road from her father's home and just a few miles from Spring Farm. She took a job at Doyle's Hardware in Utica while also working part-time for me. Gradually more and more of her chores here became those of horse care.

At the same time she was getting pressure from friends to get a job in social work, while her teachers at Brockport were urging her to get her master's degree. She qualified for "advanced standing" at Syracuse University, which would allow her to complete her master's in one year and one summer rather than two years.

Wavering, she applied for a social work position in Utica and got the job. But their funding wasn't coming through, and her start date kept getting postponed.

One day I said to her, "You know maybe there's a reason that this job is taking so long. Maybe you *are* supposed to stay outside the system."

That was all she needed. She turned her back on social work, quit Doyle's, and came to Spring Farm full-time.

"But you'll use your training in whatever you end up doing," I promised her.

Often we utter profundities without having the foggiest idea what we're talking about.

So Dawn became a constant presence at Spring Farm. Twenty-five years my junior, she became the daughter I'd never had, while my parents treated her as another granddaughter. We quickly forgot a time when Dawn hadn't been with us and got to the point where we couldn't imagine a future without her.

What a handy person she is to have around! Did Mother's washing machine cease to function? Dawn fixed it. Did we need a new phone extension installed? Call Dawn. Did Daddy need help with his TV and new VCR? Dawn could show him how it worked. A dead car battery? Dawn knew how to use jumper cables without blowing up the engine. A broken toilet? Dawn to the rescue.

"How'd you learn to do all this stuff?" I asked.

"Mostly from my father, I guess. Whenever we got anything new, he'd tell me how it worked and show me how to take it apart and put it back together."

Hooray for Dennis.

Unfortunately, Dawn hadn't taken as well to the riding lessons that Dennis had provided as well as to lessons in general maintenance and repair.

Watching Rocky Red savage me hadn't helped matters any.

So it was that Dawn thought I'd lost my mind when I arrived home from the TT.E.A.M. clinic that evening, walked into Rocky Red's stall without my Rocky armor, and, just as I'd seen Linda Tellington-Jones do that afternoon, reached up and began gently to pull, tug at, knead, and massage his nose and lips. Then I put my hands into his mouth and begin to massage his gums and tongue.

His eyes went soft. He heaved a big sigh and lowered his head, gratefully surrendering himself to my gentling hands, releasing the junk from his racing years.

He never even attempted to bite anyone after that night.

Oh, one day several months later, as Dawn was mucking his stall, he suddenly wrapped his neck around her and pulled her against himself. She thought she was going to die. Until she realized that he only wanted to suck on her ear.

By then I'd implemented another of LTJ's suggestions. We changed his name, from the flint-hard Rocky Red to something that evoked softness.

He became Sir Percival Pudding of Pie.

Puddy for short. Ever and always, our dear Puddy.

Poor Dawn. She didn't know, when she hooked up with me, that she'd accepted a ride on a roller coaster with no terminus. On the other hand, neither did I.

Three weeks after I attended the Cazenovia clinic, Dawn was sitting at Mother's breakfast table innocently eating her cereal (Mother always made sure that Dawn ate well) when I casually announced, "You're going to Maine on Wednesday."

Dawn stopped with her spoon halfway to her mouth.

"And why," she asked carefully, "am I going to Maine?"

"Because Linda Tellington-Jones's sister is giving a four-day hands-on workshop there and I've paid your tuition."

"A workshop?" said Dawn as though tiptoeing. "With horses?"

"Yes."

"No."

"You're going."

"I'm not." Hysteria entered her voice. "I don't *want* to work with horses. I don't *want* to learn this T.T.E.A.M. stuff!"

"The tuition's not refundable."

"I can't drive to Maine alone! I've never driven further than Brockport alone!"

"Oh," said Mother, "you'll love Maine, Dawn. It's beautiful. Harwood!" She called to my father in his invalid recliner in the living room. "Dawn's going to Maine on Wednesday."

"No kidding," said Daddy. "Get out my maps, Mother. I'll work out the best routes for you to take, Dawn."

"We used to take our vacations in Maine," Mother assured Dawn, "and Harwood drove dozens of charters up there when he drove for the bus company."

"I *can't* drive all that way by myself! I'm afraid!"

"Don't be silly," said Mother, as she went to search out Daddy's maps.

And so, terrified, swearing that it was a waste of my money and that catastrophe would result, Dawn went to Maine.

Only later did I learn just what a chance I'd taken. As brilliant as Dawn is with technical equipment, that's how inept she is spatially. The girl has absolutely no sense of direction. Only by dint of my father's exuberant coaching and expertly marked maps did she both get to her destination and then return to us.

She came back halfway enchanted. That was because of Linda's sister, the delightful, down-to-earth Robyn Hood. That's right. Robyn Hood. The family name is Hood, and Linda herself named her much younger sister when that sister was born.

Robyn was exactly the right person to introduce Dawn to TT.E.A.M. The two of them had an instant rapport, with Robyn sensing the treasure hiding within Dawn and Dawn realizing that she could safely put her trust in Robyn. Though Spring Farm has years since parted ways from the mainstream of TT.E.A.M., we'll never cease to think softly of Robyn. (Or admiringly of the brilliant LTJ.)

The Dawn who returned to Spring Farm was different from the Dawn who'd left. While she retained the healthy respect for, and caution with, horses that all sensible horse handlers should have, her timidity was gone. Those four days under Robyn's guidance had given her a quiet confidence around our horses that didn't amaze me—I already knew what was possible—but it certainly amazed Dawn.

The thing that *most* amazed her, however, was the fact that she'd driven to and from Maine all by herself. She couldn't stop talking about it, and it became a running joke with Mother.

"Well, of course Dawn can do anything now," she'd say. "Dawn's been to Maine."

Even to this day, when Dawn's courage falters, I can perk her right up by reminding her, "You can do it. You've been to Maine."

The next scheduled TT.E.A.M. workshop was a seven-day event, to be taught by Robyn five weeks later at Halali Arabian Farm in Willets, California. On the eighth day, Linda would be there to present a one-day clinic for the public. This was an opportunity for me to meet Robyn and for Dawn to be exposed to Linda. I signed us up and began making preparations. Jackie and Dennis would care for the horses. Mother could handle my dogs and Bonniecat. Dawn and I would drive my van, Vanessa, and Max would ride with us.

Max was a big, heavy German Shepherd who'd belonged to my niece Helen. Max had been hit by a car and lost the use of her back legs. She was in a lot of pain, but, rather than let her be put down, I had taken charge of her and found a vet who did acupuncture. It had taken months, but in the end, the acupuncture freed her of pain. For close to three years I'd been carrying my buddy Max around. I was the only one strong enough to do so, so she couldn't be left behind.

Everything was all set for the trip.

Then my father died.

Harwood Hamlin Jones was a complicated man. And a handsome one. He also, to my mother's chagrin, never seemed to age. Mother had been a pretty girl, and she became a handsome woman. But she aged early. Daddy, on the other hand, wore his hair in a youthful crew cut and always looked years younger than he was. I remember on one of our family driving vacations, we were having breakfast at the counter of a diner in Thermopole, Wyoming—Mommy, 43, Daddy, 41$^{1}/_{2}$, Peggy, 17, and Bonnie, 11. A man who'd been having breakfast nearby paid his bill, started out, then turned, came back, and touched Mother on the shoulder.

"You have such lovely children, madam."

Mother thanked him graciously. Then she cried all the way to Old Faithful.

"Deanie, he didn't think I was one of your children!"

"Yes he did! Yes he did! I wish you'd stop wearing that crew cut!"

Child that I was, I thought it was funny. Now my heart aches for her.

There was also the loss of the Jones family fortune.

"Your father was born with a silver spoon in his mouth," Mother often said, "but it got yanked out."

It was also yanked away from her. When she married Daddy in June 1929, he was the catch of the town. Not that she married him for money. Deanie was crazy in love with Harwood. But riches to rags had to have been a letdown.

Grampa Jones made a veritable fortune with his Holsteins between 1910 and 1929. My first novel was largely concerned with Francis, with the rise and fall of the House of Jones, and with the disappointment that Francis had felt in Harwood, his only child. Grampa had expected his son to share his passion for farming and Holstein cattle. Instead, Harwood planned to become a history professor and writer and to travel the world.

In the meantime, he became a virtuoso on the trumpet. And when everything including his father's fortune came apart in the Depression, with college and world travel suddenly out of the question, Harwood's musical talent saved his little family. Throughout the Depression years he played with a dance band at various Adirondack resorts. At a time when millions of people were going hungry in the streets for lack of a dime, Harwood's trumpet kept his family afloat.

During World War II, he and Mommy worked alternate shifts in a local factory, producing war materiel. And after the war the boy who'd dreamed of being a writer, history professor, and world traveler ended up where his father had always wanted him: running the family farm.

Yet he never stopped dreaming. In ways, ultimately, his dreams came true.

He was a voracious reader, of history especially. When I was nine, he began taking the family on driving vacations, even as far away as Mexico City. Then, with a boyhood pal, George Marsh, he invested in a charter bus company called Utica-Rome, appeasing his wanderlust by driving charter trips not only throughout the United States but to Canada and Nova Scotia as well.

In 1963 I gave him and Mother a trip to the Virgin Islands and Puerto Rico. In the years that followed I sent them to Europe several times, and in 1978 I gave them a trip around the world.

The year 1978 turned out to be a record year for Harwood's dreams. Because in that year, Dobson Publishing of London published his first novel, *The Forest Man*, a novel of ancient Rome.

The Forest Man was intended to be the first of a trilogy. The second book, *Bloodtied*, was in galleys and the third book of the trilogy nearly finished when Dennis Dobson died of a heart attack. His widow was unable to go forward with the publication of *Bloodtied*. Daddy was devastated.

Then, in 1980, while he and Mother and I were traveling in Europe, something snapped in his back. He'd been fine all the way through Italy. But one day as he got out of the car in southern France, he let out a cry. He was in growing pain after that but insisted on continuing, using a stout cane that we bought for him, down through Andorra into Spain. My father had the lowest pain threshold that I've ever seen. Yet this time he bore it stoically, refusing to listen to any talk of cutting the trip short and flying home. Deep within, he knew that this trip was his last.

On to Portugal, then back up into France, to Lourdes, where he bought a moss green beret that he wore almost constantly thereafter. To Chartres, then Calais, over the Channel, and up to northern England to Brancepath Castle, which Dennis Dobson's widow had purchased and to where she and Dobson Publishing had retreated.

Ironically, I'd discovered during genealogical investigations that that castle was begun in the fourteenth century by one of Daddy's ancestors, Ralph Neville. I'll never forget Daddy gamely hobbling with his cane behind Mrs. Dobson as she gave us a tour through seemingly endless rooms in the castle, down into the cellars, to the dungeons of the fourteenth-century structure, then up torturously narrow staircases to the roof, to see where thieves had managed to make off with all of the valuable lead sheeting, leaving Mrs. Dobson with a king-size roofing problem. Never once did Daddy let on to her that he was in pain. He wasn't about to miss one single moment of that tour through "ancestral digs."

In London, our friends Solveig and Anita Gray got him in to see one of the physicians who they said attended Queen Elizabeth. After X-rays, the doctor said that Daddy had a ruptured disk and told him to find a good physical therapist the moment he got home.

Instead, once home, Daddy went to his doctor, who sent him to a cancer specialist, who decided, though no such thing appeared on any X-rays, that he had cancer of the spine. Over my protests, he opted for radiation. The question of a ruptured disk was never addressed, nor was the ruptured disk treated. The radiation burned his spine so badly that he was rendered an invalid, unable to walk without crutches and finally graduating to a wheelchair.

Further tests revealed no cancer whatsoever. But there he was, an invalid, his youthful appearance finally gone. He lived another seven years and died from complications of his inactivity, not from the cancer, which all his doctors, except the queen's physician in London, insisted that he'd had.

Despite his seven years of invalidism, the end, on May 27, 1987, several weeks after his seventy-ninth birthday, took us by surprise. We buried him with his Utica-Rome Bus Company tiepin, symbol of his love of travel. On his chest we placed the beloved moss green beret from Lourdes.

I didn't know which way Mother was going to go—into depression, or into a new life for herself. After fifty-eight years of marriage—the last seven having been virtual house arrest as she cared for Daddy—she deserved the latter. Dawn and I were due in California on June 13. I wasn't going to cancel the trip, and I wasn't going to leave Mother behind. So I rented a Southwind motor home and, after frenzied preparations, bundled her and Dawn into it and off we went. With us were Max and my Australian Cattle Dog, Mr. Fraser, who was very old and suffering from endless senior moments. Foxie and Daffy went to stay with my Downey cousins, who ran a boarding kennel; Dennis and Jackie would care for the horses; and Helen would see to Bonniecat Endore right there in Mother's house.

Out of six sisters and one brother, Mother had two siblings still living, Mary in Iowa and Milly in Idaho. The three of them hadn't seen one another in several years. Mary and Milly were much older than Mother, she being the youngest in a twenty-year span of siblings, and their advancing years had put a stop to their yearly visits to us. Additionally, Mary from Iowa had used to spend winters out in Idaho with Milly. Increasing frailty had stopped those visits as well. With Mother unable to travel on account of Daddy's illness, the last three Newcomb girls had reconciled themselves to never seeing each other again in this world.

So it was that, when we picked up ninety-five-year-old Mary at her home in Randalia, Iowa, she climbed into the Southwind with as much excitement as Cinderella climbing into her pumpkin coach. Three days later we deposited her and Mother at the home of ninety-year-old Milly in Boise.

The following morning, Dawn, Max, Mr. Fraser, and I left the girls to their bittersweet last time together and pushed on for California, to that fateful workshop, where Dawn's ability to communicate telepathically with animals would finally—to my delight and her horror—be revealed in all its glory.

5

California Weirdos
and the Mare from Hell

Many easterners think that all Californians are crazies, weirdos—pot-smoking kooks wearing beads and chanting over crystals. Dawn was no exception. On top of weird, she thought that Californians would be downright nasty. She wouldn't believe that most Californians are pretty much like easterners except that they're smart enough to live where winter is something you read about in books. The fact that I'd lived in California for twenty years made no difference.

"You're an exception," said Dawn. "Besides, you're really an easterner."

Come to think of it, at that point, Dawn was an insular, close-minded little twerp.

But she'd been to Maine. There was hope for her.

Once we'd crossed the border into California, I watched her

grow ever more puzzled. Gas station attendants, waitresses, and checkout clerks were smiling, friendly, normal. As we neared the mountains along the coast our muffler pipe started to drag, and a couple of obliging motorcyclists fixed it for us, wouldn't take any money, then followed us for miles out of their way to make sure that their repair held.

"Gee," Dawn admitted finally, "people here aren't what I'd expected. They seem very . . ."

"Normal."

"Yeah. And nice."

The people at Halali Arabians didn't shatter that illusion. The normal-seeming owner, Sylvia Rust, welcomed us cordially and showed us where we could park. Nor was the illusion shattered by twenty-some other students who arrived next morning for the workshop. Some were from other states, but most were from California.

Dawn's prejudices began creeping away like chastened children.

During the morning the name Penelope Smith was often mentioned, by Robyn or by other students. Most seemed to know about this Penelope Smith, an animal communicator. Dawn and I assumed that "animal communicator" meant animal behaviorist.

"Oh no," said Linda McLain, a fellow student who joined us in the motor home for lunch. "Penelope *talks* with animals. Telepathically."

"Oh, *sure* she does." Dawn threw me a knowing glance. "Let me guess. This Penelope lives here in California."

"Yeah. Down in Point Reyes."

See? said Dawn's lifted eyebrows.

I shrugged. "I never said that *all* Californians are normal."

"Normal?" said Linda. "Normal's a figment of psychologists' imaginations. Heck, I'd be insulted if you called *me* normal. You two certainly aren't normal."

Social work training still dripping from behind her ears, Dawn bristled.

"What's *ab*normal about us?"

"How many 'normal' people would rent a motor home for taxi service from New York to Iowa and Idaho and then California, lugging two old people and two old dogs to boot, one dog senile, the other paraplegic? Especially when there'll be workshops on the East Coast in September and October both. Why didn't you just wait, Bonnie?"

"That's not the way I operate. When I decide to do something, I just do it. We'll be going to those workshops, too. We're going to be TT.E.A.M. Practitioners, and the sooner the better."

"Speak for yourself, John," said Dawn.

She had, however, enjoyed the morning training. Ironically, she was more advanced than I. She'd had four days of hands-on training, while I'd only watched LTJ lecture and perform for two days.

It was after lunch that Dawn's prejudices stopped creeping away and came rushing back.

Unlike Charlotte's place, Halali Arabians did look like horse farms in the movies, sprawling over many green acres, with a beautiful house, an Olympic-size covered riding arena, and seemingly endless neat paddock/pastures, filled with mares, fillies, and, in separate special paddocks, Halali's stallions. A couple of dozen mares and fillies, on whom we students would be working during the next seven days, were presented to us during the morning. One was six-year-old Murengay.

Murengay, Sylvia Rust explained to the group, had everyone stumped. For several years they'd been trying to train her to saddle. She would allow the saddle to be put on, and she'd allow the rider to mount. Then she'd freeze, refusing to move forward. When she finally did move, it was suddenly and at the speed of light. All riders, even cowboys and jockeys who'd given it a try, had been left on their backsides in the dust as Murengay galloped off. Sylvia had grown desperate enough to consider an overhead pulley arrangement hooked to the rider to break his fall.

Now, as we returned from lunch and sat listening to Robyn, Sylvia rushed in, her face shining.

"I know why Murengay does what she does! I just talked with Penelope Smith. She says that Murengay doesn't understand the body that she's in now or know what to do with it, because in the life just previous she was a cow."

Dawn turned to me with, oh, what a miserable, smug look.

"They've come out of their closets," that look said.

But then one of the girls taking the workshop, a Halali employee, said, "Sylvia! That's why every time . . . the cows' paddock!"

Sylvia's mouth dropped.

"Of course! Whenever Murengay gets away, she runs to the cows' paddock. We always find her grazing alongside the cows."

I turned to Dawn, with, oh, what a miserable, smug look.

"No, no, no!" Dawn said that night. "Reincarnation I understand, but telepathic communication with animals? *No!*"

I sat watching her. Why so vehement? She seemed threatened.

"Dawn, remember the night you walked into the stable and stopped at Buckwheat's stall and said . . ."

"That was a coincidence."

"Pretty interesting coincidence. You said, 'Bonnie, I think Buck's got a problem in his left fore.' We looked and, sure 'nuff, he was abscessing there. How'd you know that, Dawn?"

"I don't know."

"But you *did* know. Maybe he told you telepathically that he was hurting."

"No."

"Then how did you know?"

"I don't know!" Dawn cried out and excused herself to take Mr. Fraser for his evening dodder.

In the days that followed she alternated between ridiculing

Penelope Smith and the idea of animal communication or getting just plain angry whenever the subject was mentioned.

And another problem arose.

We'd been instructed to "tone" to the horses as we worked, to make frequent low, reassuring sounds. But on the occasions when my team was working on a horse that Dawn's team was also working on, I realized that Dawn never toned.

"Tone, Dawn, tone," I'd mutter under my breath.

Not a sound.

"Why won't you tone?" I'd ask when we were alone.

"I *am* toning."

"You're *not*. Talk to them, Dawn."

"I *do*."

The argument continued until the seventh day of the workshop. That afternoon, with just a couple of hours still to go, Robyn decided to "let the Universe decide" who'd pair up with whom. Until then friends and acquaintances had purposely been kept apart. Robyn put all our names in a bowl and drew them in pairs. Dawn and I were drawn together. The Universe had decided.

Then each of the pairs drew the name of a horse. We drew Minuet. Oh, *no!*

Minuet, a yearling recently imported from Holland, was the nemesis of the workshop. It usually took an hour just to catch her. And of course part of our training was to go to the paddocks and bring the horse on whom we were to work into the arena.

Armed with grain but not expecting much, we headed for Minuet's paddock. I went in first and was not surprised when Minuet made herself scarce while the other fillies in the paddock relieved me of the grain. I trailed after Minuet for a while, wheedling. She wasn't buying what I was selling.

I went back out.

"You try," I told Dawn. "Sometimes you have a way about you."

She hesitated.

Finally she said, "Okay. But don't tell me to tone."

She walked slowly into the paddock and out to where Minuet had removed herself.

About twenty feet from the filly she stopped. Then she just stood, looking at Minuet.

Minuet turned and stood looking at Dawn.

They remained that way for about half a minute.

Then Minuet walked up to Dawn, Dawn clipped the lead onto her halter, and led her out of the paddock.

"How did you *do* that?!" I cried.

Dawn was leading Minuet to the shade of an arbor covering the walkway. "I don't know."

"You must know."

"I *don't* know."

"What were you thinking? You *must* know."

"All right!" Dawn blurted. "I told her that Robyn had sent us to work on her. She said she didn't want to because she has a headache and besides she doesn't like the arena. I told her that if she'd let me put the lead on her we'd just bring her here to the shade and do bodywork and make her headache go away. So here she is."

"My God." I was agape. "So all this time . . . no toning. Telepathically you're . . ."

"If you tell anyone about this, I'll never speak to you again."

"Dawn! You can do what Penelope Smith does! It's real. That time with Buckwheat . . ."

"It's not! I can't! Look, can we please just do some bodywork on this filly?"

Silently then for over an hour we worked on Minuet, applying all of TT.E.A.M.'s soothing touches—TTouch. When we'd finished, Minuet was nearly asleep, head hanging low, headache gone.

Reluctantly we returned her to her paddock. She didn't leave the gate. As we disappeared from sight she was still there, watching after us.

Back in the arena for the wrap-up, we reported only that we'd caught Minuet and done bodywork on her, finessing questions about how we'd been able to catch her. Only we two knew what life-changing events Murengay, Minuet, and our visit to Halali Arabians had been.

The eighth and final day was LTJ's one-day demonstration, open to the public. I was eager for Dawn to see Linda in action. She saw only the beginning and end of Linda's presentation. Because, on that day, we lost Max.

Maxine. One of the sweetest souls ever incarnated.

Surprisingly, this trip to California wasn't Max's first. In 1984, she'd come cross-country with me in Vanessa when I'd returned to finalize the sale of my West Hollywood house. I would have flown, but with no one else able to carry Max around she'd have had to be put down. So I banked the passenger side of the cab with pillows and quilts right up to the top of the dash, creating a platform for her. To California and back, Max was my copilot. As I drove, I talked to her, explaining the sights. She took such keen interest that, even then, I believed that she understood all that I was telling her.

On the second trip, again and again she'd dragged herself up to the copilot's seat, begging till we picked her up and let her see where we were going. Each time we crossed into a new state, we'd call her to the front and pick her up.

"This is Nebraska, Max."

"This is Idaho."

With sharply pricked ears she'd survey the terrain. One of our treasures, lost in the fire, was the photo of "Max in Wyoming" taken at a roadside stop—Max, silhouetted against the desert, grinning at the camera and wearing a cowboy hat.

The evening of the day that we left Mother and Aunt Mary at Aunt Milly's, just over the border from Idaho into Wyoming, Dawn, Max, and I shared a moment of pure enchantment.

The sun had just set. We were in the middle of nowhere. There was nothing, just nothing, except sagebrush and tumbleweed and high hills out on the western horizon. We pulled off the road. Fraser was asleep, but Max was eager for adventure. I picked her up. We got out of the Southwind and walked about seventy feet from the motor home. I set Max down.

And all three of us became silent, transfixed.

Everything glowed an unearthly orange-rose, reflected off the sky from the recently departed sun. With each moment as we watched, the orange-rose deepened, turning to wine, then to deep lilac, heading for purple. And there wasn't a sound in the world. Not a single, solitary sound.

None of us moved. Except that I caught Dawn's eye and gestured down at Max, who sat with ears perked, watching it all, as enraptured as we two. We stayed there, watching, none of us moving, until it grew too dark to see the horizon anymore. Then I picked Max up. Wordlessly we returned to the Southwind and continued on our way. Words don't belong to sharings like that.

Our fourth day at Halali, Max began gagging up her food. She couldn't get it down. X-rays by Sylvia's vet revealed inoperable tumors blocking the entrance to the stomach. He recommended immediate euthanasia.

We refused, deciding to try a liquid diet. We'd try to keep her going till we got back home, so that she could die at Spring Farm, where she belonged.

For a few days she managed to swallow the gruels that we concocted for her. Then about an hour into Linda's presentation on that eighth morning I went to the Southwind to check on Max and found her hysterical. There was no mistaking the desperation in her eyes.

"Help me, Bonnie. Help me go."

I summoned Dawn, and we drove to the vet. As I carried Max in, talking to her all the way, my eyes filled with tears. That would be the last time I would carry my beloved friend alive.

"He ain't heavy, Father. He's my brother."

The motto of Boys Town.

It had been that way with my sister Max for almost four years. She'd never been heavy.

And she helped me at the end. She laid on the table, ears perked, suddenly very calm, looking straight into my eyes as the vet gave her the injection.

"Thank you, Bonnie. Good-bye," I thought she said.

The vet carried her back out to the Southwind for us, wrapped in black plastic. It's amazing how heavy bodies become when life leaves them. He'd called ahead, and we drove fifty miles down the coast to a vet who had a crematorium. There we left our dear friend Max to be consumed by flames, poured into a cardboard box, and mailed home to Spring Farm.

The return trip was equally difficult. We stayed for a couple of days at Aunt Milly's, visiting with her family. When it came time to leave, oh, how very many things the three sisters remembered that they'd forgotten to tell each other, how slow they were in packing their duds. Finally no more excuses could be found. We boarded the Southwind, and I began backing out the driveway, Milly walking alongside, waving, everyone calling.

"Bye, kiddo."

"Toodleoo, Toots."

"Take care of yourself, kid."

"Be seeing you."

"Yeah. Be seeing you."

"Drive careful."

"Be seeing you."

I pulled away—very slowly. Because I could hardly see the road through my tears.

There was yet another tough farewell to face. At Aunt Mary's we stayed overnight. She made us breakfast the next morning—

she'd gotten up early specially and made muffins. Then we sat and visited, and she poured out her distress that she might soon have to enter a nursing home. She pressed all kinds of keepsakes onto us, and I asked her to play the piano. She'd been a pianist for silent pictures as a girl. Her style was rollicking and rambunctious. Now, for the last time, she played for us, and we all sang along.

But finally we had to get going.

"Bye, kiddo."

"Toodleoo, Toots."

"Drive careful."

"Be seeing you, kid."

A couple of months later she did enter a home, and soon her mind started to go. Yet she hung in there. She died five years later, at the age of one hundred.

Three years later, Milly went into a home, where she died at the age of ninety-seven.

As for Murengay and Minuet . . .

Two years after our workshop, Murengay was doing well enough under saddle to be sold. She was a successful endurance horse and, we're told, at this writing is still alive.

Little Minuet never did come around. The Rusts worked with her for years, but they were never able to really gain her confidence. She was given to friends and, at this writing, is living in Mexico as a pet.

Halali is no more. Sylvia died after years of illness. The property was sold. The remaining horses were given away or boarded with the buyers of the property or with friends, in perpetuity. The aged stallions are living with our informant, Paul Davis, who worked for the Rusts for twenty-three years. Sylvia's husband lives in retirement on Maui and still pays his horses' board.

Halali was a good place. All horses should have such caring and wonderfully "weird" owners.

Maybe it's something in the air around Willets. For Willets was also the home of Seabiscuit.

Give me a Willets "weirdo" any day.

Dawn was determined to forget that day at Halali, but fate wouldn't allow it. Neither would the specter of Penelope Smith depart. For just before Daddy died, yet a sixth horse had come into our lives.

Deeteza.

Through the overwhelming spiritual presence that was Deeteza, Dawn's talent as an animal communicator would be coaxed to full bloom.

To completely explain the wonder of Deeteza, I must go back to 1956, when, as a model in New York City, I was taken under the wings of the enormously wealthy Phil Rubin and his wife, Marcia.

Marcia had been a Ziegfeld girl, had been a pal of Lee and Ira Gershwin, had red hair and green cat eyes, an imperious manner, a laugh like a fishwife, and, according to Marcia, no one, not anyone in the world, knew more about everything than she.

Additionally, whatever Marcia owned was the absolute best that could possibly be had.

Marcia and Kazinka had much in common. They both reminded me of Bette Davis.

Phil got me an apartment in one of his rent-controlled buildings, while Marcia taught me that it was better to have one good dress than ten cheap dresses, that I must never wear jewelry unless it was real, that Louis Seize furniture judiciously purchased at auction was preferable to Early American reproductions from Macy's, and that playing poker all night long a couple of nights a week at the Rubin apartment was the proper way to entertain oneself.

She also taught me most of what I knew about riding. She and Phil were accomplished riders, showing often and taking home the blue. They maintained their horses at Stanley's stable on Long Island, and for a couple of years I rode with them almost every Saturday.

In keeping with Marcia's determination to own the best of everything, in the late 1960s she paid top dollar for an Arab stallion named Betez, grandson of Witez II, the Arab stallion chronicled in the classic *And Miles to Go*. Betez's sire was Nitez, a son of Witez II. According to Marcia, no Arab breeding in the world, *none*, could equal Witez II/Nitez breeding.

One morning, in April 1987, I got a call from a woman out in the Finger Lakes Region. She'd accepted and was caring for and helping to sell horses belonging to a breeder friend in Virginia who was going through a divorce. And the Finger Lakes lady was distraught.

"One of these mares is straight from Hell! Please buy her. If someone doesn't take her out of here, I'm liable to shoot her."

What salesmanship.

I didn't even know this lady. I can't even remember how she got my name. At that point I wasn't even vaguely known in the horse world.

Angels at work again, obviously.

"What's so hellish about this mare?" I asked.

"She's crazy! She demolished a stall when we tried to close her in, and she fights with the other horses. I've had to give her a pasture all to herself, and I need that pasture. The other little Arab who came with her has a very sweet temper, but this Deeteza is a witch. Black really suits her."

"Dee-*tez*-a. Arab. Black."

"You know Arab breeding? She's still got a few breeding years left. She's a Nitez daughter."

The Finger Lakes lady obviously thought the line had gone dead.

"Hello?"

"How much does your friend want for this black witch of a horse?"

"A thousand."

For a Nitez daughter? Even a witch of a Nitez daughter?

"You've got a deal. I'll be there tomorrow afternoon."

"There's only one little thing. You'll have to catch her. We haven't been able to catch her since we put her in that pasture."

Now, with hindsight, I know that Buckwheat started stuffing hay into his automatic waterer to get to Spring Farm, while Deeteza found her own ways of becoming *horsona non grata* in order to get here. Yet even then I knew that there's no such thing as coincidence. Something wonderful was happening.

Dawn was in Maine at the time. Not wanting to haul a horse alone just in case, I got Jackie to drive up with me. My first trailer had been a rickety wreck purchased from Charlotte, but I was now towing a slightly better secondhand trailer purchased from Jimmy Volo—low and dark, but sturdy.

The farm where Deeteza was being kept was perched on a hillside overlooking one of the Finger Lakes, enjoying marvelous views and refreshing breezes. Once I'd backed the trailer up to a paddock gate as directed and we'd prepared the trailer—all doors open, hay net in place, grain bucket handy—the lady pointed to a lone figure out in a pasture beyond the near paddock.

"That's her."

The horse was looking straight at us.

"Oh, hell," the lady sighed. "She's onto us. You'll never catch her."

"We'll see."

Carrying my secret weapon, a bunch of carrots, with the lead line curled in my right pants pocket and its snap ready to grasp, I ran a gauntlet of eight carrot thieves in the intervening paddock and climbed over the gate into the pasture. I walked in about thirty feet, sat down, and began eating a carrot.

Deeteza watched intently for a few moments, then ambled toward me.

I paid no attention.

She walked right up to me and reached for a carrot.

I turned my back, refusing to let her have one.

She pushed at me with her nose, demanding. Still I refused.

Her shoves became more demanding.

Finally, with great reluctance, I let her begin to nibble at the carrots on my lap. As she did so, I brought the snap of the lead up out of my pocket and clipped it onto the throatlatch ring of her halter.

She gave no resistance whatsoever. (Dawn and I were to discover how very unusual that was.) I stood up and fed her two more carrots, then led her through the gang of horses in the paddock to the waiting van.

She walked right on! It was all so easy, so perfect.

Then suddenly, before we could close the lower portions of the back doors, one of the refreshing breezes from off of the lake gusted. We'd neglected to latch the top portions of the double doors back against the sides of the trailer. The gust caught the top door on the right and slammed it shut with a terrible bang. Deeteza reared and hastily backed out of the trailer.

We tried for another hour. There was no getting her back on. She wasn't being nasty about it, she simply wouldn't get on.

The Finger Lakes lady was beside herself.

"*Now* what am I going to do? We can't put her back into the pasture. Believe me, you'd never get hold of her again."

"Put her in a stall overnight. I'll be back in the morning with a professional trucker."

"She's already destroyed one stall!"

"It's the only way. She'll be good. She wants to go home with me."

"She has a funny way of showing it. Though those carrots of

yours must be magic, she didn't want anything to do with ours."

True to my word, I was back the next morning with Jimmy Volo, pulling the light and bright, new, very expensive trailer that he'd wanted me to buy instead of the one that I did buy. It was a two-horse gooseneck with extra headroom—what's called "Thorough-bred" height. A feed area with pass-through doors in front of the stalls added to the spaciousness.

I'd be true to my word with Jimmy Volo as well.

"Get this horse loaded and home safely," I'd told him, "and I'll buy the trailer."

Of course, if I bought the trailer I'd also have to buy a truck. Vanessa couldn't pull a gooseneck; only "fifth-wheel" trucks can pull goosenecks.

The lady was pathetically glad to see us. As expected, Deeteza had remodeled her stall during the night.

"If this guy can't get her on," said the lady, "I won't answer for what I'll do to her."

It took even Jimmy half an hour and lots of patience. But finally, Deeteza, Arab princess, daughter of Nitez, granddaughter of the fabled Witez II, entered her magnificent new trailer and departed for Spring Farm.

That evening I called Marcia.

"I'm the proud possessor of a Nitez daughter," I told her.

She laughed.

"It can't be a Nitez daughter. A Nitez daughter would be *very* expensive, Bonnie."

"I've got her papers right here. Deeteza, by Nitez out of Hana."

A long silence. Then Marcia said . . .

"Oh. Hana. Yes, I know that breeding. I never did like it."

Good old Marcia.

Despite the put-down, Deeteza would one day be more famous than her daddy ever thought of being.

On top of which, the day that the nice Finger Lakes lady waved us off with Deeteza ranks right up there in importance with the day that Jackie gave me the gift of Dawn.

The first week with Deeteza was touch-and-go. Mostly go. We put her in a half-acre paddock that had a newly constructed run-in shed. (Observe how insidiously the farm was growing.) Then we tried to make nice.

Carrots had lost their charm. There was nothing left except woman-to-woman conversation.

Which was very one-sided. We talked hanging on the fence and talked as we put out food and water. We told her she was beautiful, related the history of the farm, told her about ourselves and the other horses, and I told her about Marcia's disdain for her mother, Hana.

The conversation wasn't truly one-sided, however. At first from the far side of the paddock, then inching closer, Deeteza listened. Sometimes she'd stand stalk still, staring at us. At other times she grazed, but with eyes glancing always toward us and those beautiful pointy Arab ears, of which we later learned she was so proud, flicking constantly toward our words.

Was it imagination, or did those ears go back flat against her head when I told her that Marcia considered her mother's breeding to be inferior?

Meanwhile, I called Gail Nash, the breeder for whom the Finger Lakes lady had been keeping Deeteza. Gail was puzzled to learn of Deeteza's lack of sociability while at the Finger Lakes, but her dislike of stalls was understandable. At Gail's place in Virginia, Deeteza had lived outside, in a pasture and woods. Before that she'd been on a ranch in Texas. Stalls were thus horrors almost totally unknown to her. Gail related how Deeteza's Texas owners had bragged of a horse that you could pull in off the range, groom up, take to a show, and bring home the blue in Halter Class. And she told me of the many foals that Deeteza had had for her. One, named Fine Print, was currently making a name for herself as an endurance horse.

Gail had hated selling Deeteza, but her situation demanded it. And at twenty-one, Deeteza was near the end of serviceability for breeding. She'd soon be "useless" to a breeder.

Armed with a better understanding of our beautiful horse—who wasn't a true black but such a deep mahogany bay that she might just as well have been—we kept talking to her.

Then one day she was just simply there, no problems, no excuses, coming to us to be fed, allowing herself to be touched and finally led down to the stable to meet the other horses—where she calmly accepted one of the stalls as her own. The largest stall, of course.

Kazinka and Tina uttered not so much as a squeal when we led her in.

A Master Teacher, a wise and ancient spirit assuming the form of an Arab mare, had come to Spring Farm. Respect from the other horses was automatic. And as for us . . .

When the student is ready, the teacher will appear. Though she didn't know it, Dawn was ready. Deeteza had appeared.

The lessons would come thick and fast.

6

Dressage Disasters
and Talking to Four Bales

Before getting on with anything to do with Deeteza, I must tell you about another horse who'd sort of, but not quite yet, arrived at Spring Farm.

As you'll recall, at the beginning, all I'd wanted was a horse I could *ride*. I didn't think that was asking for much.

Unfortunately, once Marcia Rubin learned that I was riding again, she convinced me that dressage was the only acceptable riding discipline to pursue.

Dressage is upscale and highly demanding, mentally and physically, for both rider and horse. Think the Lipizzaner Stallions. Teachers focused entirely on dressage aren't easy to find here in the "boondocks." While searching for such a teacher I worked with Arlene Kennerknecht, a local instructor, brushing up on basic horsemanship and learning some low-level jumping. I finally located a dressage specialist at Spindletop, an hour away, and began driving there twice a week.

One morning I trucked Tina down to be evaluated by my teachers, Sally and Veronica, hoping that Tina would be suitable for dressage. Instead they discovered why she tripped so frequently when I rode her. She had problems involving the front right shoulder and the left rear stifle.

"She's certainly not the sound athlete you need for dressage," said Sally. "Actually, with that stumble, she's not safe to be ridden at all."

"Jeez! Do I have to buy *another* horse now?"

"If you're serious about dressage, I'm afraid you do."

One day Veronica called with excellent news. There was a good dressage horse for sale.

"A Thoroughbred. Country Matters. We've gone up against her often in shows. She usually wins. And they're not even asking that much for her."

I went to visit Country Matters at a small stable near Syracuse where she was kept. She was on cross ties when I came in, mahogany bay and pretty.

"We call her Lefty," her young owner told me. "Because of the white on her left fetlock."

I made an immediate mental note to call her Lady. Lefty wasn't fine enough.

"Why are you selling her?"

"We're moving to Texas. She's allergic to alfalfa, and that's the only kind of hay they have down there."

We were later to discover that Lady was allergic, violently so, to many things, including vaccinations.

The girl showed me an impressive list of Lady's wins and of course praised her to the skies, as had Veronica and Sally.

"How is she at trail riding?" I asked.

"Oh . . . okay. The last time we went out, she went runaway and brought me back to the barn real fast, but that's the only time that ever happened."

Did my "danger" antenna go up? Of course not.

"Do you want to ride her?" asked the girl.

"I'm not sure that I should without my teachers. I'm only beginning dressage."

"I'll put you on a lunge line."

She saddled Lady and led her out to an exercise paddock about sixty feet square. I mounted and the girl backed off to the center with the lunge line.

I asked Lady for a walk.

Smart and purposeful. I hardly had to ask her to collect.

I asked for a sitting trot.

Nice.

A posting trot.

Nicer.

"Try her canter," said the girl.

I gave Lady the canter depart.

She took one stride of canter and went runaway.

In a sixty-by-sixty-foot paddock I was suddenly aboard a horse traveling at full gallop. She'd never be able to cut the corners, we'd crash through the fence. We went nearly horizontal to the ground cutting the first corner, and the second, and the third. I crouched over her neck like a jockey, trying to become one with her balance. But I was going to die. This horse was going to kill me.

We made almost two circuits of the paddock before the gallop slackened. With all her strength the girl was pulling Lady inward, forcing her to slow.

At last Lady came to a halt.

The girl's face was as white as mine must have been.

"She's never done anything like that before," she said.

I should have said, "Didn't you say she went runaway on your last trail ride?"

But I didn't. Instead I said, "I must have given her a bad canter depart. I'm just not good enough for her yet."

So did I climb down and politely excuse myself from purchasing the horse?

Of course not. I bought her. Pending a soundness examination, of course.

The vet came out and listened to her heart, lifted each of her legs and moved them about in various ways, checked her hooves, watched her move, and marked her sound.

This is the routine exam given by all vets. We've come to realize that a vet exam should evaluate the entire horse, not just its legs and feet. The horse should be evaluated under saddle and at all gaits. For it's with the unnaturalness of a rider on its back, with an often ill-fitting saddle, that any problems the horse might have—of pain, temperament, spine, balance, or lameness—will become apparent.

But my teachers had said the horse was wonderful, the owner said the horse was wonderful, and the vet said the horse was sound. I made an appointment to trailer her home.

Again, red flags should have started waving when I arrived with Jimmy Volo to truck Lady. (I was in transition between my first wreck of a trailer and the medium-worthy trailer that later flapped its door and terrified Deeteza.) The girl was waiting for us, with her mother.

"Let us load her," said the mother smoothly. "We know how to do it. She trusts us."

It took about twenty-five minutes, but they finally got her onto the trailer.

I was puzzled. This was a show horse, used to being moved around frequently. Hard to believe that she was this reluctant a loader.

"She had a trailering accident before I bought her," the girl explained. "The trailer rolled over with her in it."

Ah. That explained it.

"You just have to be patient with her."

Thank goodness that during those insane years of my life no one approached me waving a deed for the Brooklyn Bridge.

Lady didn't go to Spring Farm. Instead I took her to White Fox Farm, only about a mile from Spring Farm as the crow flies, three miles by road. There in its huge indoor arena I could ride in comfort and safety and take lessons in basic horsemanship with the owner, Jeanne Raposa, an excellent rider and mother of David Raposa, an up-and-coming hotshot on the show-jumping circuit.

Lady never ran away with me again. Instead, each time I asked for the canter she tried to throw me. I felt considerably less stupid when Jeanne mounted, asked for the canter, and nearly got tossed herself. She tried again, and again. Same result.

"Well, it's certainly nothing that *you're* doing, Bonnie. This horse has a problem."

Interesting, though, that no expert could tell me what the problem was.

I also discovered, when I tried to trailer Lady without the aid of her former owner or Jimmy Volo, that she was untrailerable. I wanted to take her to Spindletop for a day, so that Veronica and Sally could figure out what was happening with her canter. I, and the boy who was helping me, gave up when Lady began rearing and kicking—*really* kicking, literally trying to kill us.

What the hell had I bought here?

I phoned the girl who'd sold her to me. She had her money now and didn't need to make excuses. She told me to get a very long rope, attach it to Lady's halter, and, with several people manning that rope, thread it through the trailer and out a forward escape hatch, and pull Lady into the trailer with brute force.

Huh?

Veronica and Sally were stunned when I told them of Lady's behavior. Yet when we really analyzed her list of wins, it became obvious that she'd almost always been shown at the same large riding establishment in Syracuse, where she'd been stabled for years. She'd seldom been trailered.

It was also obvious that she hadn't been ridden in shows for months before I bought her. During which time she'd been moved to the small barn where I met her.

Something had happened to her—or something had changed. She hadn't been sold because of alfalfa.

At this point Dawn and I could write a manual on "How to Buy—or Not Buy—a Horse." Sadly, most people selling a problem horse hope against hope that all will go well for it. Even sadder is the fact that most horse owners haven't the foggiest idea about why their horse acts up in the first place or how to fix its problems.

From out of my early, gullible, starry-eyed fog came a real understanding of horses that has benefited a lot more than just those who've lived here at Spring Farm. The prime ingredient in that understanding has been the wisdom gained through Dawn's talent. It's been a learning experience that neither of us would trade for all the rideable horses in the world.

I kept Lady at White Fox for a year, riding her almost every day at first, hoping she'd come around. I never asked for the canter, but the two of us became a well-oiled machine at the walk, sitting trot, and posting trot. Marcia would have been proud of our picture-perfect collect, our smooth halts, our impeccable ten- and twenty-meter circles.

And what a character Lady was. A clown whom Dawn and I came to love.

One night, when I hadn't had time to ride her during the day, Dawn and I drove over to give her turnout in the arena. They were having a show the next day, and multiple jumps had been erected, some banked with plastic greenery. Lady had a ball, dashing here and there, running figure eights around jumps. Dawn and I stood at the entrance to the arena, enjoying her antics.

Suddenly Lady rushed up to a jump banked with greenery. She seized one of the potted plants in her teeth and galloped straight at us. About ten feet before collision she put on all four brakes and skidded to a halt in our faces. With a shrill whinny amazingly like laughter, she dropped the plant at our feet, wheeled, and went galloping off, still laughing.

Instances such as that that caused us to begin entertaining the idea that one could have important and satisfactory relationships with horses which had nothing whatsoever to do with *using* them or riding them. That a rich life could result from regarding horses, and all animals, simply as friends with a right to . . . just live.

I rode Lady for the last time in January 1987. It was late. We were having a snowstorm, and everyone else had gone for the night, so that I was responsible for turning off lights and closing the barn. Lady and I had been having a creamy ride, just like silk. I suddenly felt so confident. For the first time in all those months, I asked for the canter.

It happened so quickly. All I knew was that I was suddenly on the ground ahead of her. I remember the pain. I remember sobbing uncontrollably. I remember Lady just standing there, allowing me to take hold of her bridle, to hang on her neck as I sobbed. I remember continuing to hang on her, allowing her nearly to carry me over to the door into the stable.

Then I remember nothing till I awoke in my bed at one in the morning. I was in excruciating pain. I could barely move. Slowly memory returned. Lady had thrown me. How had I gotten home? Lord, had I untacked her? Turned off the lights? Had I even put her back into her stall?

Crying out with pain, I got myself out of bed, put on some clothes, and went out into the night. The storm was worse. Carefully, still dazed, I drove to White Fox. I turned my lights off before pulling in, not wanting to wake Jeanne and her family.

All was well in the barn. The lights were off. I'd cared for my horse properly and put my tack away. I'd even given her fresh water and hay.

I never rode her again. There'd been the wild ride that first day. Now the dirt on my helmet showed that I'd hit headfirst. Had I not been wearing that helmet . . . well, twice was enough.

But how to get her home?

Would I try again to get her onto a trailer? Just me and a couple of suicidal helpers? Not on your life.

Maybe I could lead her home through the woods. Not much more than a mile.

I envisioned the trek and all the things that could go wrong traversing rough terrain. Uh-uh.

Lead her home over three miles of road with cars speeding by? Uh-uh again.

But I couldn't keep paying board at White Fox forever.

I called Jimmy Volo, told him my sad story, warned him of the danger. He didn't seem worried. He and a male friend arrived and loaded her. It wasn't easy, even for them. Actually, it was pretty violent. Not that Jimmy and his friend abused Lady. *Au contraire.* But somehow they got her on without getting themselves killed. And Lady came home to Spring Farm.

Two years later we found out why she couldn't tolerate the canter—or the trailer. We were presenting a clinic featuring Tony Gonzales, a farrier with revolutionary concepts involving the soundness of horses and their shoeing that take the whole horse into consideration.

We brought Lady out for Tony's evaluation and told him her history. Smiling, he reached up and felt along her withers, just in front of where the saddle would end if she were saddled.

He motioned to Dawn and to me.

"Feel this."

We reached up and felt a long, solid chunk there in the withers.

"Those are vertebrae riddled with arthritis and calcification.

What you're feeling is damage from that trailering accident the girl told you about. My guess is that Lady went along well for a few years—maybe the pain and arthritis hadn't gotten bad enough—or maybe she loved that girl enough to perform even though she was in pain. But it was finally too much. See, every time that a rider shifts her weight forward in the saddle for the canter, the saddle shifts forward, too, ever so much. In Lady's case it was just enough to touch a spot that blinded her with pain and turned her violent. You experienced the results of that violence, Bonnie. Twice. You're lucky to be alive."

He went to Lady's head and kissed her soft muzzle.

"This lady has earned retirement. Don't ride her, ever again. And don't ever again ask her to board a trailer."

With Lady's arrival at Spring Farm we had two lead mares. That was okay; we'd divided the pasture into two sections. Deeteza led the horses in the smaller section, while Lady became the leader in what we began to call the Thoroughbred Pasture.

. . . because there were suddenly more Thoroughbreds to lead than just Puddy.

As it happened, while Lady was boarded at White Fox I fell in love with yet another horse, a Thoroughbred stabled there, Lamoka Bo.

She was huge, about seventeen hands, a gentle, not-too-smart giant purchased by David Raposa as a possible world-class jumper—they like them big on the jumping circuit. But Bo couldn't cut the mustard, so she was up for sale.

I couldn't stop thinking about Bo after bringing Lady home. I talked with Jeanne about possibly buying her and went over to take a test drive.

Climbing up onto Bo was like climbing Everest. Once up it was akin to riding the bowsprit of the *Titanic*.

"I'm flying!"

Since I was still looking for a dressage horse, Veronica and Sally come up to look at her.

They were impressed. At first. But then, as the handler was leading Bo away from us, we all saw it. Even I, a neophyte, saw it. Bo had weak back "ankles." Her fetlocks buckled outward as she walked. With those weak ankles, without the solid support needed as she took off for a jump, she didn't have a prayer as a world-class jumper—or any kind of jumper.

David must have been tossing dice when he bought her, betting on her sire, American History, a Thoroughbred stallion who'd sired some excellent jumpers.

Naturally, Veronica and Sally advised me not to buy Bo, considering her unfit even for the rigors of dressage. Just as naturally, I bargained with Jeanne and bought her anyway. Bo had no future except, eventually, in light of her size and the price of horsemeat, a ride to the slaughterhouse. I couldn't let that happen.

Once I got her home I called Al Berlieu, the owner of Lamoka Stables, who'd sold Bo to David.

"Bo's the sweetest horse I ever had," he told me. "I bred her. Raised her up. God, I'm glad she's found a home with someone like you. David begged me not to race her, but I did, just once. I had to be sure. I didn't think there was any danger. I was right. She couldn't run *fast* enough to hurt herself."

With those ankles, no wonder.

But there was more to Bo than just Bo.

"Hey, how'd you like to have her mother as well? Four Bales. War Admiral breeding. Eighty-four starts, a lot of finishes in the money. She's had about twelve foals. I'll give her to you. She's just as big and sweet as Bo. She's twenty-one, but she might have one more breeding left in her. Come on. How about it?"

He was actually pleading with me. I realized then how much he cared. But he was a businessman. Four Bales had become "useless," a financial burden. He couldn't bear the thought of meating her, but financial wisdom said that he should.

Before I knew it, I'd agreed to take her.

And here I must confess to a crime. That of ignorance.

On second thought, ignorance isn't a crime. Ignorance is merely the lack of proper knowledge regarding a particular situation. Ignorance isn't stupidity. Stupidity occurs only when one has been given the proper knowledge regarding a particular situation but then fails to adjust one's behavior as a result.

Proper knowledge, however, can take a long time to sink in. While it's being sopped up, one can act very stupidly.

In those first years I accepted the belief that horses have to have some use in order to justify their existence. The use of mares, aside from being raced, ridden, driven, or shown, is to have foals. What those foals are "for," what their future use is to be, is often ill perceived. I'd begun dimly to understand the abuse heaped on many horses by our society and to contemplate the callousness and lack of sensitivity so often accorded these beautiful creatures. But I'd not yet really "gotten" it.

Dawn was light-years ahead of me. Because, though she hadn't yet admitted it when Four Bales came to us, she had been getting it, "straight from the horse's mouth," all her life. Not only could she hear an animal's cries for help, she experienced its pain, understood its point of view. Quietly, gently, in situation after situation with an animal, she'd make certain remarks. I'd suddenly know that she was right, and I'd hang my head in shame.

People such as I hear with ears and see with eyes. Dawn both hears and sees with her heart, hearing things that no ears can physically hear, seeing what no eyes can physically see. That's meant literally. And just as it would be nice if every racehorse had Al Berlieu for an owner, it would be nice if everybody had a Dawn in their lives, to bring them more quickly to compassion and sensitivity.

I'm ashamed to say that before Four Bales came to Spring Farm, I allowed her to be sent to Graywood, a Thoroughbred breeding establishment, to be bred yet again to Bo's father, American History. Dawn and I drove up to meet her the day that she was bred.

She was almost as big as Bo—sixteen and a half hands. Before her twelve foals, she'd probably matched Bo's seventeen hands. And yes, she was just as sweet-tempered.

She remained at Graywood for fourteen days after the breeding, the length of time necessary before a sonogram can detect a viable fetus baking in the oven.

The news, when Gail Gray called, was negative.

"It didn't take. Should we try again?"

Dawn was listening on an extension. Her eyes clouded. When she looked at me, I had my answer.

"No. I declare Four Bales permanently retired. We'll pick her up this afternoon."

Gail Gray is an Al Berlieu kind of breeder. She's a sharp businesswoman, but she cares. I heard the relief in her voice.

"It's for the best, Bonnie. That old gal's done more than her bit."

The reunion between Bo and her mother that evening was an eye-opener. Never listen, not for a second, to those who say that animals have no souls, minds, emotions. If Bo and Four Bales had had human bodies, they would have been able to hug, kiss, and sob for joy less awkwardly. They did a pretty good job of it anyway.

There's always a reason for everything. One has only to decide what that reason is. To see the elation of those reunited mares, to understand more profoundly the depth of love that can exist between horses, seemed an excellent reason for the addition of Four Bales to our herd.

An even greater reason was soon apparent.

One morning about a month later, Dawn arrived for work in a truculent mood.

"What's the matter?" I asked.

"I had a stupid dream last night."

"What did you dream?"

Dawn grumbled to herself for a moment then said, "It was just a voice. It kept saying, 'Go talk to Four Bales.'"

I shrugged. "So go talk to Four Bales."

Dawn exploded. "What the hell am I supposed to say to her?"

"Wing it. Go talk to Four Bales."

Dawn stared at me for a moment, then, still grumbling to herself, set off up the hill to the shed and paddock where we were keeping Bo and Four Bales. Five minutes later she was back.

"Well?" I asked. "What did she say?"

"This is stupid. Really stupid."

"*That's* what she said?"

"No! That's what *I* say."

"Well what did *Four Bales* say?" Egad, pulling teeth would be easier.

"She says that she's pregnant and we should feed her more hay and grain."

"She can't be pregnant, she's been sonogrammed. Go tell her that she's only imagining that she's pregnant."

"I'm supposed to go up there and tell a horse that she's only imagining that she's pregnant?"

"Yes."

Dawn threw up her hands and departed yet again. Five minutes later she was back.

"What did she say?"

"She still insists that she's pregnant and that she needs more grain and hay."

Was it possible? Dawn didn't yet believe in her abilities, but I did.

It so happened that one of our vets, Fritz Koenneke from Cazenovia Animal Hospital, or "Caz" as we call it, was coming that afternoon to do some dental work. I waited until he'd finished, then said, "Dr. Koenneke, Dawn had a strange dream last night."

Dawn's head jerked up. Her face turned beet red. Don't you dare tell him! her eyes warned.

But fools rush in, and I can be the biggest blabbermouth in town when it suits me.

"Her dream told her to go talk to Four Bales. She did. Four Bales says she's pregnant and needs more to eat."

Until that moment we'd never said a word to Dr. Koenneke about animal communication. But his eyes began to twinkle, and his response was one of the reasons that we came to love the man.

"She's in her twenties, as I recall. You had the sonogram at fourteen days?"

"Yes."

His eyes were positively dancing with mischief now.

"I'd like to check her. No charge."

So up the hill to the shed we went, Dawn trailing behind, fuming.

Four Bales came to us, seeming eager for the exam. I held her head. Dawn hung around outside the door of the shed, I couldn't even see where she was. Dr. Koenneke put on a long glove and reached in to check the uterus.

Silence. Punctuated by "Hmm." "Ah." "Oh?"

Then he began to laugh.

"This is one smart horse. She's got a very nice pregnancy going here."

"She *can't* have!" cried Dawn, appearing in the doorway. "The sonogram!"

"I've seen this before," said Fritz. "Sometimes an older mare's pregnancy doesn't show on a sonogram at fourteen days. Well, old girl"—he stripped off his glove and patted Four Bales's rump—"you'll be getting those extra rations now."

He never said a word about Dawn's dream or her supposed conversation with Four Bales. He just kept grinning all the way back to his van. He was still grinning as he drove away.

Dawn wasn't grinning. "You shouldn't have done that! You shouldn't have told a vet!"

"Why not?"

"He must think I'm a kook. Vets don't believe in these things."

"Who says? And how else were we going to know whether we *should* be feeding her more?"

I called Gail Gray, assuming that we now owed the breeding fee.

"Let's wait and see," said Gail. "If you get a live foal, I'll be glad to take your money."

Dr. Koenneke checked Four Bales again a month later. Her system had reabsorbed the fetus.

Blessed little soul, you who enlivened that fetus just long enough to make us aware of its existence. Thank you. You made it increasingly difficult for Dawn to deny her talent.

Yet deny it she still did.

Dawn does this thing that I call "digging in her heels." She gets this look on her face. This here-I'm-staying-for-the-rest-of-my-life-and-I'll-destroy-anyone-who-tries-to-move-me look. One senses her entire body turning to lead, sees her heels dig deep into whatever she's standing on. The definite impression is that not even a bulldozer could budge her.

And she's such a *little* girl!

It remained for Deeteza—the Great Voice, as the other animals began to call her—to work patient, persistent alchemy and transmute the lead to gold.

7

The Great Voice and
the Philosopher and Architect

A few days before we set off for California, we'd trucked Deeteza to a horse farm near Syracuse, to be bred while we were gone to an Arab stallion named Raffons Tomesyn. "Tommy" was a champion in the show ring, had the temperament of a pussycat, and excellent breeding—a worthy match for our Deeteza. Again I was thinking automatically, which is not to think at all. Mares were to be used, bred. It took several more years before I realized how very wrong that thinking is, during which time many of the mares at Spring Farm were bred.

In Deeteza's case one could say there was good reason. Deeteza was a rare chalice, carrying what in Arab circles amounted to royal blood. With time marching on, there weren't many Witez II-by-Nitez granddaughters left alive. The great Arab stallion Raffles was also in her pedigree. Those lines "should" be continued. Or so the thinking went.

The first day home from California, we called the farm for a report on Dee's sonogram. We had a healthy fetus! The next morning, we went to fetch her. She'd put up only a modicum of fuss when we'd taken her there. Patience was all that had been needed. It should have been the same coming home. Instead we had a catastrophe.

I paid the woman who ran that boarding establishment, and she directed us to the shed where Deeteza was living in a large pipe corral stall. We tiptoed in, eager for the sight of her, wondering if she'd remember us. She'd been with us for only a couple of months before we'd brought her here. Now we'd been separated for more than three weeks.

She remembered and whinnied a glad hello.

Then she thought better of it. She turned and stomped to the back of her stall.

"Oh-oh. She's mad at us. Deeteza," I wheedled, "we got back only yesterday and now we're here to take you home. Spring Farm. It's home for life, Deeteza."

She swung her head and looked at me. Then she walked back to us. We reached up to stroke her. She beat us to it. Twitching her top lip like Samantha's nose twitched in *Bewitched*, she covered our hands with the velvet-lipped "twitchy-twitchys" that would become her trademark.

"All's forgiven," said Dawn with a laugh. And we led her out to the waiting trailer.

It was the new trailer, Thoroughbred height, wider than most, with lots of windows. Claustrophobia was further banished by the fact that the wall between the trailer proper and the tack room and bunk space up in the gooseneck was only about six feet high. To the horses, that airspace seemed a continuation of their own. There was a centerboard, which kept horses from swaying into each other's space, plus well-padded breast and butt bars, which gave horses something to brace against in front and in back and which also kept them from moving forward into the walk-through or from backing out while the back ramp was being raised or lowered.

A coach fit for a royal princess.

We commenced our patient attempts to walk her on, now employing techniques learned at Halali. The proprietor stood watching. A girl who was bathing a horse over beside the barn watched also. That horse was not cooperating, and I noticed that she handled it roughly.

I should have paid better attention to that fact.

The lady proprietor was patient for only a few minutes; then she began to offer advice. Before we knew it, she and the girl had taken over the loading.

We should have said thanks but no thanks. Frankly, though, we were intimidated. These were "real" horse people, in the business for years. Surely they knew more about loading than we.

"Go get another horse," the woman told the girl.

The girl disappeared into the barn.

"This should do it," the woman told us. "They usually go right on when they see another horse walk on."

The girl came out leading another horse, which walked on with no fuss, into the space on the right.

"Come on, mare," said the woman, giving Deeteza a whack.

Deeteza wouldn't budge.

"Get the fly spray," the woman told the girl.

Dawn and I exchanged glances. Why did she want fly spray?

We found out all too soon. The girl returned with the aerosol can, handed it to the woman, and took Deeteza's lead. Before we knew what was happening, the woman was spraying Deeteza unmercifully from behind and the girl was yanking on the lead and shouting at her. Shocked and terrified, Deeteza ran up into the space on the left.

Rapidly the lady got the butt bar into place as the girl tied Dee's lead rope to the breast bar and backed the other horse off of the trailer. Dazed, I walked up into the vacated stall, meaning to go to Deeteza's head and comfort her.

"See?" the woman was saying as they raised and locked the ramp. "You've just got to be firm with them."

Then all hell broke loose. Deeteza had been standing stock still. Suddenly she came out of her shock and reared. The lead rope— which the girl had tied to the breast bar instead of snapping the side tie to Deeteza's halter—went taut. As she felt that restraint under her chin, Deeteza went ballistic.

This was the first indication we had that one should never, ever put downward pressure on a rope under Dee's chin. Wham! She'd go straight up and almost over backward.

Now she reared again and again, out of her mind, fighting the restraint. It's all a blur. But at one point she tried to get her front legs up over the center divider to climb into the stall with me. As on the back of runaway Lady, I was sure I'd be killed, for the back ramp was up and I couldn't escape that way. Then Deeteza was trying to climb over the breast bar; I couldn't even go forward in safety. The metal interior was a place of clanging horror as Deeteza's hooves lashed in every direction.

Then she collapsed onto the breast bar.

Everything went silent.

The back ramp came down. The woman, the girl, and a horrified Dawn stood staring up into Deeteza's stall. Equally horrified, I peered over the center divider.

Dee's back legs were under the breast bar, in the walk-through. She was curled around the bar, on her chest, head hanging down into the walk-through, looking more like a helpless kitten than a horse.

"My God," I said. "I think she's dead."

"Get her untied!" cried Dawn.

I can't remember who did what. Someone got the centerboard swung back into the stall where I'd been standing to give Dee more room while someone else started sawing at the tautened lead with a knife. I just remember crouching in front of her, trying to hold her head up.

"*Is* she dead?" someone asked.

"She's still breathing," said someone else.

"She must have fainted."

But surely our precious horse had grievous injuries. Surely she'd been destroyed.

As the knife sawed through the last of the rope, Deeteza came to. She threw up her head and, to everyone's further horror, did a complete backward somersault, out of the stall, down the ramp, and onto the ground, where she landed splayed out, her front legs straight out in front of her, her back legs straight out behind.

Somehow she struggled to her feet and started to run.

"*Deeteza!*" Dawn shouted.

Miraculously Dee stopped, turned, looked at Dawn, and went to her. She buried her forehead against Dawn's breast, hyperventilating and trembling violently. Dawn put her arms around that poor head, lowered her face into Deeteza's mane, and began to take slow, deep breaths. Little by little Deeteza's hyperventilation slowed until she was breathing in rhythm with Dawn.

In the meantime I was still standing in the trailer, watching them and being harangued by the two "experts."

"Make her get right back on. You can't let a horse get the better of you."

"You have to show a horse who's boss. Get her right back in there."

"You can't let her win, or you'll never get her into a trailer again."

Win? What a strange word to use after what had just happened. Their actions might have killed Deeteza. We still didn't know but what she was injured.

Win?

I kept watching Dawn and Deeteza, conjoined, like a statue except for Dee's shaking. Finally Dawn lifted her head. She looked at me for a long moment. Then she shook her head ever so slightly.

At that moment Dawn crossed her Rubicon. I knew that she was talking to Deeteza and she knew that I knew she was talking to Deeteza. Between us two there would never again be any foolish hiding. And the bond that was forged between Dawn and Deeteza in those moments was eternal.

"Dawn says not to put her back on," I told the women. "I trust her judgment."

They turned and looked at Dawn as at some worm.

"You'll never get that horse onto a trailer again," said the woman.

"Yes, we will," I said. "But we'll do it our way."

We led Deeteza gently back to her stall.

"What did she say to you?" I asked.

"She just kept saying, 'Please don't make me get back on.'"

"Oh God, Deeteza, we're so sorry."

Deeteza reached over and gave me a twitchy-twitchy.

We laughed. What a relief to laugh.

"I take it you're feeling better," I told Dee. "Want some TTouch? It's even better than massage."

Twitchy-twitchy.

We stayed with her for a couple of hours, soothing her with bodywork and checking her over. It was hard to believe that she'd come through without injury.

Of course she hadn't. Several weeks later a sonogram revealed that she was no longer pregnant. The vet agreed that the trauma of the loading had caused the loss. Those two women hadn't killed Deeteza. Only her baby.

Writing this sixteen years later, anger floods my heart. Then the anger fades as I realize how seminal that episode was and how much we learned from it.

For one thing, we learned to trust ourselves, not "horse people." We learned that having been in the horse business for years doesn't make one an expert—nor wise, nor kind, nor does it necessarily bestow sound judgment. From that point on, we'd stick with TT.E.A.M. and our own judgment. Did we need horse experts, we'd met them. And they were us. Our horses would be handled by expertise as we understood it, not by the standards of the "horse world."

God sends us nothing but angels. Those women were two of the most important angels we ever met.

Driving home, we made our plans. We'd make the three-hour round trip to that farm every day. We'd school Dee in TT.E.A.M. groundwork, not even going near the trailer for a week. Then we'd get to trailering lessons. It might take weeks. But when Deeteza got onto that trailer again, she'd walk on of her own accord.

We got advice for those trailering lessons from an unexpected source. For, once home, Dawn said . . .

"We need to call Penelope Smith."

. . . and the walls come tumblin' down.

It was all very easy. It wouldn't be as easy nowadays, Penelope is no longer that accessible, but back then Dawn just dialed her number, Penelope answered, they talked, and afterward we sent Penelope twenty dollars for the consultation.

Dawn was in a frenzy after that call.

"Bonnie, it's all true. I'd already gotten most of it myself, but I didn't trust it. I didn't trust myself." She was walking in circles, gabbling, not always articulately. "Oh, Penelope had her. She had Deeteza. 'She's a princess,' she said. 'You have to treat her as such.' Isn't that just Deeteza? She's told me that a hundred times. 'I'm a princess. I must be treated accordingly.' She even got that Dee's vain about her ears. 'Have you noticed how beautiful my ears are?' Dee keeps asking. And her mane. 'You must never cut my wonderful mane,' she tells me. She told Penelope the same things! Bonnie, all that Penelope asked me was Deeteza's name, breed, and sex. That's all she had to go on. And she *knew* the horse. She had her on the line! It's real. This stuff is real!"

Then the trailering tips.

"You mustn't treat this horse like 'a horse,'" Penelope had told Dawn. "She's *extremely* intelligent, a very special soul. But she doesn't understand the trailer. She gets on, the thing goes, and she doesn't know how, and she doesn't know where you are, and it frightens her. You need to show her how things work. Show her the truck, show her where you sit, show her everything. Then she won't be frightened."

For more than a week, beneath the jaundiced eyes of the proprietor and the girl, we did TT.E.A.M. groundwork with Dee. They thought us fools.

Let them. We had to shrug off what others thought and said about us and move forward in our own private vision.

After the first week, we started leading Dee over to the trailer at the end of each lesson, not asking anything of her, just walking her around the rig, then back to her stall.

Finally one day we began trailering lessons in earnest. We'd found a spot over near the barn where the rig was out of the way. The back ramp was down, and we'd removed the centerboard, turning the trailer into a roomy box stall, invitingly bedded with fresh straw.

For we'd done research and discovered that, given their druthers, horses prefer being trailered loose in a box stall and that they then ride backward, on a diagonal.

First we led Deeteza up to the truck. It was a fifth-wheeler—that is, it had no box on the back, only a large metal ball that received the connector of the trailer's gooseneck. We'd named the truck

Tiger Lil. She was red, with a red velvet, red leather, and wood interior, plus all sorts of special amenities. Another Jimmy Volo special, she'd been his own truck, outfitted for his comfort on long hauling jobs.

The window was open on the driver's side, and we led Deeteza to it.

"Okay, Dee," Dawn began. "This is where Bonnie sits. She uses this wheel to make the truck and trailer go where she wants them to go. Down on the floor . . . see those things sticking up? They're called pedals. One pedal makes the truck go forward, and another makes it stop when Bonnie wants it to stop. And here beside the wheel, these gizmos make it so that Bonnie can see where she's going in the dark or the rain."

Dee stuck her head in through the open window. She touched her nose to the seat, touched the steering wheel, and looked around the cab.

"Usually," said Dawn, "I sit there on the other side."

We then showed her the tires on the truck and explained how they worked. Then we showed her the hitch, explaining how it safely attached the trailer to the truck and made the trailer do everything that the truck did. She was especially interested in that. We drew her attention to the doubled tires on the trailer and explained the electrical system. We opened the door to the tack room and bunk area and showed her what that was all for.

Then we arrived at the back. We told her how the ramp works and pointed out its sturdiness and nonslip attributes. We explained why we'd removed the centerboard and extolled the virtues of the box stall that she would enjoy on the ride home.

Then we snapped a fourteen-foot lead rope onto her halter, went into the trailer, scattering grain on the floor just beyond the ramp, made ourselves comfortable in the straw up near the front, and commenced chatting about this and that, ignoring her.

She grazed for a while, her hooves sometimes bumping against the ramp. A couple of times she tentatively put a foot onto the ramp. Finally she stepped up onto the edge with both front feet. And off again. And on again. With each try she edged farther up the ramp, stretching her neck toward the grain, but with her back feet still on the ground. We continued our conversation, oblivious.

She knew what we were up to, and we knew that she knew, and she knew that we knew, for communication between Dawn and Deeteza was now firmly established. She knew we were letting her do it at her own speed.

Finally she was standing with her front feet just inside the trailer and back feet on the ramp.

"Want some more grain?" said Dawn nonchalantly. She put the pan of grain down on the straw, out of Dee's reach. Dee backed away down the ramp but came right back up, reaching for the grain.

At that moment a little head peeked up over the side of the ramp.

"Hi!" we both heard.

A yellow-and-white, long-haired kitten, about ten weeks old, scrambled onto the ramp and came bounding through the straw, purring a mighty purr.

Dee forgot the grain and stared at the kitten.

And suddenly Dawn was talking to Dee out loud.

"I don't know if we can, Dee."

"What? What's she saying?"

"She wants the kitten for her own. She wants it to come home with her."

"Lord, what a purr!" I laughed as the kitten climbed up my chest and kissed my face. "Well—we *could* use a cat in the stable. I'll see if the people here will let her go, Dee. Are you female, honey? Yes, you are. Girls are the best mousers."

Suddenly the kitten jumped off of my chest and went bounding back through the straw, out of the trailer.

Dawn laughed. "She says she wants us to meet her friends."

Soon the kitten was back. Gamboling along behind her were two younger kittens. One was long-haired, bright orange, the second was short-haired, black tiger with white. They struggled through the straw as far as the grain dish, climbed into it, and commenced to play a tumbling game. Dee came fully into the trailer, reached down, and gave them each a twitchy-twitchy.

"We're being ganged up on," said Dawn. "Dee and Princess Purr say we need to take these two as well."

"You've named her already?"

"I suggested it, and she likes it. She says we can call her Prinnie."

Well—a princess for a princess. And the proprietor was delighted to be rid of some of their many kittens.

Deeteza was all for leaving immediately. We said no. We hadn't planned to take her that day anyway.

"But why?" asked Deeteza.

"Because we'll have our hands full with the kittens," Dawn told her. "We'll get them home today and be back for you in the morning."

It was a most reluctant mare who was returned to her stall.

"Let her stew," I muttered as we walked away. "She'll be that much more willing in the morning."

Prinnie rode home in Dawn's lap. The younger two sat on my lap, playing with the steering wheel.

"What shall we name them?" said Dawn.

At which point they told me.

"The orange one says she's Sonya Pia. The other says he's Captain Zero."

That communication had to be real. *I* would never have come up with such outlandish names.

*   *   *

|

We were back bright and early the next morning. Dawn got Dee while I paid the proprietor for the extra board.

Then Dawn led Dee up into her box stall. I closed the ramp and the top doors; Dawn left through a walk-through door and got into the tack room and up onto the bunk, where she could see Deeteza and Deeteza could see her; I got into the cab, started the truck, casually waved to the girl and the watching proprietor, and we were off.

And yes, it's illegal for people to ride in a horse trailer, but what's legal and what people sometimes do are two different things.

Dawn had a flashlight with which to signal me out the window in the front of the bunk if anything went wrong, but it wasn't needed. Deeteza remained totally calm, riding facing backward, on a diagonal.

It was Dawn who was the nervous wreck.

"The trailer lurches and sways so!" she said afterward. "I kept expecting it to flip. It's a wonder that *any* horse who's ridden on a trailer will get on again. I was terrified."

So their roles had been reversed during the ride.

"Dee kept looking back up at me and saying, 'Are you okay? You're *sure* you're okay?'"

There was a hairy moment that scared me as well. We were on I-90, the New York State Thruway. It's a four-lane toll road, the east- and west-bound lanes divided by a wide green strip. I was in the inner, passing, lane, sandwiched in between other vehicles that were also passing a long line of slow-moving vehicles in the outer lane. In other words, there was no place for any of us to go except straight ahead.

Suddenly, from way behind, a siren was heard, coming fast. *Very* fast. I could see in my rearview that it was a state trooper, streaking along in the passing lane. He must be doing at least ninety, and he was overtaking us. He couldn't pass us, he must be crazy!

Back in the gooseneck, Dawn was having the same thoughts. She couldn't see the trooper, but she could gauge his velocity by the sound, and she could see that we were boxed in.

Even Deeteza reacted. She went to the window and looked out at the green strip, sensing that the noise was on that side.

The trooper never slackened speed. Overtaking our line of vehicles, he tore off onto the shoulder that edged the green strip and passed us all going, yes, at least ninety, spewing stones and gravel in every direction.

It took a few moments for everyone to begin breathing again.

Then Deeteza turned and looked questioningly at Dawn.

"That," said Dawn limply, "was a policeman. And he was in a hurry."

One day, months later, we heard a siren coming up Route 12. Fast. *Very* fast. Dawn ran to the window at the barn's south end and looked out. A police car streaked by, shrieking at the top of its lungs. In the pasture beside the road Deeteza lifted her head and watched it pass. Then Dawn heard her say to the other horses, "That was a policeman. And he was in a hurry."

How Dawn and I often yearn for the peace and simplicity of the stable in that summer of 1987. Just six horses, Kazinka, Viva, Tina, Buckwheat, Puddy, and Deeteza—Lady, Bo, and Four Bales would not arrive on the premises till the fall—and just four cats.

Yes, four. George Kigercat joined us shortly after the arrival of the first three.

Into eternity I know that the spirit that animated George Kigercat will travel with me—for, in my current lifetime, that spirit had already taken incarnation as the original George, cat patriarch of Spring Farm back in the 1940s and '50s—as my beloved Georgie Girl, queen of our Hollywood home—as a cat unrecognized as George and thus called Lackadazeycal, Dazey for short—and now appearing again as George Kigercat.

He was a four-month-old stray when brought to us by my niece Wendy Kiger, who'd rescued him from a pack of neighborhood kids who were throwing stones at him. Wendy's love of cats wasn't shared by her husband, so to Spring Farm George came. He was just the right age to fit in.

Chores were a breeze in those days, just five stalls and the run-in shed to muck each day, just six horses to feed, six horses to groom. And after chores each evening, we had "sit-down time" for the stable cats. We had a little TV and two rocking chairs that we'd bring out into the aisle of the stable. Making themselves part of things, the horses would stand with their heads hanging over stall doors and the Dutch door from the pasture. The kittens would climb onto our laps, and we'd just relax for a while. I can still feel those lazy, wonderful summer evenings, with the doors wide open and a sweet breeze wafting down the aisle to cool us as we rocked and petted our kittens, watched TV, and talked.

George Kigercat had the cocky attitude of Mickey Rooney mixed with delightful cuddliness. His behavior during sit-down time will never be forgotten. He'd climb inside one's shirt and then down a sleeve. There he'd fall asleep, snoring gently. As he grew and found it harder to fit into sleeves, he'd still push his head in as far as it would go, then start to snore.

Another vivid memory of George is an incident that took place in January 1988. In the fall of 1987, I'd had Bob bulldoze a pad in front of the stable, preparing for the erection of the arena. Winter closed in before building could begin, so we were left with a large, flat area in front of the stable. We'd had a thaw, then a freeze, so that a veritable ice-skating rink covered that space. One sunny afternoon Dawn and I were standing in the open stable door when George Kigercat dashed out of the stable past us, chasing invisible quarry. He hit the ice and went into a long, uncontrolled skid. We laughed. And kept laughing. For George picked himself up, looked down at the strange, slippery stuff, and tried to run again. He spun his wheels for many seconds, then realized that he couldn't get going that way. He gathered himself and walked, on slow, careful cat feet, over to solid ground. He kept walking away, away from the ice.

Then, to our amazement, he turned and ran back at the ice full speed, hitting it and sliding for many yards.

"My God!" I cried. "He did that on purpose. He's ice-skating!"

He repeated the performance, making an even longer run, this time down an incline. He hit the ice at top velocity and managed to slide all the way across.

At which point he did something even more astonishing. He ran back into the stable and got Prinnie, Sonya, and Zero. He led them out to the ice and actually showed them how to run and slide. And they *did*. For nearly twenty minutes those cats had us convulsed with laughter as we watched their happy skating.

There's never a cop or a video camera when you need one. If we could have captured that process of discovery, the teaching of others, the intelligent, purposeful play, on film, we'd have been able to blow out of the water anyone who says that animals don't have intelligent, creative thinking processes, camaraderie, communication, humor, souls.

Magic. Just magic.

We began calling George our "Little Philosopher" after Dawn spotted him sitting atop a fence pole one evening, staring at the sunset.

"What are you doing?" she asked.

"I'm considering the manner in which the rays of the sinking sun seem to blend with the earth and become one with it," he replied.

George never gave a pedestrian answer to anything.

His architectural abilities revealed themselves shortly after the arena was finished. Dawn found him sitting in the middle of the arena staring up at the trusses.

"What are you doing?" she asked.

"I'm analyzing the construction of this building and calculating the vertical and horizontal stresses on those trusses."

"Naturally. How silly of me to have asked."

"The trusses are not done right," George continued.

"George, H&L Builders specialize in this arena package. Surely they calculated the stresses."

"Your builders are long gone, and you can't even get them on the phone to fix the faulty front door. Luckily I'm a great architect, and I'm telling you that the trusses are spaced too widely. I'm convinced, however, that they will bear the load if you brace them diagonally. You *must* put in diagonal braces."

A couple of days later a visitor to the arena, a man in the building trade, looked up and said, "Hey! You've got no diagonal braces between those trusses. Better get some in before you lose that roof."

We paid close attention to George's pronouncements after that.

Life had changed. Totally. For both of us.

It was easier for me than for Dawn. My memories of this life begin at eighteen months of age. From that age I was a prodigious, and conscious, dreamer. One of my novels was actually inspired by a dream that I had when just eighteen months old.

And I come from a family of clairvoyant dreamers. As for instance, my cousin Garry Leonard, the only son of Aunt Milly from Idaho, was killed while navigator of a B-17, on his first mission over Germany, February 6, 1945. He was nineteen. Another of Mother's sisters, Pearl, was the first of our family here locally to receive the news from Aunt Milly. When she did, she called her sister Ida.

"Ida, it's Pearl."

"Yes. Garry's dead."

"Oh. Milly phoned you, too."

"No. I've been sitting beside the phone waiting for this call.

Last night I dreamed that we were all at your house. Suddenly there was a terrible sound. A plane crashed on your lawn. We all ran out. The plane was in flames, and we ran toward it. But then Papa came out of the burning plane. He was carrying Garry in his arms."

William Newcomb, "Papa," had died in 1943.

"Papa raised a hand and said to us, 'Stop. He's mine now.' And then he just disappeared up into the sky, carrying Garry in his arms. So I've been sitting by the phone. Waiting."

That's but one of the incidents the details of which were told and retold in Mother's family. So that clairvoyance, prophecy, and telepathy were par for the course to me. While my own life up until meeting Dawn and awakening to animal communication had been filled with enough psychic and telepathic, UFO, reincarnational, and ghostly experiences—plus everything else in the "things-that-go-bump" spectrum—to leave me open to anything.

To me, nothing is an impossibility and the words and phrases "can't," "can't be," and "can't do" aren't in my vocabulary.

For Dawn it is, or, to be fair, *was*, quite different. She came out of her formative years with a negative rather than a positive charge. Her first response was always to say that a thing couldn't be so or couldn't be done. Whereas mine was to proceed full steam ahead, saying "We can do this. Okay, there might be problems. We'll figure a way around them."

Which made us the perfect team. I lifted her out of her "can't do" mode, while she tempered my more exuberant excesses.

She finally admitted that, as long as she could remember, she'd been "picking up telepathically." As a child she'd assumed that everyone saw, heard, and knew all the things so naturally known to herself. Then at some point she realized that they didn't and she must be crazy. If people knew, they'd laugh at her. She didn't want to be different. She wanted to be . . . normal.

So she closed the doors. And hid from her own self.

That was finished now. We both understood that we'd entered a brave new world.

It was a private world to start with. We needed to let others in easily, gradually.

Because, egad. What would the neighbors think?

8

The Girl from Paris Hill Road Meets Mr. Magoo

What will the neighbors think?"

A cliché usually reserved for comedy routines. Yet they were the first words out of Mother's mouth back in 1961 when I called to tell the folks that I was divorcing my first husband.

"Oh, Bonnie! What will the neighbors think?"

How very far out onto the limb of understanding Mother shinnied before her days were done.

She was even our first convert to animal communication. Not that she knew she was being converted. She was just sort of swept along, a bemused, often confused, and sometimes amused expression on her face.

But then, animal communication was not the only bemusing, confusing, and amusing thing going on at Spring Farm. The place was growing and changing like Topsy.

For one thing, I was making improvements to the interior of the barn. The milk house, the previous site of my sauna, cold-water faucet, and chamber pot, was extended five feet into the old calf pen and remodeled into a pine-paneled, carpeted, state-of-the-art bathroom containing shower, vanity sink and mirror with makeup-table lighting, toilet, sauna, and Jacuzzi tub.

Rising up in the corner of this monument to luxury, over the cemented-in milk cooler, was a spiral staircase just thirty-six inches wide, leading to the floor above. On that second floor Kubla Khan did decree something only vaguely resembling a "normal" bedroom/living space.

That space occupied the north end of the haymow. The main room was twenty by thirty-five feet, with fifteen-foot ceilings. It had only one window, left over from the original barn structure, but spaces for future ten-foot-high windows over built-in window seats had been left on each side of the room as it was paneled in pine. On the haymow side of this room were twin closets, eight by twelve feet and ten feet high. Between the closets, leading to the haymow, was a divided arched door, six by nine feet, purchased at auction. It was from an old Grange hall and bore the inscription "Hang your shooting irons here."

Looking at this structure from the haymow side was the most fun. It was in two steps. The roofs of the two walk-in closets formed the first step. A wrought-iron spiral staircase led to the top of one of those closets. The wall surfaces on that level were lined with bookcases; the edges were guarded by banisters. Between those two decks over the walk-in closets a miracle of staircase construction occurred, contrived by a local carpenter, Doug Hughes. His staircase, again with banisters, joined the decks over those closets into a landing over a Romanesque arch, then stairs led up to the roof over the bedroom/living space, also lined with bookcases. Those two levels housed the library I'd spent a lifetime collecting.

Meanwhile, Dawn's living arrangements changed as well. She

was still renting the house over on Paris Hill Road near her parents. It was smallish, circa 1820, with its original woodwork and wide-plank floors. On the walls of a second-floor bedroom a child of the occupant just previous to Dawn—a lady confined to a wheel-chair—had drawn beautiful, but emotionally tortured, pictures. That upstairs was a bit creepy; Dawn never actually used it. And at night, as she sat with her cats watching TV, they often all suddenly looked up, as someone, or something, began walking around up there. Whatever or whoever it was sometimes came down the stair-case, thankfully stopping at the door at the bottom.

Dawn took it in stride. She was accustomed to living with ghosts, having dealt with a ghost named "Katherine" in the home of her uncle Karl Fredericks, and then with the ghost of my nephew Chris Miller, Peg's youngest boy, who was electrocuted in a freak ac-cident in 1976, at age nineteen. Chris had been raised in the house that the Haymans rented from Peg and Bob. Eventually every mem-ber of the Hayman family saw and experienced the mischievous Chris, who obviously preferred his old home to the dairy barn that Peg and Bob had converted into their home after his death.

Dawn's cats were Timothy Tyler Butts, Julie, Rikki, Otto Sharie, and Heidi.

Timmy was gotten purposefully from the dairy barn of my niece Jodi Scalzo. The "Butts" was in honor of Rob Butts, the husband of *Seth Speaks* author Jane Roberts.

As to Julie, one night I received an SOS from Dawn and rushed right over. One of Dawn's neighbors was nearly hysterical with fear. She'd found a kitten in her garage. We finally managed to corner the even-more-terrified eight-week-old Julie and rescue her from that overwrought person.

Like Julie, Rikki and Heidi were kittens who'd been born to one of dozens of stray/feral cats on Paris Hill Road. They found their way to the cat kibble that Dawn left out for strays, then allowed themselves to be lured into the house.

Otto Sharie was found by Dawn's young stepsister Nicki in the Hayman garden. Nicki named the kitten Sharie and brought her to Dawn. But Sharie told Dawn that her name was really Otto.

Otto Sharie was a vocalist.

"I think she's having her first heat," said Dawn one day. "She talks, Bonnie. She runs around the house screaming, 'I'm here! I'm ready!' And last night she ran through the living room, took a flying leap, plastered herself onto my screen door and shouted, 'Air raid! Air raid!'"

I assumed that Dawn's imagination was working overtime. But then she took her fabled trip to Maine. In order to give her cats some company, I slept at her house each night and was repeatedly awakened by well-enunciated cries of "I'm here! I'm ready!" Then there'd be the occasional *splat* as the cat plastered herself onto the screen door, screaming, "Air raid! Air raid!"

Dawn had her spayed once she returned from Maine. The vocalizations ceased. Neither of us, though, can deny that we heard them.

Timmy, Otto, and Heidi became normal, friendly, cuddling cats. Rikki never did tame down, remaining untouchable. Julie was touchable, sort of. She wasn't wild, but she remained forever strange, in endearing, often amusing ways.

Came the day when Dawn's landlord informed her that she and her little family must leave. The house was to be demolished. That wonderful old house, which had sheltered close to two centuries of people, generated those sad-but-beautiful drawings on a bedroom wall, and set some spirit to walking, walking, was to be bulldozed and buried so the landlord could erect a modular home for one of his kids. Dawn had less than a month to vacate.

But to where? She'd lucked out with that house. Rental houses in our area are like hen's teeth, but there it had been, a treasure for a girl just out of college and only two hundred dollars a month.

We started looking at apartments. Most wouldn't accept pets.

And we were stunned by what she was going to have to pay. Everything was four hundred dollars a month and up.

"That's ridiculous," said Mother, settling the matter in one easy lesson. "You've plenty of room in your barn, Bonnie. Let her live with you temporarily until she finds something."

So to Spring Farm Dawn came, bag, baggage, and cats.

Soon it was obvious to all of us that temporary made no sense. It was never verbalized. We all just knew. Dawn had come home. To Spring Farm. Where she belonged.

Shortly after my father died, there was another addition to our family. Andrew Magyar. Andy was Hungarian, born in Romania. After World War II, escaping communism, he hiked over the mountains into Germany carrying forty pounds of salt, said to be worth its weight in gold in Germany. When he got there, he found that Germany had all the salt it needed. His was worthless. That's sort of the story of Andy's life.

He emigrated to Australia in 1950. I met him in 1976 while living in Australia and taking flying lessons—he was in my flying club. Our relationship was platonic. I could trust him not to put the make on me, and we became friends. So it was that when, in 1986, he started making noises in his letters about committing suicide because he had no reason to live, I foolishly supplied him with a reason. He was to retire from Honeywell in 1988.

"Come to Spring Farm, then," I told him. "You can live upstairs in my parents' house."

Ann Landers would have had pithy advice on this subject, but I've always been a sucker for underdogs and strays.

So in early 1988, to Spring Farm Andy came, bag, baggage, and personal idiosyncrasies.

In a way, after Daddy's death, it was good having Andy living upstairs from Mother. It was someone there in the house with her in case of emergency.

In other, more important ways, Andy was a catastrophe. He was very set in his ways, and those ways were pretty strange. Before things were finished, he'd driven Mother nearly out of her mind and catapulted Dawn and me into the Twilight Zone.

Early on, Dawn and I began to compare Andy to Mr. Magoo, that comic figure who wanders about oblivious to danger, never getting hurt himself but wreaking havoc on everyone else. (Come to think of it, Andy even looked like Mr. Magoo.) He considered our rules, our dos and don'ts, to be ridiculous and was shockingly careless around the horses—of his own safety and of theirs. I paid his tuition at a seven-day TT.E.A.M. workshop, given by Robyn over in Cazenovia. Which made things worse. After that workshop he considered himself an expert. And experts are impervious to injury or to injuring.

Another mistake was to designate him our Handy Andy and assign to him minor repair and building jobs. It turned out that he'd studied with Rube Goldberg and Mickey Mouse. The things he came up with were awesome in their impracticality and lack of function. Anything he did had to be redone by Dawn.

To make things worse, he became obsessive and possessive about the tack room, where we let him set up his workshop, guarding its door with a vengeance. We took to sneaking in when he wasn't around to get things that we needed, or to saying "Pretty please" when he was there.

Then he tried to take control of the stable itself, arranging things to his own liking, complaining when we moved or rearranged anything.

One evening I totally lost it.

He set me off with "Bonnie, I just can't work with all of that tack in the tack room."

"I beg your pardon?"

"I need space for my work. You need to do something with all that tack and horse stuff."

For a moment I stood speechless. Then Andrew was greeted with what felt to me like *Hurricane* Andrew, suddenly welling up from my insides and exploding all over him.

"Great! Out! All out!"

I went into the tack room, grabbed a saddle, brought it out into the aisle of the stable, and dumped it. Back for another saddle, and another.

"Bonnie, you don't have to do it now!" he exclaimed.

"No! It *has* to be now!"

Riding a wave of fury, with Andy and Dawn standing dumbfounded, I emptied the tack room, piling everything—tack, trunks, blankets, pails, feed buckets, and supplies—in the aisle of the stable.

"Now are you happy?" I asked when finished. "Now you have the workspace you need. Forget the horses. We're not here for the horses, we don't need a room for their stuff. Only for Andy. We built that room just for Andy."

He'd been standing with bowed head.

"I'm sorry," he said and left. It was the end of his tenure in the stable.

"Terrific," said Dawn. "Now we have to carry all this stuff back."

"It was worth it."

Another problem was his driving. Andy's passion was airplanes. He expected the same performance from his cars. Andy could get from Chuckery Corners to the George Washington Bridge in three hours flat, a drive that takes sane people five hours when obeying speed limits, four hours when not. Three hours was averaging eighty-five miles an hour. And not on the Thruway. This was on state and county roads, "shortcuts" that he'd figured out.

Yet in the seven years that he was with us, he got just one speeding ticket. Maybe that was because he traveled too fast to be seen. Or policemen thought they'd only imagined that something had just whizzed by. Mother rode with him just once before refusing to do so ever again. Dawn and I made the same decision after riding with him one winter's day in icy conditions and discovering that icy roads didn't slow him one bit.

Even when she wasn't riding with him, Andy's driving nearly got Dawn. On one occasion, as she was driving home, a car peeled out of a parking lot and came at her head-on. It was Andy, having forgotten that he was in a country where they drive on the right side of the road. On another occasion, in the parking lot of a mall, a car came speeding toward her, again head-on. It was Andy, his mind on anything but his driving. Dawn took to scanning roads and parking lots far ahead, lest Andy be out and about, subconsciously wanting another shot at her.

Andy's absent-minded, and often thoughtless, ways took a toll on Mother more than on us. She had to live in the same house with him and share bathroom, kitchen, and laundry facilities.

Andy was a clean freak. He changed his clothes twice a day and never wore anything twice without washing it. Hence, he did two loads of washing and drying each day.

Each morning he took a fifteen-minute shower (Mother timed them), then spent another half hour shaving or whatever. He'd march down the stairs, usually as Mother herself was just getting up, and take over the bathroom, never asking whether she needed to get in there first. In self-defense, she kept a chamber pot in her room.

He also took over the kitchen three times a day to cook his Hungarian and Romanian dishes. They were all fried, in lard, and filled the kitchen with smoke. Sometimes, at lunchtime, Mother got a break. On those days Andy had cold sandwiches filled with his favorite sandwich makings, raw bacon and sliced onions. When he wasn't cooking, he was baking bread in his bread maker. That, at least, smelled good.

Cooking tools were forever missing. Andy would come to the door between the living room and kitchen.

"Deanie, where did you put the eggbeater?"

"I haven't used the eggbeater in weeks."

"You must have, it's missing. You've used it and just forgotten."

Mother would get up, go to the kitchen, and find the eggbeater in whatever strange place Andy'd left it the last time he'd used it.

"And *I* didn't put it there," she'd tell him.

"Humph" was all Andy would say, never admitting that it had been he.

Or he'd put the teakettle on, go upstairs, forget it, then accuse Mother of forgetting it.

"Andy, I did not put the teakettle on! I've had no reason to do so."

"Well, neither have I, so you must had done it and forgotten."

After several years of hearing "You must have done it and forgotten," Mother began to wonder if she were the one doing those things, if she were getting Alzheimer's. We assured her that she wasn't. He'd done the same thing with tools in the stable and in the barn whenever he was working there for some reason. We three girls formed a support group, to protect ourselves from his onslaughts.

One day Mother came hurrying to the barn.

"Dawn, please come in and look at the toilet."

Dawn went with her and found a five-gallon pail filled with water sitting beside the toilet. Taped to the tank was a sign saying "Each time you use the toilet, pour in a pail of water."

"The toilet won't flush," Mother whispered, glancing toward the stairs to make sure that Andy wasn't coming. "So he insists that I pour water into it every time I use it."

"That doesn't make sense. It'll overflow the bowl."

"That's what I *told* him!" Mother whispered urgently. "He says no, that's what I must do. He thinks the toilet needs to be replaced."

Dawn took the lid off the tank.

"The chain from the ball to the gasket's broken."

She went to the hardware store for a new chain, came back, and installed it.

"Honestly, that Andy!" said Mother. "I *knew* he was wrong,"

Shortly thereafter Andy came to the living room door.

"Deanie, where's the pail? And why did you take the sign off the toilet?"

"It's working again."

"How?"

"Dawn fixed it."

"Humph," said Andy and went back upstairs.

One day Mother came looking for Dawn yet again.

"My dryer's running really hot, and I'm afraid to use it. Andy says he knows how to fix it, and he's gone to the store for parts."

"The dryer vent's probably plugged," said Dawn.

Sure enough, not only was it plugged, it was packed, from end to end.

"It's a wonder we haven't had a fire."

"It's that damn Andy and all his washings!" said Mother.

Dawn detached the vent, cleaned it out, and reattached it.

At which point Andy arrived with his bag of parts.

"It's all right," Mother told him smugly. "Just a plugged vent. Dawn fixed it."

"Humph," said Andy and went upstairs.

He played mind games with Dawn and me as well, more sophisticated than those that he played with Mother. And eerie.

Andy had an amazing telepathic connection with me. That was demonstrated hundreds of times. I'd have a thought, and Andy would voice it out loud then comment on it. A couple of times over the years it had disturbed me so much that I'd vowed to break off contact with him, thinking of him as a psychic vampire—appropriate since he'd been born in the Romanian district of Transylvania. Somehow, though, he'd always kept me feeling too sorry, and somehow responsible, for him to end the friendship.

I never did know whether Andy knew that he was picking up my thoughts or whether he assumed that those thoughts were his own. Just as Dawn and I will never know whether what began to happen to us multiple times each day was Andy's telepathic ability getting stronger or whether he'd bugged our office and was listening to our conversations.

Again and again the door to our office would open, Andy would walk in and say something in direct answer to whatever we'd just said.

He certainly had the know-how to bug us. His second passion after airplanes was electronic gadgetry. His rooms were filled with electronic stuff and catalogs regarding the same.

We actually did begin, periodically, to search the office for bugs. The thing is that technology had gotten so sophisticated he didn't have to physically bug us. There were listening devices that could hear through walls or hear what was being whispered many yards away. If he really wanted to listen to us, he could. Especially since, after that explosive night in the stable, to give him something to do, I'd set him to cataloging my library. His workstation was on the second tier of the library—the roof over our apartment. So that, for almost a year, he'd spent most of his days out there in the barn with us, but upstairs.

Our suspicions were pretty well confirmed the day that Dawn and I were sitting in the office discussing a Rube Goldberg repair that Andy had done on a door in Mother's house.

"We're just going to have to tell him that it's no good," I said.

At which point the haymow door, some fifty feet away from us, opened. Andy came down the stairs and said, "If you girls don't like that repair, I'm sure that Dawn can make it right."

Coincidence? Not after hundreds of such instances.

Telepathy? Perhaps.

Listening devices? We'll never know.

But Dawn and I took to whispering into each other's ears whenever we had anything to say regarding Andy. It was a creepy way to live, for Mother and for ourselves.

And bless Mother's heart, that two-faced little darling. By various tendrils of the grapevine we discovered that when Mother went out for breakfast with Peg and Bob each Sunday morning and she was asked about Andy, she'd say something like "Oh, Andy is wonderful. Yes, I just love Andy."

Mother had been raised not to speak ill of the Devil. And I guess that she didn't want Peg and Bob to worry. But the result was that Peg and Bob really, really liked Andy and felt that Dawn and I were lax in our appreciation of that terrific guy.

As I said, Ann Landers would have had a field day with this one.

And Sheridan Whiteside would have been a stroll in the park compared to our Andy.

9

Passengers and Ghosts on Spring Farm's Ark

Naturally, our animal family was growing as well. Spangles was a noteworthy addition. He appeared, framed by our picture window, running here, there, and everywhere out in Deeteza's pasture in the winter of 1987–88. For a while we paid no attention. Neighbors had a black dog that was allowed to run loose. He was often in our pasture.

But finally Dawn looked up from her desk, studied the dog running to and fro, and said, "That's not the neighbors' dog. This one's been dumped."

"Dumped" meant that someone who didn't want a particular animal anymore had taken the animal in a car and dumped it out in front of a likely-looking place in the countryside. Dozens of such abandoned animals had ended up plastered all over Route 12 in front of Spring Farm.

I stopped work and studied the dog as well. "No, that's the neighbors' dog."

"Humor me," said Dawn, rising from her desk. "I'm going up there to get him."

"Humor me" was a signal. Dawn used it especially when we were doing TT.E.A.M. work on a client animal whose person was not open to animal communication. "Humor me" signaled that she was getting special information from the animal. I went to the window and watched her walk up the hill.

As she approached, she realized that the dog was running hither and yon because he was searching for horse manure under the snow. No, certainly not the neighbors' dog. This was a desperate animal, staying alive on the only sustenance available.

So intent upon his foraging was he that he hadn't noticed her approach. She called out softly, not wanting to startle him into running out into Route 12 in front of cars.

He froze, looked up, bared his teeth, and growled. A long, slow, meaningful growl.

Oh, boy. With pounding heart she got down on her knees, held out her arms, and said most jovially, "Here, puppy!"

The dog hesitated . . . then charged. Right into her arms, knocking her over, tail madly wagging, tongue joyfully kissing.

"Yuck! Not after horse manure!"

He appeared to be a teenage Labrador mix. We placed "found" ads and canvassed the neighborhood. To no avail. In the meantime, he moved into the barn with us, joining Fraser, Foxie, and Daffy.

Spangles, by the way, had his own version of what had happened in the pasture that wintry day. Other animals subsequently told us that Spangles told them that he'd found Dawn wandering around lost. He'd led her down to the barn, and Bonnie had been so grateful to him for finding Dawn and bringing her home that she'd let him stay at Spring Farm.

Quickly we learned that our search-and-rescue dog was severely neurotic. He couldn't be left alone, he shrieked, he destroyed things, he chewed furniture, he barked constantly, he wouldn't stop chasing cats, he ran in endless, mindless circles, he urinated and defecated indiscriminately. Probably why he'd been dumped. Even Robyn, presenting a T.T.E.A.M. clinic for small animals at Spring Farm, said, after trying to work with Spangles, that he was the most difficult dog she'd ever encountered.

To keep him from destroying the place, we chained him to one of the iron pillars that supported the floor of the haymow, the office roof.

"Are you going to keep that dog chained there for the rest of his life?" Gail once asked.

We certainly hoped not, but at that time it was the only way to stay sane.

Little by little, he calmed down. The chain forced him to contain himself, and Dawn's love gave him security. Whenever we sat down to relax, Spangles came off the chain and straight onto the couch with Dawn. She was endlessly patient with him as he desperately cuddled with her, napped with her, watched TV with her. And poured his heart out to her.

"I can't believe it!" he told her. "I can't believe that I got myself born as a dog again! I'm helpless as a dog! I meant to be born as a person so that I could *get* them!"

In the life just previous, he explained, he'd been a dog in a research lab, where they'd repeatedly injected stuff under his skin. When his body had become so sick, hairless, scab- and pus-covered that he was no longer useful, they'd disposed of him by using him in a drowning experiment. He'd wanted to be reborn as a person so that he could go get the people who'd done those things to him.

We could only commiserate. Like it or not, he was a dog again. He was going to have to come to terms with that.

Secretly, we were relieved that, fourteen or fifteen years hence, some rage-filled kid wouldn't be out tracking certain "scientists" with a high-powered rifle.

Spangles's coming to terms was so gradual that a year after his arrival we could hardly remember what a nut he'd been. He became a joy. Anal compulsive, but a joy. After months of chasing cats he instead appointed himself Keeper of Cat Safety and Barn Peace. Anytime he imagined danger to a cat from another dog (and it was always imagination), he'd chase that dog away. Anytime the animals had a spat, Constable Spangles came running, barking, and growling to break it up.

And he loved his toys. Dawn has always been big on toys; they're a part of her childhood that she refuses to relinquish, so that her first thought when we get a new animal is to get it some toys. Spangles was compulsively neat with his. He kept them in a row on the lower shelf of our library table. When he wanted to play, he'd stand before them for a moment, then delicately pick up the one that he'd decided on. Just as delicately, when he finished, he'd return the toy to its proper spot.

Shortly after he arrived, his skin problems surfaced. He lost much of his hair, and the skin got scabby and gross. We tried everything we could think of: homeopathic, allopathic, herbs, additives, salves. Vets tested him twenty-five ways from Sunday. We could find no cure. Additionally, he was hysterical about his rear end. One had only to walk toward that back end, and he'd yelp and run.

We remain convinced that his many problems were holdovers from his previous lifetime. His memories and emotions surrounding that lifetime affected the body that he inhabited in this one. Yes, he eventually released overt anger, but the energy of emotional memory remained to sicken him still.

Yet while we recognized what was going on with his skin, great animal communicators that we are, we'd forgotten the last part of his message. Until we tried to give him a bath. We had an old stainless-steel Jacuzzi tub that was three by five feet and three feet high, in which we bathed dogs. One sunny spring day we set it out in the driveway with warm water about a foot deep. I picked Spangles up and started to lower him in.

He went berserk. He bit at me, clawed, screamed, fought, and snarled, teeth bared, eyes wild. He'd gone to another time, to a place where humans were lowering him into a vat to kill him. How ashamed we were not to have remembered.

We never again tried to bathe him in a tub. Instead, one of us would get into a bathing suit and hug him while the other gently wielded the lather and hose. He hated it. He trembled and cried. But it didn't send him into the mindless frenzy produced by the tub. Taking him out when it rained was another ordeal. And he'd go to any lengths to keep his feet from getting wet.

How droll that he'd gotten himself reborn as a Labrador Retriever, a water dog.

Remembering the gentle, quiet, but playful, kind, and intelligent dog with whom we had the privilege of living for fifteen years, we think of all the other hyper, just-plain-nuts young dogs that people call us about and want to unload. We wonder how many potential solid citizens of dogdom are dumped or euthanized before they get a chance to settle down. What a shame that dogs aren't accorded the same long suffering that we humans usually accord to our own incorrigible, often destructive and out-of-control youngsters. Dogs don't mature till between two and four. How different are puppies from human kids, who are the bane of their parents' existence while young, especially as preteenagers and teenagers, then pillars of the community when adult?

Back at the old corral, my "riding" arena was finished in the spring of 1988. By the next spring we'd installed seven horse stalls along the east end. We had to, to house the new arrivals.

"Lamoka Babe. You'll love her, Bonnie." Al Berlieu again. "I bought her as a foal, when Bo was a foal. I turned her in with Bo and Four Bales. Bo and Babe grew up together. You'll have a nice little family group. She won a lot of money for me at the Finger Lakes. The thing is, Bonnie, she's still sound. I want to retire her sound. There's new talent coming in at the Finger Lakes. Babe's getting outclassed. This season coming up—she won't be able to outrun them. But she'll ruin her legs trying. I can't let that happen. Please take her."

How can you say no to a guy like that?

Of course it was love at first sight when we saw her there in her stall—a pretty chestnut, sweet-tempered, refined, almost dainty, only fifteen and a quarter hands. An iron will, not stature, had made Babe a winner.

"Here, you lead her out to the trailer," Al told Dawn and me. He followed, leading a second horse. Must be Babe had a loading problem.

But Babe walked right on. And Al walked the second horse on.

"This is Lamoka Gypsy, Babe's sister. You'll love her, too."

"Al!"

"Please?"

So we returned home with *two* more retired racehorses. They were virtually the same age, both sired by Murtaugh, bought by Al as weanlings, foster-mothered by Four Bales, and nearly identical, except that Babe's blaze was cockeyed and Gypsy's straight.

And except that, while Babe had been winning big for Al, Gypsy had never won a race until the last one she had run. At which point Al had retired her.

Once home, we put them in the outdoor arena to let them work out the kinks and sat up on the railing, admiring them.

At first they just walked about, investigating this new place. Then they met in the center of the ring and literally put their heads together.

For a few moments they just stood like that, staring at each other.

Then, shoulder to shoulder, they started trotting, counterclock-wise, along the rail of the oval. As they trotted, they gathered speed.

"What the heck are they up to?" I said just as they reached the far end of the ring, about where a starting gate would be, and—

—they were off! bursting out of that imaginary gate.

There on the railing Dawn and I sat paralyzed, watching those two Thoroughbreds thundering toward us. Déjà vu—Lady all over again. They'd never make the turn. They'd go right through the fence.

But they made it, banking expertly.

And they kept going, round and round, faster and faster.

We'd seldom experienced anything as exhilarating, sitting there as, again and again, those magnificent, powerful animals thundered past just inches from us. One could sense what it must be like to ride one of those wonderful creatures full out in a race.

More important, we could feel the joy of the horses, their love of what they were doing.

It was the last race that Lamoka Babe and Lamoka Gypsy ever ran. They ran it as a gift, not only to themselves but to us.

In the weeks to come, we discovered a lot about our new residents. For one thing, Babe was nuts. Sweet but nuts, inclined to explode at any odd moment. One memorable day, she freaked as we were turning her out into a new pasture and went through the fence. (God help us, at that point we still had wire fencing.) She took off, dragging wire and posts behind her that ripped a vertical section out from under the roof of the nursery wing that Doug Hughes and his crew were building, leaving them clutching for support as Babe galloped mindlessly on. It was Dawn who ran after her and finally got hold of her, Dawn who calmed her and led her safely back to the stable.

As to Gypsy, we figured out why she'd never won any but that last race. According to Al, she was fast. She'd generally take the lead. But then, as horses began to catch up, she'd slow way down.

The others would pass her at full speed, leaving her unable to regain the distance. Al couldn't figure out why that always happened.

We figured it out very quickly. With the exception of Bo, Four Bales, and Babe, Gypsy *hated* it when other horses came near. Once turned into the pasture, she'd attempt to kick the stuffing out of Puddy and Lady if they approached. In her stall she'd kick viciously at the wall that separated her from Puddy.

What was happening in a race, we realized, was that the moment that other horses approached from the rear, Gypsy slowed down to try to kick them! In the one race that she had won, obviously no horse had gotten close enough to tempt her to kick.

To save our stalls and protect the other horses, Dawn had a talk with her.

"Gypsy, why do you kick the boards between Puddy and yourself?"

"He comes up to that wall. So I have to kick him."

"Why do you have to kick him?"

"He comes too close."

"Gypsy, he's in his own stall. He has to be able to move around his own stall."

"He comes too close! I have to kick him!"

"So it's just that he's too close to you? You don't feel that you have to kick him when you're by the wall that separates you two and he's at the other end of his stall?"

"No."

"Does that give you an idea as to how you can handle this situation?"

"No."

"What if, when Puddy just happens to come near that wall between the two of you, what if you walked to the other end of your own stall?"

There was a long silence. "I never thought of that," Gypsy said finally.

"Could you give it a try?"

"Well—I guess."

And she did! Her stall kicking subsided to a minimum.

"Okay," said Dawn some days later, "you're doing a wonderful job of walking away. I'll bet your feet aren't half as sore since you stopped kicking the wall so much."

"I guess."

"So let's work on not kicking at Puddy and Lady in the pasture. You don't like it when they get too close to you, do you?"

"I hate it."

"Well, let's think about this. You know how now, when Puddy gets too close to your wall, you just walk to the other end of your stall?"

"Yeah."

"Well, do you think when Puddy or Lady get too close to you in the pasture you could just walk away from them?"

There was a long silence. "I never thought of that," said Gypsy finally.

That day, when we turned the Thoroughbreds out, Gypsy simply walked away from Puddy and Lady and began to graze.

Oh, she had many lapses over the years. She remained a kicker—at other horses, never at human beings—but, all in all, most of the time, she just walked away.

We'd finally have peace on Earth if human beings would try as honestly as Gypsy.

Spring Farm continued to grow. Our total layout consisted of the house, garage, and barn, the outdoor ring, the new arena with adjoining paddock, two large pastures containing run-in shelters that were accessible from the stable, two large paddocks with run-in shelters on the hill behind the arena, a new tack room on the east of the stable, and, on the west, the twenty-by-thirty-two-foot lean-to shed called the nursery and its two small exercise yards.

We had to keep adding accommodations, because the horses kept coming.

After Halali, we attended TT.E.A.M. trainings on a concentrated basis. As I'd planned, we earned the status of Practitioner I in a little over a year and began working and earning money as such. Every penny went toward maintaining our growing stable of unusable horses. Unfortunately, as we worked, clients unloaded more unusable horses onto us.

Scherry and Dulcie were next, from the stable of Carol Northrup over near Cazenovia. During school hours, Carol taught fifth grade at the Enders Road School. After hours and on weekends, with her stable of twenty-one horses, she conducted the Carol Northrup Pony Club. Carol cared deeply about her horses and was open to new ways of curing their problems. For about a year we went almost weekly to her place, to work with this horse or that and to demonstrate TT.E.A.M techniques to her students. Obviously we were doing things that helped, else she wouldn't have kept calling us back. But Carol had two horses who'd become unusable.

Scherry was a delicate little chestnut, somehow seeming more like an oversized doe than a horse. At fourteen and three-quarter hands, she just made it into the official category of "horse" rather than "pony." Her breeding was Anglo-Arab—Thoroughbred and Arab—and though temperamentally a bit "schitzy," she'd been one of Carol's best eventers, eventing being a show category in which horse and rider must perform in jumping, cross-country, and dressage. Scherry had carried many a student to the blue in eventing. (Of course, after any event, her rider had to virtually run her into a wall to get her to stop.)

One day, after returning from a show, Scherry's rider hung her garment bag beside Scherry's standing stall and commenced to groom her. As the girl worked, Scherry swished her tail. The tail became entangled with the hanger of the garment bag, which ended up hanging on the tail. The startled horse broke loose and, pursued by the garment bag, ran out of the stable and through a split-rail fence. A rail drove straight into her chest, just missing her heart. Scherry's young rider and other youngsters ran after her, got control of the frantic horse, pulled the rail out of her chest, and stuffed their own clothes into the gaping wound, stemming the bleeding until a veterinarian arrived.

By the time we met Scherry, the wound had healed, leaving just an indentation in the left chest where muscle would never grow again. But neither would Scherry's confidence ever grow again. At least, in Carol's estimation, not enough to be entrusted with a young rider.

So to Spring Farm Scherry came, there to become one of our most fabled occupants.

Dulcie was a Welsh-Arab pony, white, fourteen hands, who developed a fear of things around her feet and hence a tendency to shy. She came along beautifully with TT.E.A.M. groundwork and exercises such as "pick-up sticks," where a horse learns to pick its way calmly and judiciously through a welter of crosshatched poles and branches. Actually, after TT.E.A.M., Dulcie was probably okay to be ridden. But Carol wouldn't risk "probably" with her kids.

So to Spring Farm Dulcie came.

There was a third horse, Holly, whom Carol hoped to make her own personal mount. But although she was amenable as long as people remained on the ground, once a person mounted her, Holly shied, bucked, reared, and/or bolted. Carol trucked her to Spring Farm a few times for clinics—Centered Riding, Tony Gonzalez, TT.E.A.M.—but despite her expert horsemanship and all that help, Holly remained incorrigible.

This, unfortunately, was in the days before Dawn and I—or almost anyone—realized that chiropractic was available for horses. Holly's problem might have been pain. A chiropractic vet might have solved the whole thing.

Carol's heart was heavy. She loved Holly dearly, but, like most riding stables, hers operated on a shoestring. She couldn't continue to provide for and give stable space to an unusable horse. Holly had no future except as a pet. Even then, she would have to be protected from herself. Any new owner must never, ever try to ride her.

Carol had just about decided to send Holly to us.

Then, at Christmas 1989, we, along with Carol's friends and students, were stunned by Carol's sudden and completely unnecessary death.

On the morning of December 24, her friends Lou and Doug Bombard called an ambulance for her. She'd been throwing down hay for the horses, had pulled something, and was in pain. Doug rode with Carol in the ambulance. She must have had a premonition. Inexplicably, as witnessed by the ambulance attendants, she willed her horses to the Bombards.

"If anything happens to me," she said, "my horses are yours. Find them good homes."

The emergency room doctor gave her muscle relaxants and painkillers and dismissed her.

He neglected to take into account the medicines and inhaler that Carol routinely used for asthma, obviously lethal when taken with what he'd prescribed.

In late afternoon of that Christmas Eve day, when friends and students who were doing chores for Carol went to the house to check on her, they found her near death. Once again an ambulance was called. To no avail. Just fifty-eight, active, and vital, a first-class horsewoman, beloved by friends and students, dedicated to her animals—dead because of the carelessness of an emergency room doctor.

But how dead was Carol, really?

Knowing Carol's wishes, the Bombards sent Holly to us. And after darkness one night in early spring, Dawn made her way up to the hillside paddocks to check on Holly and the other horses there. She thought herself quite alone as she went into the shed, got a few chips of hay, and put them out for the horses. On emerging, she looked down at the gate and saw that a woman was standing there. She wore dark pants and a dark jacket. She was stroking Holly.

"Bonnie? Is that you?"

There was no answer.

"Who's there?"

Still no answer.

Dawn felt a chill. Thinking suddenly that someone was sneaking up behind her, she looked around. No one. She turned back to the gate.

Holly stood alone. The dark figure had vanished.

"Holly," Dawn asked silently. "Who was that?"

"Oh," said Holly, "that was just Carol. She comes to see me a lot."

Then there was the case of Gigi. Gigi was thirty-nine, an incredible age for a horse. A neighbor of Carol's had been keeping her, but the accommodations weren't really comfortable, not for a horse that old. So to Spring Farm Gigi came.

She was a brown-and-white pinto, *just* over fourteen and a half hands, and so, like Scherry at fourteen and three-quarters, she just squeaked into the classification of "horse." She'd been born into Carol's barn and raised and trained by Carol. Together in their younger years, she and Carol had won a lot of races at Central New York shows.

Bright-eyed and bushy-tailed, Gigi came quickly to be loved by us all. On her fortieth birthday, August 22, 1991, more than two hundred people attended a birthday open house, bringing bushels of carrots and other gifts for Gigi and her stablemates. Guests partook of a donated three-foot-long cake, shaped and colored like a carrot, while Gigi basked in the adulation.

The only hint of her impending death was a remark that she made to Dawn.

"Carol wanted me to make forty. I've done it."

Yet she seemed perfectly fine. Until, late on the afternoon of October twenty-third, I looked out and saw her rolling violently in her exercise paddock, colicking. I shouted for Dawn, and we got her down to the arena. One of our vets, Leigh Lain, was summoned. Living only about four miles from us, Dr. Lain was here within minutes. We also called Cassia Holstein, Gigi's last rider in the pony club. Cassia's parents drove her over, and Cassia, Dawn, and I spent the night in the stable with Gigi. We didn't walk her much. Walking seemed too much of an effort for her.

Dr. Lain had given as much aid as she was able. Colics are terrible beasts that leave vets, owners, and horses virtually helpless. Colic is a general term, used when a horse evidences pain somewhere in its gut. A simple gas colic is relatively easy to relieve, especially with TT.E.A.M. techniques. Or there might be an impaction in the bowels. Vets use various methods to break up the impaction. Walking, walking, walking the horse can sometimes do the trick.

But there are more sinister possibilities. It may be a twisted gut. Or a rupturing gut. In aged horses it might be a cancer that's suddenly reached a vital organ.

When Leigh had done all she was able, we could only watch— and hope it was only gas or an impaction.

The end came abruptly on the morning of the twenty-fourth. Gigi had been standing in the middle of the arena dull-eyed, as she'd been for much of the night. Suddenly she let out a scream and began to stagger. I ran to her and tried to steady her, but she collapsed, dying. Her friends crowded around—Dawn, Cassia, and myself, and volunteers who helped us with barn chores at that time—all of us sobbing.

Hers was the first equine death at Spring Farm. None of us had ever seen a horse die.

There is just something so . . . huge about the death of a horse.

Suddenly I shouted for everyone to get back. Because Gigi's legs began to thrash wildly.

But then it became obvious that there was nothing "wild" about her movements at all.

Lying on her side, Gigi was galloping.

She galloped and galloped.

Then suddenly she stopped. And she was dead.

Dawn was visibly shaken. When we'd said our good-byes and covered Gigi with blankets, I took her aside.

"What happened there?"

Dawn could scarcely speak through her tears.

"I saw that she was dying. Mentally I called out to her to look around, that there'd be a friend there waiting for her. She said, 'I see her! It's Carol!' That's when she started galloping. 'Run to Carol,' I told her, and she said, 'I'm running, I'm running!' Then she started laughing and said, 'Oh! I forgot to leave my body behind.' . . . That's when she stopped galloping. And she was gone."

We were silent for a while.

"Carol and Gigi raced together when they were young," I said at last. "They won a lot of races."

"They will again," said Dawn.

A reader of our Spring Farm CARES newsletter, *All That Is*, once wrote, "It's so comforting to read your descriptions of the deaths of your animals. You make death seem—joyful."

How could it not be? How could we not be joyful, seeing in our minds' eyes Gigi and Carol together again, galloping joyously through some beautiful field just beyond the horizon?

Gigi was the first of our equine friends here at Spring Farm to further convince us that death is only that. Just . . . the horizon.

10

More Passengers and the Birth of Spring Farm CARES

There came a day when Dawn turned to me and said, "Bonnie, am I an employee or am I your business partner? I need to know whether or not I have a future here at Spring Farm."

My mouth dropped. The effrontery! The unmitigated gall! A jumped-up little chit only years out of college, actually proposing, assuming, that she could be my business partner. Me, the great BJR, dancer, model, actress, author, Hollywood escapee, woman of the world, TT.E.A.M practitioner, horse-owned village idiot.

Oh no, little girl. I do a single. And you haven't put a penny into what's being built here. I'm the one who's spent her every cent, ruined herself financially.

Like Tevya, I turned and stalked away. Like Tevya, I turned and looked back. At my "offspring," who dared to have her own agenda.

Of course . . .

An employee, yes. Who was seldom paid since I seldom had anything to pay her with. She worked for a roof over her head and three squares, most of which squares were provided by Mother.

Of course . . .

I *had* been paying the installments on her red Toyota truck, Effie. On the other hand, Effie was used almost exclusively to haul feed, hay, and manure for the farm. I'd also been paying her student loan lest she be led away in handcuffs, for what would I do if that happened? How could we get along without her?

But a business partner? No! *What* business? There was no business here, only insanity. More and more heads to shelter, more mouths to feed. I must be completely out of my mind, how had I gotten into this mess?

Of course . . .

As T.T.E.A.M Practitioners, we worked together. So she was contributing actual earnings. Yes, I'd paid for her training, but she worked hard caring for the animals, while her communication skill made her more important to them than I!

Her communication skill.

Gingerly at first, among friends, she'd begun to do consultations for their animals. The results were good. She gained confidence.

Came the day when she actually began to charge for her services. Ten dollars per animal.

But those were face-to-face consultations, with client and animal sitting in front of her.

It was her first telephone consultation that will remain in my memory. The client was a friend of Dawn's sister Janice, down in New York City. The client had a remarkable problem. Her cat, Kitty Kat, kept banging her head against walls.

I had butterflies as we waited for the phone to ring, like a producer at the back of the house, waiting for the curtain to rise.

The show was a smash. When the phone rang and Dawn answered, I watched a new, quite magnificent entity emerge. No longer little Dawn, afraid of driving to Maine. I witnessed a star being born.

Her face was placid and beautiful. Her words flowed effortlessly. The information was just there, as from a spring. Truth and honesty radiated from her every word.

Kitty Kat told Dawn that she was banging her head because she couldn't stand the rock music that her owner listened to. The lady even left a rock station playing for Kitty Kat when she went to work. The cat liked classical music. And less volume.

This drew an "Oh wow" of understanding from the lady. Now she knew why, as she showered each morning, the dial of the transistor radio that she left blaring on the floor outside the shower kept mysteriously slipping from her rock station to a classical station.

Dawn brokered a deal between lady and cat. The lady would leave a classical station playing while she was at work. The cat would let the lady have uninterrupted rock while showering.

Janice reported a week later that her friend was delighted. Both she and the cat were keeping their bargain. And Kitty Kat no longer banged her head against walls.

Word spread quickly. Our phone started ringing, and the ten-dollar checks rolled in, every penny going to support our animals.

Did I hear a fiddler, playing up there on the barn roof?

Deaf I'm not.

A single. I'd been kidding myself. I hadn't been doing a single since Dawn came into my life. She was an indispensable part of everything happening at Spring Farm. She deserved to share equally in the outcome.

And what would that outcome be?

The neighbors assumed that I was filthy rich. They assumed that, as the ex-wife of a Hollywood producer/director, I must be taking daily baths in molten gold and toweling off with hundred-dollar bills. To this day many of them still believe that. Nothing could be further from the truth. Ask my banker. Hollywood isn't like it is in the movies. Hollywood is only like Hollywood *in* the movies. Producer/directors aren't always millionaires, and their ex-wives get, proportionately, as good or as bad a deal as any other ex-wives. My five years of alimony ended in 1981. I'd had a house on the market in West Hollywood, mortgaged to the hilt, on which I took a bath in the real estate crash of the mid-1980s. Beyond that, I owned Spring Farm, also mortgaged. I received paltry royalty checks from my books, even more paltry residual checks from television performances, and sporadic checks when community property assets made distributions or were sold. It was with this occasional income, and an additional mortgage on the farm, that I'd been able to finance all the construction, remodel the barn, take care of the animals, and live my eccentric life. I guess the neighbors can be forgiven for thinking that I had millions as, over the years, they'd witnessed the farm grow and horses begin to sprout from every bush.

By 1989, I'd shot my wad. To keep going, I began to sell off chunks of the farm.

What was I doing? To where was all of this leading?

Well . . . wherever it led, I suddenly understood that Dawn would be walking beside me.

"I guess you *are* my business partner," I told her.

She just nodded. "Okay."

But we needed income!

One day the mail brought a flyer from an organization called Hypnodyne, announcing a weekend course in hypnosis, with certification to practice hypnosis professionally.

I'd had remarkable experiences with hypnosis. In 1957, my dentist had extracted all four of my wisdom teeth in one sitting using hypnosis. I had felt no pain, and that night I had eaten normally, again without pain or complications. In 1972, I had stopped smoking with hypnosis. It had taken one session, and not only had I stopped smoking, I had never again even craved a cigarette. I had sent my father to the same hypnotist. After fifty years as a heavy smoker, he had had the same experience.

But certification in one weekend?

Again we were sitting at Mother's breakfast table when I announced, "We're going to Boston next weekend. We're going to become hypnotists."

Dawn was used to me by now, and, after all, she'd been to Maine. Plus California. We made arrangements with Dennis and Jackie, loaded a mattress and bedding, food, and whatever into good old Vanessa, and, the next weekend, with Mr. Fraser as passenger, went to Boston, returning home Certified Hypnotists.

One shouldn't be alarmed by the fact that it took just one weekend. Very few of those taking the course actually attempt to practice. Even fewer practice successfully. You've got to have what it takes. As always, natural selection prevails.

Those who are serious about the matter also do a lot of follow-up reading and studying.

For the next two years Dawn and I practiced, successfully—receiving clients at first in the barn, later in offices in a professional building in Clinton.

The greater part of our practice was "stop smoking." Our success rate with men was about 90 percent, with women about 65 percent. We attributed this to a sociological difference between the sexes. Men have generally been taught to just *do* a thing. Women, on the other hand . . . well, "It's a woman's right to change her mind." Society insists that women are weak-willed, indecisive creatures. Unfortunately, many of them believe it.

Then there were the weight loss people. No statistics regarding the sexes could be determined there, as most weight loss clients were women.

Occasionally we got really interesting cases. We helped agoraphobics go back out into the world and claustrophobics go into their closets. We helped people overcome test anxiety, fear of heights, animals, and any manner of bugga-boo. We still get calls from old clients, hoping that we're still practicing, while several clients became good friends. We're proud of the work we did and grateful for the income it provided.

But each day our bills mounted. More and more got piled onto credit cards. If we couldn't generate more income, we'd go under.

We couldn't go under. We'd promised our animal friends a home for life.

We scheduled more clinics, workshops, and lectures—TT.E.A.M. with LTJ or Robyn, Sally Swift's Centered Riding with Mitzi Summers, and Proper Balance Movement with Tony Gonzales. We gave Reiki workshops, Creative Writing workshops, and lectures on myriad topics. Penelope Smith started coming once a year to teach her Beginning Animal Communication Workshop. She and Dawn hit it off, becoming confidantes, and we began sending Dawn out to Penelope's home in Point Reyes for advanced training. (So much for California weirdos.) Dawn and I began teaching TT.E.A.M. workshops ourselves, at home and as guest instructors around the state, and we took students privately.

On top of all that, we began to board problem horses for extended TT.E.A.M. training. There were the Morgans, Symphony and her daughter, Serenade, both of whom needed to learn manners; Bobby, a young Trekhaner stallion with both medical and behavioral problems; Lady, a Morgan filly and undisciplined hussy; and Flash, a Quarter Horse stallion with the dangerous habit of crowding.

Still we got further behind on the mortgages, utilities, and property taxes, while the combined amount on my credit cards was staggering. The possibility of bankruptcy, of losing the farm, became real. At one point the bank even sent a man to measure the buildings, anticipating foreclosure. Loans from Mother and my friend Jerry Kenion came to our rescue at that point. But the respite was temporary. I began to have trouble sleeping. Mostly I just tossed and turned, worrying, worrying.

Throughout all this, Dawn's uncle, Karl Fredericks, a tax accountant from New York City, kept telling us, "You've *got* to go nonprofit. It's the only way you'll survive."

He might as well have been telling us to become panhandlers on some street corner.

"We can't ask people for money," we said.

"No, you don't understand what nonprofits are all about. The IRS grants tax-exempt status to organizations that intend to legitimately provide services to the public. When you solicit donations, you're not soliciting for yourselves, you're soliciting for the animals, you're soliciting support for programs and services that a certain segment of the public wants and needs. Look, you already *are* a charity, except that you two are making one hundred percent of the donations!"

By then we'd taken in more horses—Deelight, daughter of Deeteza; Tara, an Arab mare being retired from breeding; Topaz and Toby, retired from a riding school; Gigi's son Raja, again from Carol's stable and elderly himself; Iron Isle (Ginnie), a Thoroughbred mare from Graywood; and Riago, a two-year-old Bavarian Warmblood given too much stress too soon. Then there were the colts and fillies: Bo's Tutti, Deelight's Meloudee, Babe's Breezie, Gypsy's Mariah, Ginnie's Ember and Story, and Tina's TLC.

Kazinka's TLC, really. With that foal, Kazinka took her revenge on Tina, stealing TLC's affection to the point that he spent all his time with Kazinka, going to Tina only to nurse.

We also had another dog, Buddy, a white German Shepherd stray, hit by a car out in the road one Sunday morning. The first vet we took him to felt that, like Max, he'd never again have the use of his back legs. We got a second vet, Steve Abel. An operation and

Steve's acupuncture put Buddy back on his feet. He had epileptic seizures, but Bach Flower Rescue Remedy helped to control them.

Then there were a dozen new cats and two goats, Roo and Rosebud.

"What's going to happen to these animals when you go under?" Karl kept asking. "Euthanasia? The meat market?"

"Of course not! We'll never let that happen!"

"Then wise up! You *must* become a nonprofit."

I finally went out and bought a book, Mancuso's *How to Form a Nonprofit Corporation*, which walked me through the process.

Not that it was easy. I spent months acquainting myself, and Dawn, with the realities of not-for-profit corporations, understanding what we were letting ourselves in for, the enormous responsibilities, legally and morally, that we were taking on. We had to make decisions about what kind of not-for-profit we wanted to be, come up with a statement of goals and programs, come to terms with the enormous turn that life was taking.

After those months, using the forms in the book, I submitted a stack of paperwork to the IRS.

To our astonishment, only weeks later, in January 1991, the IRS answered.

We were no longer Spring Farm. We were Spring Farm Center Alternative Research Education Sanctuary, "CARES" for short, a 501c3 not-for-profit. It remained only to register our corporation with New York State.

The whole thing cost the price of the book, my time, and $150 in the required fees.

But oh, the vast new responsibility.

Yet with 501c3 status came powers that we hadn't had before. The power of raison d'être. Of delineated intentions. The power to hold fund-raisers to help support the animals, to approach media, get stories and information about ourselves and our animals out to the public, to apply for grants, to solicit donations, to speak up in public as a legitimate haven for animals, to begin educating people about the humane treatment of animals.

And the power to look to the future and dream big.

The Universe always knows what's going on. Because the Universe, All That Is, participates in each and every "becoming" of any happening. The moment we became a 501c3, word flashed to the world via invisible tendrils—"They're open for business!"—and we began receiving calls regarding abused animals.

Hence, into our lives on May 5, 1991, by means of a phone call, came Nancy McElwain, executive director of the Stevens Swan Humane Society.

"Do you people happen to have a horse trailer?"

Tiger Lil and our Thoroughbred trailer had long since gone byebye to help pay bills, but we knew a woman with a trailer who'd help.

"And could you help us move the horse?" asked Nancy.

That morning, glancing into an overgrown pasture where he was working, a telephone lineman had noticed a clump of something that he thought was a dead bush. Then it moved. He didn't know what sort of animal it was, but he knew it needed help, and he called Stevens Swan.

Bob Wokowski, the society's humane officer, nearly had an apoplectic fit when he entered that field to investigate. It was a Shetland pony, encrusted with burdock. No face was visible. Just one soft little eye was visible through an open space in the burdock-matted ropes of mane. The tail was indistinguishable as such. The body was a mass of burdock-plastered hair that hadn't shed out for years. We later weighed the burdock that we took off her. It weighed twenty pounds.

Her hooves hadn't been trimmed in years. And she'd foundered repeatedly. The hoof of the left fore grew forward for about eight inches, upward for about eight inches, then backward, the jagged end actually cutting into her leg just below the "knee." The hoof of the right fore doubled under so that she was walking on the front of the fetlock (roughly equivalent to an ankle), and the backward-trailing hoof was fourteen inches long. The hooves of the back legs were a foot long, growing forward and upward.

The field in which she stood was solid weeds. Only in a circle about twenty feet in diameter around her were the weeds eaten down. There was a pond a hundred feet away and trees for shade a hundred feet in the opposite direction. But that pony hadn't been out of her twenty-foot circle in quite some time. She couldn't walk on those feet, all she could do was ski. So she'd had no shelter, had had only the weeds in that circle for food, and for water . . . what? Morning dew?

Even by the inadequate standards of our state, it was a clear-cut case of animal abuse. We later learned that her owners had "put her out into the field to die"—three years earlier.

For three years that pony had stood there, refusing to cooperate.

Bob swung into action, getting an order from a properly indignant judge for the pony's immediate removal from the premises, while Nancy called for our help. It was the beginning of a warm and fuzzy, mutually beneficial relationship between Spring Farm and Stevens Swan that lasted through Nancy's tenure.

We made arrangements with Lori, the girl with the trailer, to meet us at that farm in an hour. Then we loaded Effie with every piece of equipment we could think of—various-size foal and yearling halters, every description of lead and rope, baling twine, stall guards and sheepskin girths with which to fashion a sling, a sheet of one-inch plywood, a platform used in TT.E.A.M. training that was three by six feet and eight inches high, a feed pail, grain and carrots, a jug of water—because if we couldn't drive into the field to load the pony, we'd have to walk, drag, or carry her out. And we didn't know how sick she might be. Or how ornery.

The place was directly across the valley from us. Bob Wokowski and Betsy, Stevens Swan's assistant director, were in the yard when we arrived. The pony's owners were sequestered in the house. Waiting for the trailer, we assessed the situation. The terrain was too rough to drive into the field. Somehow Sugar, as Bob had learned that she was called, would have to be brought out over a distance of about 150 feet.

"Let's go take a look at her," I said.

Dawn and I gasped as we got near.

"I'm seeing it," I said, "but I don't believe it,"

"She can't even lie down normally," said Dawn. "She can't curl her feet up under herself."

Sugar never moved as we stood there trying to decide what to do. That one kind little eye peered up at us through the hole in the burdock. She didn't seem able to lift her head.

"Well," I finally said, "let's see if she can get out on her own power."

We got a halter onto her burdock-laden head and attached a lead, then hooked a couple of fat rope leads together, looped them around her butt, and waved some carrot pieces in front of her

She got a bite and reached for more. Gently urging, with pressure on the lead rope and support from the butt ropes, we helped her slide, ski, awkwardly forward. A few slide-skis, then she'd rest. That poor little head never lifted. A few more slide-skis, and rest again. It was going to be a long, hard trip. But it looked as though she could do it.

Bob led, trampling the weeds to give her a path.

Slide . . . slide . . . slide. Slowly we covered a hundred feet.

Then new energy enlivened that little body. Sugar later told us that that was when she saw the open gate and realized that she was leaving that terrible field. Suddenly Bob couldn't trample weeds fast enough. Ski ski ski ski ski ski ski! Straight out the gate.

The trailer had just arrived. That little eye grew brighter as Lori backed it to the spot where we waited. We opened the back doors and put the platform under the back lip as a half-step up.

"This will be hard. We'll probably have to lift her."

Wrong. Without hesitation, Sugar scrambled up onto the platform, then up into the trailer.

That pony *really* wanted to leave.

We slung the stall guards under her belly and fastened them to either side of the trailer with baling twine. I rode home beside her, bracing her from the bumps, starts, and stops.

Once home, with the trailer backed up to the door of the arena and the back doors opened, I cut her loose from the sling. The others were just about to put the platform in place and were discussing ways to lift her down, when Sugar simply leaped headlong out of the trailer. Luckily they were there to halfway catch and steady her.

Again she didn't hesitate. She skied straight into the arena—straight to a chip of hay laying there. God only knows how long it had been since she'd had hay. She lit into it passionately.

She told us afterward that she thought she'd died. She thought we were angels who'd brought her to Heaven.

We yearned to attack with scissors and clippers, but Sugar was a crime scene. Only after evidential photos and videos were taken were we free to clean her up.

That miserable, burdock-matted mane went first.

And there she was! *Two* eyes now, so bright! And a beautiful little face.

We had to cut all the hair off of her tail, leaving just a cute, stumpy little puff. We clipped her coat down only partway. Dr. Lain warned that since she'd been used to a dense coat for three years, it would shock her thermostat to take it all off at once. Later, with proper nutrition, she'd shed out naturally. All cleaned up, she was gray-blue rather than dun brown.

And what a radiant little girl we had. Getting that junk off must have been like jumping into a clear, cool pool after years in the desert, while the loneliness she'd endured became apparent as she skied happily around the arena, nickering to all the other horses.

We'd have understood even better had we known that she thought she was in Heaven.

What a survivor. She was eighteen, middle-aged for ponies who've been cared for. For a pony who'd endured the life that Sugar had, it was getting on.

She literally couldn't lift her head. That heavy burdock had been there so long, and for so long she'd had to peer upward in order to see, that the muscles in her neck were trained that way. As manes tend to fall naturally to one side, the crest of her neck lay limply over to that favored side, having for so long been pulled downward by the weight of burdock. And once we got her tail trimmed off, we realized that she couldn't move it.

We set immediately to work with TTouch on neck, crest, and tail, reconnecting her nervous system to the brain, reminding her muscles that they were alive.

The tail responded quickly. How it tickled us to see that dead stump finally twitch. Then swish. Then swish swish. Then engage in an orgy of joyous swishing.

After a couple of days of TTouch, she started to lift her head. Only that folded-over crest took months to regain muscle tone and return to its proper position.

People who'd known Sugar for years later gave us heart-wrenching accounts: of Sugar standing out in that pasture in snow-storms, a foot or more of snow accumulated on her downcast head, neck, and back; of children from the family being allowed to ride her, even whip her to run, with her feet in that condition; of baby after baby being pumped out of her during prior years; of watching her try to lie down and get comfortable with those lobster claws.

Why hadn't those people called the humane society? Some of them had. Sugar's owners had had a pony-breeding operation. Sugar was the only one left. Details of the way that the ponies had been treated, and the way in which some of them had died, were nauseating. And the abusers *had* been up on charges of animal abuse before. But each time, judges had given them nothing more than a slap on the wrist. These people were feared. Feared by their relations, by neighbors—and, we discovered, by the judiciary. Because the judge who had at first been so angered, who had issued the writ and been ready to throw the book at them—which could have meant a thousand-dollar fine, a year in jail, and orders never again to own animals—that judge had obviously been talked to by someone. He backed down. In the end, Sugar's abusers were required only to relinquish her and to pay $350 in vet/farrier bills.

It didn't matter to Sugar. Not anymore. When we asked her what punishment she'd have given her abusers, we expected a harsh reply. Instead, her mild, almost wistful response told us that, to her, the worst part of what she'd endured had been the loneliness.

"I'd lock each of them in a room for a year and not let anyone go near them," she said.

And when, months later, the obituary of one of her former owners appeared in the paper and we told her about it, all she said was "He's going to have a hard time of it over there."

Life had become too beautiful to harbor grudges. The simplest things were treasures to Sugar. Even a feed dish and water bucket of her very own sent her into paroxysms of delight.

Two days after her arrival, our then farrier, George Buell, came to do her feet. He stood open-mouthed at the sight of her.

"I've never seen anything like it. I'm not sure what will happen if we try to trim her back to normal. I'm not even sure there's a 'normal' left to find."

He'd have to use a hacksaw to get most of the length off, then rasp and file to start re-forming what was left back into hooves. There was no way that Sugar could stay upright while all that was being done.

But we attacked the problem.

And attacked is the right word.

Nancy McElwain, Betsy, and Bob were there to help with the "great foot restructuring," along with Dawn, George, and myself. Our first thought was to just lay Sugar over on her side and hold her there while George worked. Easy. She probably weighed only two hundred and fifty pounds.

Have you ever watched six big, strong adults attempt to lay on her side a pony who doesn't care to be laid on her side?

Back to the old drawing board.

A sling. We trussed her up with one side of the sling attached to a gate. The other side was held up by Nancy, Betsy, and Bob. Dawn held her head, and I brought up the rear, literally, since, with alarming frequency, Sugar attempted to sit down.

We told jokes as George worked, to keep from thinking about how heavy a pony can be. The process took more than two hours. Midway through we reversed her in the sling, so that George could work on her other side. By then Sugar was pretty disgusted with the whole process—perhaps this wasn't Heaven after all.

When George was finished, her skis had been shortened to clubby-toed skates. Not knowing where the quick was now, he hadn't dared cut any further. The new feet weren't pretty, but what a joy it was for Sugar the first time that she lay down and discovered that she could fold her feet under herself.

It would be many more months before she had anything even faintly resembling normal hooves. If even that was to be. Because X-rays taken by Dr. Koenneke the next day revealed some amazing things. Inside the left fore, whose hoof had curled up and grown back into the leg, Sugar had *dissolved bone*, creating a gelatinous mass that allowed for cushioned movement. Inside the right fore, where she was walking on the front of her fetlock, she'd developed a sort of internal hoof. She'd grown new bone on which to walk!

"*That* is survival at work," murmured Dr. Koenneke as he studied the pictures.

Nancy later confessed to us that they at the humane society had been afraid that we, the "horse experts," would decree that Sugar should be put down. While we'd been afraid that the humane society would decree the same thing. After seeing Sugar's joy just to be alive again, putting her down shouldn't have been in question.

Yet it was.

Dawn and I assumed that she must be in terrible pain. There was no way, we thought, with these rapid changes in her hooves and in all the muscles of her body, that she wouldn't be. Were we being cruel not to put her down?

And what would people think, coming into the barn and seeing that misshapen little creature? Would they be scandalized, thinking that we were terrible people to be so cruel? Would people pressure us to put her down?

What will the neighbors say? I wish that that question could be blotted out of the collective mind of the species.

This was early in our spiritual becoming, early in our understanding of the fact that many animals are Master Teachers, angels even, come to show humanity the way back to its spiritual core— that, additionally, most animals are no more eager to be "shown the kindness of death" just because they're experiencing pain than we would be—and that they have as much right to continue living, and dealing with their pain, as we have.

When Sugar came to us, Dawn and I hadn't yet found our spiritual cores; we didn't yet understand the validity of our own authority or comprehend the enormity of the spiritual message that Spring Farm CARES had come into being to give to the world. We still sometimes looked to others for guidance, afraid to follow our own hearts and souls and to heck with what other people said.

So we called Linda Tellington-Jones for advice. To our distress, she recommended euthanasia.

Our goddess had spoken.

Luckily, our trust in our selves came quickly to the fore.

And we realized that we'd been unfair to both Linda and Sugar. Linda had had only our description of Sugar's condition to go on. And that description had been appalling. Had Linda been able to see Sugar's shining eyes, she would never have suggested putting her down.

Just as when we'd allowed those two women to try to load Deeteza, the fault was ours, for failing to trust ourselves, for seeking authority outside our own hearts.

No, we wouldn't kill that joyous little creature who'd overcome all odds to survive, who'd rebuilt her own body. Sugar's exuberance filled the stable. She was so obviously enjoying the company of the other animals, chowing down with gusto, proud of her own stall with private dish and bucket, greeting all comers with happy nickers, loving the attention she was receiving.

Pain? Well, if she was in pain, she wasn't even giving it the time of day. The vets whom we consulted agreed. Leigh Lain, Fritz Koenneke, the chiropractic vet Sue Ann Lesser, and the homeopathic vet Joyce Harmon all joined Sugar's cheering section.

Thank God. Had we killed Sugar, we would have killed a Master Teacher who'd come expressly to help show us the way. We'd have robbed Spring Farm CARES of part of its soul.

. . . while robbing Sugar of her own fulfillment in this lifetime.

~ II ~

Spring Farm CARES and the Universal Party Line

Throughout the years, visitors have said again and again, "It's so peaceful here."

Often things don't seem peaceful to us as we go about our fourteen-to-sixteen-hour days, often contending with hassles and emergencies. But the people who come here understand what has been created, and they soak it up.

Because Spring Farm CARES is a place where not only do animals and people communicate, but trees, flowers, bushes, and rocks as well. It's a place where no one looks askance if someone sees a troll in the garden, or elves, fairies, ghosts, angels, or extraterrestrials. It's a place where no one judges the realities that others create and perceive.

And we've had some wonderful realities created here. Our intent, Dawn's and mine, allows minds and spirits to open to things that our culture forbids us to consider "real." Our intent has created a special little universe, covered by an invisible dome and guarded by angels.

Spring Farm was special before either Dawn or I came onto the scene. In our pasture is a tree that experts say is more than four hundred years old. The God Tree. This place was sacred to the Indians long before whites decimated the continent. The sacred quality remains, announces itself to visitors, and opens portals to other wavelengths—allows other worlds to see us and us to see them.

We have a small army of ghosts, human and animal, all benevolent, all welcome.

The most prominent human ghost is my grandfather Francis Merritt Jones.

He first made his presence known one day in 1987, as Dawn, Mother, Gail, and I were trying to move furniture up the stairs in Mother's house. That furniture had belonged to Grampa and Gramma Jones. I'd intercepted it as Peggy was about to sell it at a garage sale. There were two pieces, a settee and the armchair in which Grampa had died. I planned to put them in the large central room upstairs. That seemed appropriate. The house had been Gramma and Grampa's before we moved there in 1945, and that central room had once been their bedroom, where my father had been born.

The stairwell, though, is narrow, and there's a bend at the bottom. It's always been difficult to get anything bigger than a bread box up or down those stairs.

I was determined, however. We worked with the chair first. We took the door off its hinges to allow another inch or two and tried the chair up, down, sideways, every which way. We worked and worked at it.

"It's not going to go," said Mother finally.

Suddenly Dawn, up on the staircase, said, "Humor me."

I looked at her sharply.

"Turn it to the right," she directed. "Now slip that corner in here and flip it toward me."

Voilà! Up the stairs it went. Dawn repeated the performance with the even larger settee.

"Does anyone smell pipe tobacco?" she asked once we'd gotten the pieces into place.

None of us did.

"Gee," she said, "I sure do."

Mother had begun to notice Dawn's psychic talents. "What *kind* of pipe tobacco?"

"A very sweet smell."

"Oh." Mother's matter-of-factness amazed me. "That would be Mr. Jones, Harwood's father. The only way Mrs. Jones would let him smoke was if he smoked really sweet-smelling tobacco."

And what we'd been trying to move up the stairs was the chair in which he'd died.

"How did you do that?" I asked Dawn afterward.

"I don't know. All of a sudden I seemed to be hovering overhead in the stairwell. I could see exactly what had to be done to make the chair go up."

Grampa continued to make his presence known to Dawn. At that point she did the closing chores in the stable while I did the chores in the barn. One night, shortly after the furniture episode, she was dragging the hose around, topping off water buckets in the nursery, when the flow stopped, as though someone were standing on the hose somewhere along its length.

"Bonnie?"

There was no answer. The flow of water resumed. Must have been air in the line.

Then it stopped again.

"Who's there? Get off the hose!"

The water started again. Then it stopped again.

Dawn dropped the hose and went storming out into the arena to confront the trickster.

There was no one there.

Only some *thing*.

The distinct aroma of sweet pipe tobacco.

These "appearances" became frequent. The water would stop, and Dawn would smell that tobacco. She took to calling out, "Hi, Grampa. Nice evening, huh?"

It made sense for him to be taking an interest in what we were doing. His Spring Farm had revolved around his Holstein cattle, but his second pride and joy had been his horses. He was taking pleasure in his granddaughter's version of Spring Farm.

And perhaps he was sending me a message.

Throughout my childhood I'd repeatedly been told of Grampa's disappointment that I hadn't been a boy, who'd continue Spring Farm.

Then, one summer day when I was thirteen, we were out in a field loading hay. Mother was driving the truck, Daddy and Grampa were picking up bales and throwing them onto the flatbed, and I was stacking them, five and six tiers high, easily tossing sixty-pound bales over my head.

I'd just tossed one such bale and turned back for the next one. Grampa was leaning on the tailgate, wiping sweat from his brow and watching me.

"Bonnie," he said, "you're as good as a boy any day."

No accolade that I'd ever receive would match that given to me in those few words. No other words could have given me as much confidence in myself, in my right to exist and to be me, whatever "me" would turn out to be.

Would that all kids could have such words spoken to them.

Now Spring Farm *had* been continued. By a girl. Who knew herself to be as good as anyone else on the face of the earth.

Dawn and I take comfort in Grampa's visits, and our employees, many of whom have found themselves suddenly surrounded by that sweet aroma, take it in stride.

"Hey Bonnie," I'll hear over my walkie-talkie. "Your grampa's down here in the tack room. Got any message for him?"

Yes.

"Grampa, you're as good as a girl any day."

One visitor from another wavelength was more disconcerting. Again, Dawn was alone in the stable one night, getting feed out of a bin. Suddenly a pail sitting on a nearby bin crashed to the floor, and behind her a young male voice said, "Good evening."

Dawn spun around. There was no one there.

Yet she "felt" who it was. She came to the barn and said, "Garry was out in the stable just now."

Garry, Aunt Milly's son, the one carried off by Grampa Newcomb in Aunt Ida's dream.

Dawn's "feeling" was confirmed later that evening. She was working at her desk when she glanced toward the main entrance. We kept that eight-by-eight-foot overhead door up in the summer. Fitted into the opening were screened panels and a screen door. Standing just outside that screen door was Garry Leonard, in full-dress uniform.

Dawn knew his appearance well. I kept his picture on my desk.

He was looking straight at Dawn, relaxed, hands in pockets. She "felt" his words.

"Don't be scared. There's nothing to be afraid of."

Then he was gone.

As though to validate Dawn's experiences, the next night a female employee, with no knowledge of what had happened the night before, was in the stable getting feed out of the bins when, again, a pail was suddenly knocked to the floor and a young male voice behind her said, "Good evening."

She came running to the barn, declaring that she'd never go near the stable again.

Garry made no further appearances. But we've learned that it takes a lot of energy for those from other dimensions to even impinge on our senses, much less knock objects to the floor and become visible. Garry must have felt a pressing need to make himself known.

Why to Dawn?

For a multitude of reasons, long before Garry's appearance, we'd come to suspect that Dawn was the reincarnation of Garry Leonard. It's interesting that, in this life, seemingly against odds, Dawn visited Aunt Milly in her home in Idaho and has met both of Garry's sisters. Interesting, too, that Garry's fiancée was named Janice—as is Dawn's sister.

Coincidences.

But there's no such thing as coincidence.

One visitation was fleeting and mysterious.

We were having a celebrity auction, arranged by our friend Cissy Wellman, the daughter of director William Wellman, with our friend Werner Klemperer, "Colonel Klink," and the radio personality Jack Baxter donating their talents as auctioneers. There was to be a buffet before the auction, laid out in the center of the haymow. I was racing back and forth, up and down the stairs from kitchen to haymow, bringing the food and arranging it on the tables.

On one trip, as I emerged into the haymow, a tall, slender man with long hair and a beard, wearing a long white robe, was just walking into the granary, where, at that time, we had our thrift shop.

I'd put a sign outside the door saying that no one was allowed into the haymow until the dinner bell rang. I plopped down my tray and ran to the granary to ask the intruder to leave.

Except that there was no one in the granary.

That one has remained a puzzle. More than anyone, the man resembled various depictions of Jesus. But what Jesus would have wanted in our thrift shop is beyond me.

In all the buildings, old and new, there've been "ghostly" happenings. Disembodied footsteps. Cold spots. On one occasion someone invisible came up behind an employee and hugged her. Toilets are flushed by invisible hands. Something very large but unseen often crashes against one of the buildings. Unseen hands throw things down stairways. There's a little man who sits on the roof over my bedroom. Inexplicable things happen with electricity and electronic equipment. A gray cat has been seen by most of the employees. That's probably Bonniecat Endore. Several weeks after her death I saw her curled in Mother's lap as Mother slept in her recliner.

Then there were the ghost horses. There was a spot just at the top of the stairs leading into the haymow—just at the spot from where I saw the man in white—where the scent of horses was sometimes unmistakable. We thought we were imagining things until Dennis happened to be going up those stairs one day, stopped at the top, and said, "I smell horses." There hadn't been horses in that barn for fifty-five years. When horses *had* been in the barn, their stalls had been downstairs, and at the other end. Additionally, during all the years of my growing up, there'd never been the scent of horses anywhere in that barn.

Why would that scent suddenly be there? Was the spirit of Gigi visiting? Or did the horses now living on the property somehow attract equine spirits from out of the past?

One interesting point is that Grampa had built my barn only in 1932. He'd lost two barns to fire, his cow barn in 1929 and a smaller barn in 1930. (He, too, had been caught flat-footed with no insurance. It's another sickness that runs in the family.) This last barn replaced the small barn that had burned in 1930. That small barn had been located just slightly down the slope from the new one. Its east side would have overlapped the location of those stairs.

It had been Grampa's horse barn.

Then there were the galloping ghost horses. We haven't heard them in years, but they used to gallop at night, from about the present arena, behind the barn, and straight onto the field beyond. They'd often bring us running, thinking that we had horses loose. One night they even brought workshop students, camping out in that yonder field, bursting out of their tents in the middle of the night, thinking they were about to be trampled in a stampede.

And there were the UFOs. By UFO I mean an airborne object that is unidentifiable to the understanding of the observer. I'd seen two "unidentified" craft at Spring Farm, while the neighbors up the street, just beyond Burmaster Road, had grown accustomed to the airborne lights that often appeared over the fields behind their homes at night. Griffiths Air Force Base, a major SAC base, was fifteen miles away. Maybe what we were all seeing had to do with secret goings-on at Griffiths.

Coming to work before sunup one morning, when she still lived over on Paris Hill Road, Dawn encountered a UFO. Her first thought was that it was a search-and-rescue helicopter, for it was hovering over our next-door neighbor Walt Savicki's strawberry field, shining a light down onto the ground. Looking closely at what was shining the light, however, Dawn saw that it was a whitish cloud. And there was no sound. She didn't stay around to ask questions.

One day Peggy, who's not one to indulge in flights of fancy, was driving along near the spot where Dawn had seen the mysterious cloud when the front end of her car rose several feet off of the ground. She drove along for some seconds like that, doing a sort of back-end "wheelie"; then the front end gently settled back down onto the road. Peg related the incident matter-of-factly and has never mentioned it again.

She reminds me of Martha Axelrod, a friend who told a group of us one day about an incident in a manor house inn in Scotland, where she and her husband had stopped for the night. Once into bed, he dropped off immediately, but she lay counting sheep. As she did so, a door in the opposite wall opened. A man came and stood at the foot of their bed. She described him in detail: his physique, countenance, and dress from an earlier age.

"What did you do?" we asked.

"What *could* I do? I said, 'Go away!' and I pulled the covers over my head, huddled up against Bernie, and went to sleep. The next morning I looked at that wall. There *had* been a door there, but it was bricked up."

Martha then said that what she had seen hadn't happened.

"But you saw him," we all said. "And you were awake."

"Yes, I saw him. And I was definitely awake. But it didn't happen."

"Then you're making it up," we persisted.

"No. It happened. But I don't *believe* that it did."

It's an attitude that afflicts many of us. Oh yes, we saw it. But we don't believe we saw it. Things like that aren't allowed to happen—to other people, maybe, but not to us. So we consign the incident to a locked room in memory and forget it until someone happens to be relating something that happened to them. Then suddenly we say, "Gee. Now I think about it, something like that happened to me once, too." We tell the story and then put it back into that locked room. Because the things in that room don't jibe with the reality that we've accepted, the reality that our society tells us we *must* accept—or else be thought weird, unstable, foolish, or even insane.

At Spring Farm CARES we unlock those hidden rooms and bring unofficial experiences out into the light of day. With their help, we expand our experience and understanding of "reality," our idea of what is possible, even normal, if only we'll open our minds to those possibilities.

Some of our visitors have been treated to UFO sightings. Or, in one case, hearings. A UFO was heard on two separate occasions by people sleeping over for clinics, some in the bunk room, others out in the field in tents. All were roused from sleep by the approach of what they thought was a single-engine plane, a real putt-putt, the engine sounding sort of like a riding lawn mower. It was coming down the hill from the direction of the Savicki farm, slow, very loud, and low. Those who came hastily out of their tents and the bunkroom thought that the plane was crashing. It flew directly over the house, at a height that witnesses said was not more than a couple of hundred feet.

Except there was nothing there. Only the sound.

That sound flew on toward Utica, until it could be heard no more.

Just as everyone had finished exclaiming and comparing notes and gotten back into bed, the mystery craft was heard returning. Again everyone piled out and strained to see what it could be. It went right over them again, at the same height, in the same line of flight, back up the hill toward Savicki's, where the sound faded till it could be heard no more. And that was that.

All in all, on those two occasions, about a dozen people witnessed the "invisible flying rider mower."

Then there were the inquisitive lights witnessed by Barry Greco, who accompanied his wife, Thurman, to a workshop. (And cooked for us!) The summer nights were balmy, so he and Thurman decided that it would be nice to sleep on couches out on our porch.

Sometime during the first night Barry awakened, looked over at the edge of the porch, and realized that he was being watched. By a light. It was about the size of a mango. It was just hanging above the porch railing, observing him. He doesn't know how he knew that it was observing him, he just knew. He felt no fear. He understood that it was benign, and he began to observe *it*. Several more lights joined it, all watching him as he watched them. Finally they all flew away.

Like Peggy with her car doing wheelies, the next morning Barry mentioned the episode with an almost ho-hum attitude.

After all, he was at Spring Farm. What was there to be surprised at?

From the moment of their arrivals, Deeteza and Sugar stood out from the rest. They communicated easily and often forcefully with us and with visitors, and quickly established themselves as Master Teachers.

Let it be said that the other horses weren't jealous of them. Horses, we've learned, are noble beings, despite disparaging remarks made about them by much less noble humans who try to ride or use, and all too often abuse, them. Were horses less noble, there'd be a heck of a lot more dead or damaged human beings lying around.

But souls incarnate in the form of horses for as many reasons as souls incarnate as humans or any other animal, and their personalities are as varied. As are their strengths and weaknesses, their desires and aspirations, and their tendencies to perfection or defection. Yet it's interesting to note that, while we humans often kill the Masters who appear among us, horses graciously make way for theirs.

Deeteza.

How to describe her? She was vain. Vain of her ears, her mane, and her bloodlines. And she had her fears and phobias, as evidenced by the trailering trouble.

I don't think that Deeteza knew until she'd spent time at Spring Farm that she was a Master. I think it came to her. We, and Spring Farm, helped her greatness to blossom while she helped us to blossom, Dawn in particular.

I can hardly remember a communication from Deeteza after we got her back to Spring Farm that wasn't a declarative statement. Hers was a strong, commanding, and often demanding personality, never any ifs, ands, or buts. Although when she was in the process of teaching you something, she did it in easy steps, often with sly humor, until you came by yourself to the realization that she intended you to come to. If Kazinka was the Bette Davis of horses, Deeteza was the Katharine Hepburn.

Sugar was as different from Dee as oranges from lemons. Quietude, gentleness, joy, and gratitude are word portraits of Sugar. Sugar lived lightly on the world, like a stirring of air that is the softest of breezes, expecting nothing for herself, lovingly stroking all that she touched.

She told us that in a previous life she'd been an Indian medicine woman, Nicohee. Soon her communications validated that statement. If a horse in the barn was ill or injured, Sugar would dictate a remedy for it. And gosh darn if Sugar's remedies didn't work. Soon the first question from the veterinarian Leigh Lain when she was called in to help a horse was "What does Sugar say?"

There was one particular remedy that we shared with anyone who asked for it. Some months later we learned that the remedy had made its way to Pennsylvania, where it was being used to good effect by a popular vet there. That vet told people that she'd gotten the remedy from an Indian medicine woman—without mentioning that the Indian medicine woman was now a Shetland pony.

Deeteza, on the other hand, was a seeress. The Great Voice, the animals called her. She had a meditation spot up on a hill overlooking the stable, where she spent hours each day, head lowered, her spirit voyaging. Deeteza was the one who announced the changes, made the proclamations—for Deeteza was in communication with the birds. The birds, she explained to Dawn, were the bringers of news, of wisdom, and especially of change.

"Watch the birds," she told Dawn. "And listen. The birds encircle the globe. They carry messages from Mother Earth herself, if only you'll grow the ears to hear what they have to tell you."

Daily Deeteza talked with Dawn, teaching, advising, encouraging, teasing, upbraiding—and loving. The bond between them grew steadily, becoming a solid and beautiful bridge seemingly between two species, but really between two hearts.

I really do think that, out of the whole Universe, Dee loved Dawn the best.

She didn't seem to give a hoot about any of her children. When Gail Nash called and asked us to take Dee's last foal, Deelight, Dee just shrugged.

"You might like her. Of all my foals she *looks* the most like me."

Deelight did indeed look like Deeteza—so much so that when they stood together, the uninitiated wouldn't have been able to tell them apart.

Of course, they almost never stood together. Dee made it plain from the get-go that she was happy with her pasturemates and would vehemently object to having Deelight added to that company.

Dee had been forced to give birth repeatedly, all at the whim of us humans. She'd done her duty. That, as far as she was concerned, should be the end of it. She had another calling now, that of the Great Voice. Her progeny had no place in that destiny.

Yet she remained proud of her royal bloodlines. She understood that we, too, valued the blood of Witez II and Nitez and that we'd have Deelight bred. But she showed neither interest in the pregnancy nor in Meloudee once he was born. Being a boy, he'd be gelded, so there was no continuation there.

She only chimed in as we were trying to choose his name.

Arab owners usually include part of the name of a prominent parent or ancestor in the name of a foal. Like Dee*teza*, Ni*tez*, Wi*tez*. To us, though, Dee was the prominent ancestor, so we were looking for a name to incorporate "Dee."

One day Dee called Dawn down to the pasture.

"I've been thinking. I have some favorite flowers. They're purple. A lot of them grow up near my meditation spot. It would be nice if his name could be Dee's _____, the name of that flower."

"Okay."

"There's a problem."

"What?"

"That favorite flower is an aster."

She turned and walked away.

Dawn thought about it for a moment, then realized.

What a snot!

Without Dee's help, we decided on Meloudee, incorporating the "dee," then "lou" from his sire, Louki.

We subsequently learned that the purple flowers that grow in profusion near Dee's meditation spot are, indeed, wild asters.

In the meantime, Sugar was directing the remodeling of her own hooves. Our farrier, George, was a student of Tony Gonzales and totally into animal communication, hence willing to accept Sugar's assistance.

Making Sugar's new feet was a matter of paring back the hooves carefully. At a certain point in a horse's hoof you reach living tissue, much like the quick of a fingernail. With each slice of his paring tool, George risked "quicking" Sugar, causing sharp pain and possible infection.

Here Sugar took the lead. With Dawn interpreting, she'd tell George whether to stop for the day or continue. When George was unsure, she'd have the last paring held up to her nose. She'd sniff it, bite on it, and then say whether or not to proceed.

The procedure was risky for George. Though Sugar had gotten strong enough to stand with each foot raised to be worked on, George was tall and Sugar was short. And her hooves were like rock. The only way for George to comfortably trim her was to lie on his back under her. The thought of quicking her, having her jump in pain and rearrange his face, was unnerving.

On one particular day he was ready to stop. But Sugar bit on the paring and insisted that he continue. Through Dawn she promised

(a) that he was not about to quick her and (b) that she wouldn't trample him if he did. So he kept paring. Then he let out an exclamation.

"I'll be damned. I just found a healthy frog in here!"

A frog is the soft, cushiony, normal inner bottom of a horse's hoof, not some croaking little prince magically imprisoned.

We were mightily impressed, not only with the discovery of a healthy hoof waiting to happen but with Sugar's unerring insight.

Nicohee, medicine woman. She dictated stories of some of her previous existences, wrote poetry, counseled any who asked, and generously helped to heal.

And one day we found her a friend, another Shetland mare. Stevens Swan found Bubbles wandering as a stray. Her owners were located. They didn't want her. Bubbles was old, thirty-three, they said. So to Spring Farm came Bubbles, a useless, unwanted old pony.

Sugar was ecstatic, Bubbles delighted. With Sugar's enthusiastic permission, Bubbles moved into Sugar's own private pipe corral stall and the two of them happily set up housekeeping.

12

Reincarnated Cats
and Pet Mice

Our philosopher and architect, George Kigercat, hadn't remained in the stable for long. Though Prinnie, Sonya, and Captain Zero never attempted to change their status—a status that, we came to understand, is one of great honor among cats, that of Barn Cat—George Kigercat had other career plans. After his first summer and winter with us, we found him following us every time we left the stable and went to the barn.

"George," we told him, "if you come into the house, you're going to *stay* in the house."

"Why can't I go in and out with you?"

"You just can't. We're nervous enough that we have to have any outdoor cats with that killer road."

"I promise not to get killed in the road."

"No. In or out, no in-betweens."

He chose to come in. He was good for about a year; then he started trying to slip out anytime the door opened. By then he'd become so dear that we couldn't bear the thought of losing him.

Ah, the joys of holding George. The way he melted into the arms, the way he'd look up into one's face so adoringly, his little nose so pink, as he watched his chance to play the game that we all knew, to quickly reach up and nip the tip of one's nose.

"Ha! No, George, I saw that one coming."

The way he'd cuddle in my arms at night—in the early days, when I still slept downstairs in the barn, before the apartment was finished—his head on the pillow beside mine, the two of us face-to-face, his topmost paw laid over my neck, snoring softly.

He was suddenly desperate to get outside and eat green grass. Recognizing that he must need it, we started taking him on a leash. That sufficed for only a short time. Then he began not only to beg to be let out but to threaten.

"If you don't let me out, I'll sicken and die."

We kept him in.

About a month later he sickened and nearly died.

It was a serious urinary blockage. Each time the vet got him unblocked, he blocked again. It appeared that he'd just keep doing that. The vet, Steve Abel, suggested operating, "making him a girl" by creating a female-type urethra to prevent future blockages. We opted, before taking that drastic step, to try the homeopathic preparation cantharis. Luckily, Steve, who'd already taken Max out of pain with his skill in acupuncture, is a progressive vet. We delivered the cantharis, and he administered it for us.

The following morning when we called to find out how George was, we were told, "Come get him. He seems totally recovered."

Of course George had won. He was allowed in and out at will. Obviously he was wiser about his own health than we, as there were no more urinary problems for nearly four years.

But how we suffered when he went out. And how he put us

through it. Again and again he'd be gone for hours, sometimes all through the night.

"Geooorge!" Dawn would wail mentally. "Where are you?"

"I'm fine. I'm hunting."

"What are you hunting?"

"Big game." (George always insisted that mice were beneath his dignity.)

Sometimes, though, the answer would be "Leave me alone. I'm sleeping."

"Where are you sleeping?"

"On the big blue thing."

On that occasion we found him asleep on a blue couch in the haymow.

"On the yellow thing."

That one was embarrassing. He must have run in with a visitor. He was there in our living room area, asleep on our yellow couch.

Sometimes he'd take pity on us.

"Please!" Dawn would call. "Come home for just a minute. Let us know you're safe."

Big sigh. "Jeeez! Oh, okay. I'll meet you at the front door of the stable in five minutes."

Sure enough, in five minutes he'd come trotting from this direction or that, interrupting his safaris to calm our anxious hearts.

He told us that he spent a lot of time with a Mr. Peabody, an owl. But when he told us that Mr. Peabody envied his flea collar and wished that someone loved him enough to give *him* a flea collar, we wondered. It never occurred to us, though, when finally we got our hands on the large, long-haired, gray-tiger-and-white stray cat who'd been skulking around the property for a few years, that he was the famous Mr. Peabody.

We knew that he'd been living under Mother's front porch, but we'd never been able to get near him. Then one day we heard a cat fight in the tack room. We could smell "tomcat in distress" well before we got there. Captain Zero had been attacking an intruder, who was hiding behind a chest. We expelled Captain Zero from the room, and gingerly I reached down behind the chest and took him by the scruff of the neck. He allowed me to lift him out and set him on my lap. There he huddled, accepting our soothing. He gave no problem when we put him in a carrier and took him up to the hay-mow of the barn.

He stayed in a cage there for a couple of days. We had to get him neutered, but we wanted to make sure he was healthy enough first. During those days any sort of tomcat odor disappeared. We found ourselves with a totally peaceable fellow; it was getting very cold . . .

. . . and one day, I'll never understand why, I just up and took him into our apartment. We expected fights and more "eau de tomcat." Instead, he looked at the other cats, they looked at him, he found a place to curl up and sleep, and that was it. He'd come to stay.

George Kigercat, who lived downstairs, immediately told us, "You've got Mr. Peabody up there."

"You said Mr. Peabody's an owl."

"He is."

"Are you Mr. Peabody?" we asked the new cat.

He lifted his head and gave us a basilisk stare.

"I'm Archibald Peabody the Third."

"George said that Mr. Peabody is an owl."

"I *was* an owl. In the life just previous."

After watching Archie in action for a couple of weeks, we didn't doubt that he'd been an owl. Aside from his unblinking gaze, if ever there was a cat who couldn't maneuver a cat's body, it was Archie. Again and again in the middle of the night we'd be awakened by a crash. We'd stir and mutter to each other, "Archie." The cat couldn't so much as leap a two-foot length, horizontally or vertically. It wasn't that he had a problem in the hindquarters. He took off with real power. The problem happened just after the takeoff. He never used the *front* quarters. Instead, he seemed to expect to *fly*.

He never seemed to figure it out. He kept trying—and crashing. His method of getting up onto a windowsill was to crawl, hooking in with the front claws, scrambling with back feet until he'd hauled himself up. His method of coming down was, you guessed it—crash.

Yet for all the laughter he provided, we held Archie in unique respect. He was almost unworldly. He was a total pacifist. He'd allowed himself to be driven into a corner of the tack room by neutered Captain Zero and, once up in our apartment, never displayed a hint of aggression. If the other cats had altercations, he walked away. His face never showed an expression, nor did his body. Archie just *was*—solemnly, splendidly.

Another strange thing was his celibacy. After that tomcat odor faded, we thought he must already be neutered. Examination, though, found him intact. Yet he'd have nothing to do with females.

When he arrived, we had one unspayed female, Julie, of the neighbor's garage. Julie never grew beyond the size of a six-month-old kitten, and she was sickly. We'd decided not to stress her with spaying. Living in that apartment, we'd reasoned, she'd never meet any intact males.

Then along came Archie, and we prepared to neuter him.

Until we saw his reaction to Julie's heats.

When Julie was in heat, a cat who normally couldn't be touched was suddenly all over us. And she was suddenly all over Archie.

Memory of his reaction still makes us laugh. He drew away as from a leper and looked at us with the first emotion that he'd ever displayed. Pure disgust.

"I don't like girls!" he said.

If he'd been human, that would have been uttered through clenched teeth.

Poor Archie; Julie's heats tried him badly. To relieve his distress, we always put her in another room for the duration.

The second unspayed female was Sylvanna. She came to us as a kitten and grew up alongside Archie. He seemed fond of her, never resenting her kittenish exuberance. Occasionally he even cuddled with her, something he *never* did with any of the others. We teased him that she was a girl. He said that in her case he'd make an exception.

Would he also make an exception when she came into heat?

No. Though he didn't treat her like a leper, he firmly ignored her advances.

We talked with him about neutering many times. He begged us not to do it. Actually, he said that he wouldn't want to stay in his current body if we did. It seemed almost a religious thing with him.

"I promise you, I'll never act like a tomcat."

We honored his wishes. He never betrayed our trust, remaining our only intact tom.

Ever the loner, he usually slept down in the bathroom instead of joining Keisha and the cats who blanketed us each night. Yet the moment we woke, there he'd be, climbing onto Dawn's chest or onto mine, where he'd stretch out Sphinx-like, virtually pinning his victim, regarding her with his basilisk stare, waiting to be petted and told how handsome he was.

A puzzling spirit and great gentleman was our Archibald Peabody III.

Keisha came to Spring Farm CARES at about six months of age, a stray. There were already enough dogs downstairs, so we put her in the apartment, where she settled in nicely with the cats. She was jet black with pointed ears, probably a miniature German Shepherd mix.

Her habits, however, were those of a pack rat.

Things in the apartment kept disappearing. Large items were

easily found. They'd be under the bed or the bedding or sofa cushions. Small items such as dishes, cutlery, cans, bottles, pens, pads, and rolls of tape, however, disappeared as into a black hole.

Then one day we heard a "clunk" under the bed. Something had fallen. Dawn got down and pulled forth an unopened can of dog food.

"What in the world?"

I should mention that the bed was a *pair* of beds, antique three-quarter brass beds, pushed together. Antique beds being shorter than modern beds, only six feet long, a king-size mattress placed sideways across two three-quarter box springs fitted perfectly.

I got down on my knees beside Dawn. Under the bed was the usual stash of stuff that had gone missing in the last days, but where had the can of dog food fallen from?

Looking at the underside of the box spring on Dawn's side, we saw a big hole. Reaching into that hole, tucked up in the springs, we found dishes, cutlery, cans, bottles, pens, pads, rolls of tape, and all manner of treasure. Not only that, Keisha had begun pulling stuffing out of Dawn's mattress above the box spring to tuck stuff up in there.

"It's a wonder that I haven't fallen through," said Dawn.

By periodically removing things from out of the box spring, we forestalled more ambitious excavating. And when items subsequently went missing, we knew right where to find them.

On July 24, 1992, Princess Purr, Head Barn Cat, Director of Mouse Removal *extraordinaire*, had a seizure and died in our arms. Only five, Prinnie had been living on borrowed time, due to, we think, having been stepped on by a horse two years before. Veterinarians at that time had diagnosed her problem as a liver shunt and predicted her imminent death. But Prinnie hung in there, limping proudly on about her duties, purring her extraordinary purr.

Her death threw Sonya Pia into a panic.

"Prinnie was Head Barn Cat! Who'll do her job? Who'll take the morning and evening report?"

Dawn and I had referred to Prinnie as Head Barn Cat as a fond joke. Now Sonya explained to Dawn that the job was very real indeed.

"Prinnie was the one who assigned the patrols!"

"Patrols?"

"The fence lines. On this side of the road, of course. Prinnie made sure we never crossed the road."

"You cats patrol the fence lines?"

"Day and night. Except in winter, one of us is always out there."

"I thought you were hunting mice."

"Oh, we do that, too. But mainly we keep watch. We warn the horses if there's danger. Ask Deeteza. But now what shall we do? Prinnie was the only one who could keep the boys working. Boys are really lazy, you know."

"The boys" were her brother, Captain Zero, and the new arrivals Captain Mystery and Hey Meow, both of the latter yellow and white.

Captain Mystery was so named because he had mysteriously appeared in the stable the night that Uncle Warren died.

Hey Meow we found sitting in the haymow one night, waiting for us. He explained that he'd been in the area for years, living in various dairy barns, moving on as, one by one, the dairies went out of business. Our neighbor, Walt Savicki, the last dairyman in the neighborhood, had just called it quits, so Sonya Pia brought Hey Meow to Spring Farm, showed him the kitty door that at that time led into the haymow, and told him to make himself known to us.

At which point we could guess how Captain Mystery had also just suddenly appeared.

At first Hey Meow kept to the haymow, and we called him Haymow. His talkative nature quickly altered that name. After a couple of weeks he grew bold and edged out into the stable. There were

BUILDINGS LEFT TO RIGHT: Deanie and Harwood's house, the barn, the arena with Nursery attached in the foreground, the old garage run-in shed, and the pasture run-in shed.
Photo by Andrew Magyar

June in January. The eight-by-eight-foot main door to the barn, bathroom windows to the right of that. The second set of windows on the far right were windows to the kitchen.
Photo by Andrew Magyar

Bonnie and clinic students in front of barn bridge and door to haymow.
Photo by Andrew Magyar

Looking from our office area, through the living room area, to the south end of the barn. In the center is the "Good Girl Spot." At far right are the stairs to the haymow.
Photo by Ed Mitchell

When the brass bed was in the old horse stall at the north end of the barn.

The bathroom.
Photo by Doug Hughes

LEFT: Staircase, two-tier library, and vault of haymow ceiling at barn's north end. Note the ladder on back wall and the braces running the length of the barn. A similar arrangement was at the south end. *Photo by Ed Mitchell*

RIGHT: Two-tier library and arched entrance to the apartment. *Photo by Ed Mitchell*

Behind the sofa is the sliding door to the granary, as seen from the haymow door.
Photo by Ed Mitchell

M idnight, Halloween
1993.
Photo by Andrew Magyar

T he morning after.
Photo by Andrew Magyar

T he Millers install the
new water line.
Photo by Andrew Magyar

Looking across the ruins to the barn bridge and arena.
Photo by Andrew Magyar

A volunteer examines the "miracle drawer."
Photo by Andrew Magyar

Daffy Doggie.
Photo by Harwood Jones

Daffy wiggling on his back.
Photo by Harwood Jones

Keisha.
Photo by Barbara Linsley

LEFT TO RIGHT: Pazazz Purr,
Sidney, Sylvanna.
Photo by Barbara Linsley

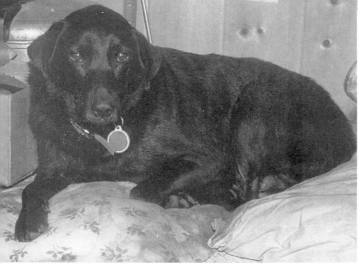

Spangles.
Photo by Ibi Hinrichs

Cookie.
Photo by Ibi Hinrichs

Spring Farm's favorite haunt, Francis Merritt Jones—Grampa Jones.

Pink Flower on one of our card table desks.

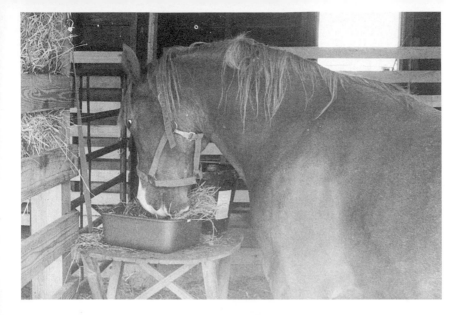

Kazinka eats hay from a pan on a table the day she was trucked to Cornell.
Photo by Harwood Jones

Excuse the poor quality, but this photo somehow survived the fire. It shows some of Kazinka's scarring and still-open sores the day she returned home to Spring Farm.
Photo by Willa Dean Jones

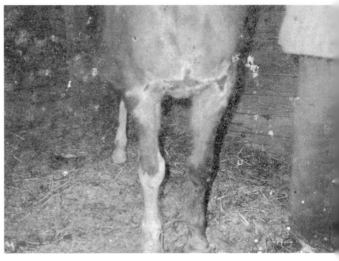

LEFT TO RIGHT:

Bonnie, Buckwheat, Kazinka, Dawn.
Photo by Andrew Magyar

The Unsinkable Buckwheat
Hayman.
Photo by Harwood Jones

Buckwheat and Jackie and
Dennis Hayman.
Photo by Andrew Magyar

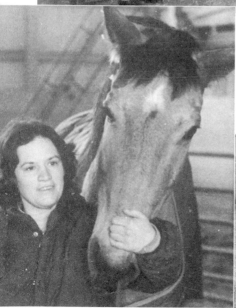

Buckwheat enjoys the right to lie down.
Nearby is Bonnie's bed.
Photo by Andrew Magyar

Dawn and Buckwheat.
Photo by Andrew Magyar

Dawn and Bubbles in Utica Park.

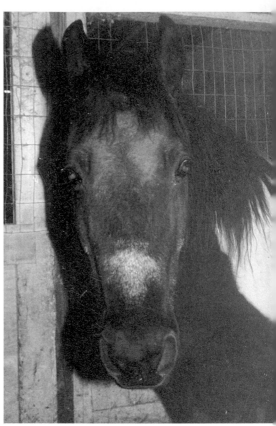

Toby.

LEFT TO RIGHT: Sugar, Dawn, Bubbles, Bonnie. *Photo by Donna Membrino*

Esther Billiams.

LEFT TO RIGHT: Tyrone Shower, Pearl, Emerald. *Photo by Lynn E. Hervey*

Sonya Pia.

Captain Zero.

Deeteza.

Left: Deeteza; RIGHT: Scherry.

Babe and Mariah in the foreground; Bo, Four Bales, Gypsy, and Puddy behind.

Lady. *Photo by Barbara Linsley*

Amber and Gigi's son Raja.

Left: Missy; right: Dream.

Carol Northrup's Holly.

Snowie and her twins,
Tippicanoe and Tyler Too.

Max.
Photo by Harwood Jones

Lamoka Bo.

George Belinda, Clarisse, and Elvis.

Dawn and Phoebe.

Chubby greets an admirer, and
Mr. Bubbles horns in.

Pookie.

Harwood and Deanie Jones.

Archibald Peabody III.

some verbal confrontations, but Hey Meow was mellow and well on in years, while Sonya Pia stuck by his side, angrily yowling down Captains Zero and Mystery.

Sonya remained Hey Meow's champion for life. It was she, we later learned, who'd convinced Prinnie that Hey Meow was not up to patrol duty. Instead, Prinnie appointed him Head Greeter and Grain-Area Mouse Manager, which duties Hey Meow performed proudly, always there to greet staff and visitors alike, while no mouse was ever seen in the grain area. Well, almost never.

"We all have our mouse areas," Sonya told Dawn proudly. "You'll notice that you seldom see a mouse."

Well, yes. But over the years we'd discovered that cartoons such as "Garfield" and "Heathcliff" are close to the mark. Dawn first realized that cats sometimes keep mice for pets while still living on Paris Hill Road. She came home one night to find her cats sitting in a circle on the kitchen floor staring at a mouse. The mouse was sitting quite calmly staring at the cats.

Dawn sprang into action and saved the mouse. She shooed the cats away and drove the mouse, which seemed most reluctant, out the kitchen door.

"What did you do that for?" asked Timmy. "He's our friend."

"Oh, sure," said Dawn.

The next night she came home to the same scene: the cats sitting in a circle around the mouse, the mouse calmly communing with the cats.

"Timmy, what's going on?"

"I told you, he's our friend."

"You won't try to hurt him?"

"No! He's our friend!"

Dawn stopped interfering. The mouse socialized with the cats for months.

Then it disappeared.

Dawn never asked why.

Then there was Hector, the tack room mouse. In those days, for the comfort of the cats, the tack room was heated with a kerosene heater on winter nights. Once the evening chores were finished, the cats would settle down around their heater. They looked like worshipers gathering at its base, worshipers of the Great God Kerosene.

One night Dawn returned to the tack room for something she'd forgotten. They were all there, sleepy and comfortable around the heater. They looked up lazily as she entered—Prinnie, Sonya, Zero, Mystery, Hey Meow, a new cat named Boo Pooh, Hector . . .

Hector?

There he was, his drowsy attitude indicating that he was a charter member of the club.

He was very old as mice go, his coat patchy and scaly, with lots of gray. He joined the cats in worship of the Great God Kerosene each night for months. Then he, too, disappeared. Again, we didn't ask why.

Perhaps, when the time comes, cats perform quick, merciful euthanasia for their pets. Just as we do.

And how strange is it that cats should make pets of animals that they hunt and/or eat? Do we not do the same?

There was also the day when we walked into the stable and recoiled in shock. There were mice everywhere! Running all around the floors, scurrying along the tops of stalls, scrounging in the horses' hay, very definitely scrounging in the grain area.

The cats were there, too. Lounging.

"What the hell is going on?" said Dawn to Prinnie.

Prinnie yawned, stretched, and recurled herself.

"It's Mouse Appreciation Week," she said.

Sure 'nuff, the mice had the run of the place for a week. Then, suddenly, the cats were back on duty and mice were nowhere to be seen. When questioned, Prinnie's explanation made perfect sense.

"If we just keep killing them, pretty soon there won't be any left to kill. Mouse Appreciation Week gives them a chance to fatten up and have some fun without being afraid of us, then there are lots more baby mice to grow into big mice so we can hunt them and eat them."

Sounds like our own environmental conservation.

So it was that, when Sonya told Dawn, "We all have our mouse areas. You'll notice that you seldom see any mice," Dawn and I could only wonder just how many mice there actually were around the place, and what interesting deals are sometimes struck between cat and mouse.

Now, however, Sonya was really distraught.

"What shall we do without a Head Barn Cat?"

"Why can't you be head cat?" said Dawn.

"Oh no! I couldn't. I'm not good enough."

"Well then, one of the boys will have to do it."

"No!" said Sonya, aghast, "Boys are—well, they just don't make good Head Barn Cats."

Dawn came to me with the problem.

"You're a girl," I told her. "And you speak fluent Cat. Ask Sonya if you can be Head Barn Cat."

"That will be wonderful!" said Sonya when Dawn proposed it.

At five the next morning we were awakened by an insistent meowing outside the barn.

"That sounds like Sonya. Something must be wrong."

Still half asleep, Dawn stumbled out into the haymow and opened the haymow door.

Sonya was sitting there.

"What's the matter?" said Dawn.

"I have the morning report. All's well."

And Sonya scampered off.

"What was that all about?" I mumbled as Dawn returned.

"I'm not sure. But I don't think I'm going to like being Head Barn Cat."

That evening at seven, as Dawn was working in the stable, an exasperated Sonya came to her.

"Where were you?"

"For what?"

"To get the evening report."

"I didn't know about it. Where should I have been?"

"Up at The Fort, of course."

The Fort was a pile of rocks in some bushes behind the stable where the cats often hung out.

"I'm sorry, Sonya. What was the report?"

"All's well."

"Thank you for the report, Sonya. I'll try to do better in the future."

At five the next morning came the insistent meowing under our window.

Dawn staggered to the haymow door.

"All's well," said Sonya.

"Thank you for the report," said Dawn.

That evening at seven Dawn dutifully went to The Fort. No Sonya.

Then Dawn heard an impatient meowing out in the pasture. She followed the sound.

Sonya was sitting beside a woodchuck hole.

"Where have you been?" she said.

"At The Fort."

"The Fort? Why?"

"Isn't that where I'm supposed to get the evening report?"

"That was last night. We never give the evening report in the same place twice."

"Well how am I supposed to know that!" cried Dawn.

"Ohhhhh—forget it," said Sonya. "I'm just going to have to be Head Barn Cat myself. Anything will be better than you."

Dawn was actually crestfallen when she returned to the stable.

"What's the matter?' I said.

"You want to know real failure? I've just been fired. By a cat."

*   *   *

The death of Prinnie Purr on July 24, 1992, was not, however, really the death of Prinnie Purr. What appeared to be her death took place in a grassy area outside the door of the arena. She had a sudden seizure and just went. As we knelt sobbing over her body, two visitors walked up behind us, a woman who came several times a week to take dictation on herbal remedies from Sugar and a new supporter, Pat O'Connor, who would become an important player in the story.

Within an hour of her death, Prinnie told Dawn that she was already back in a uterus and that she'd return to Spring Farm as a kitten by September 24. She thought her mother would be killed by a car and she'd be brought to us for nursing. If she hadn't managed to return by the twenty-fourth, we were to canvas area humane societies and find her. We'd be sure to know her. She'd be grayish and have really unusual markings.

A cat's gestation period is two months, just the time period that Prinnie was giving us. If the soul that had manifested itself as Prinnie had gone straight into a uterus, it would have had to enter a fetus already developing in a womb somewhere in order to be a viable kitten that could return here by September 24, or that could be found at a humane society on that date.

Prinnie shrugged away those details.

"I'll be there. Name me Pazazz, please."

We waited, receiving frequent updates from Prinnie, developing in the womb.

On September 21, we got a call from Juno at Seven Rays Bookstore in Syracuse.

"I remember being told about you by one of our customers. A Pat O'Connor."

. . . who'd "coincidentally" arrived as we knelt sobbing over Prinnie.

"Friends had a mother cat killed by a car last night. There are three kittens, ten days old. My friends work nine to five, they can't nurse them. Could you take them?"

Dawn was in Effie within minutes, heading for Syracuse, confident that Prinnie was back. It was appropriate that there were two siblings. She'd come to us the first time with two "sibling" friends, Sonya and Zero. And from the Syracuse area, at that.

We kept them in a cage in the apartment. As they grew, they joined the cat family there.

We weren't disabused of our expectation that Prinnie was one of them. One kitten was black, one was white, and the third was grayish with unusual markings, gray-to-beige smudges all over the body.

Additionally, the grayish kitten was half the size of the other two. The eyes of the others were already opening. It took another week for the grayish kitten's eyes to begin opening. It had trouble sucking. We thought at first we'd lose it. It lagged behind the other two in everything, crawling, walking, litter box—a real Prinnie-Come-Lately, late into the fetus she'd chosen to inhabit. But there she was.

She did goof on one thing. She'd intended to be a girl again. She was a boy. But as she told Dawn, "If you think it's hard telling boy cats from girl cats when they're born, you should try it with embryos."

We named him Pazazz Purr. That extraordinary purr was still the same. He remembered and responded like Prinnie for several months.

Then, gradually, the memory of Prinnie faded—as our doting God-parent has arranged, as it should be, lest we risk torment such as Spangles suffered, haunted and sickened by memories of a previous life. Laurence Olivier, playing *Henry V* but with dialogue from *Richard III* still filling his thoughts, would not have been a satisfying Henry. So it was that Prinnie Purr tiptoed graciously away from Pazazz Purr's memory.

There was another oddity to the story, again involving Pat O'Connor. She'd been drawn emotionally into Prinnie's death, arriving for a pleasant hour of feeding carrots to Spring Farm horses but stumbling across Spring Farm's sobbing founders. So we'd told her of Prinnie's predictions for return, and even as Dawn was heading for Syracuse to get the kittens, I was calling Pat with the exciting news.

"Do you suppose maybe they're Himalayan kittens?" asked Pat.

"I hardly think so," I replied, thinking the question naive. "Himalayans don't exactly grow on trees."

"I want a cat, but I'm allergic to them. I've heard that sometimes people who are allergic to cats aren't allergic to Himalayans."

Lo and behold, as the weeks went by, while the black kitten, Sylvanna, remained just a plain, black, short-haired kitten, the white kitten, Sidney, turned into a gorgeous long-haired, blue-eyed, flame-point Himalayan type, while Pazazz Purr turned into a spectacular blue-eyed, long-haired, lynx-point Himalayan type. That gray-beige mottling had been his Himalayan coloring going out to happen.

We called the people who'd owned the mother. She'd been a brown tabby.

Then why, we asked, did we have a couple of Himalayan crosses?

Oh, yeah. The neighbors had a Himalayan tom who was always hanging around.

In the end, Pat decided against chancing an adoption. So we kept all three.

How we loved them. How sweetly they snuggled with us.

And how sadly we lost them on Halloween Night 1993, along with so many others.

Why, one might ask, did Prinnie return that way? If she, or the oversoul of which she's a part, could foretell her coloring, her mother's death, and the approximate date, could she not have known that she'd die so young? Why had she even bothered?

Maybe she was able to foresee the possibility of the fire, maybe not. But animals have a different attitude toward life and death than we do. They know that all of us now living are as dead as we'll ever get. Prinnie had already had two years of borrowed time in her former body, and she, Dawn, and I were specially bonded. Perhaps it was worth it all just to get back to us again for another year of cuddling and purring and to assure us, "I love you. Our souls are friends forever. We'll meet and love, again and again."

13

Lord Love a Duck
and Other Watery Critters

The Stevens Swan vehicle visited us most every day.

The neighbors would think we were under investigation.

But it was really only Bob Wokowski or Nancy McElwain, dropping by to visit Sugar or conduct business.

Nancy began placing hard cases from the shelter with us. There was a gray-and-white feral cat named UPD, who'd had kittens in a drawer at the Utica Police Department. Then there was a sweet gray tiger who we named Marsha Mellow. She'd been a stray, brought to Stevens Swan with her kittens. Their babies weaned and adopted away, both mothers were due for euthanasia, UPD because she was wild, Marsha Mellow because she was a common tiger who probably wouldn't be adopted. The shelter was overcrowded—no room for a "probably not."

We gave them the run of the haymow.

Then there was Zoe. She was tallish, long and lean, possibly a Greyhound mix. She was also blond. *Really* blond. She'd been rescued at the age of six months from an owner who'd thrown her against a wall and broken two of her legs. He'd also broken the arm of his two-week-old daughter—a perfect example of what we who work with animals keep trying to impress on the police, the judiciary, the press, and the public: that those who abuse animals are already abusing, or will eventually abuse, their fellow humans. Virtually every serial killer or kid who's gone to school and blown his teachers and fellow students away has a history of abusing animals.

Animals are the canary in the coal shaft. We ignore the canary's death at our peril.

Once Zoe was nursed back to health, Nancy found her what she thought was the perfect home. She visited us the day that Zoe was adopted, and we'd never seen her happier. Only days later she arrived in tears, Zoe with her.

"She was too much for them to handle. Bonnie. Dawn. I can't take her back to the shelter after what she's been through. I just can't."

So to Spring Farm Zoe came.

It's hard to decide who was the most neurotic at first, Spangles or Zoe. Left alone for even two minutes, Zoe devoured something. Not small stuff. Zoe ate chairs, tables, sofas, everything in sight.

We had to chain her to one of the barn's iron columns whenever we went out. The length of the chain allowed her a soft rug to sleep on while keeping her away from furniture. We'd summon her to that spot with a happy "Good Girl, Zoe! Come to your Good Girl Spot."

She'd run eagerly to that place, for, more than anything, Zoe wanted to be good.

After a year she lost her appetite for furniture. We seldom used the chain anymore, but we kept the Good Girl for emergencies, and she'd go there to eat. After all the others were fed, she'd run happily beside me as I carried her food to the Good Girl. Whenever she was in doubt about anything, she'd run to the Good Girl and stand wagging her tail. And she slept in that spot.

To Zoe, the Good Girl was the place where she was completely safe.

It hurts even to write about it.

One afternoon in February 1993, Nancy called to say that Stevens Swan was about to execute the rescue of abused farm animals. We agreed to give them temporary shelter.

We were in the midst of a blizzard that had gone on for a week. Snow lay four feet deep, with drifts over the head. Nancy and her crew would be breaking through massive drifts to rescue the animals.

"Don't expect us till we get there," she said.

In preparation, we called our plowing people and got the driveway plowed, then set to work creating stalls and pens for we knew not what kind of, or how many, animals.

Late that night a stock trailer pulled in, followed in cars by Stevens Swan staff. More snow had fallen since we'd been plowed. The driver couldn't get the stock trailer near the arena. So we made a human alleyway from the trailer to the door of the arena, and the driver loosed the animals.

Noah's ark all over again. Cows, calves, sheep, goats, pigs, ducks, and geese went running up the chute and into the arena. Our horses reacted in horror, snorting and stomping. Most had never seen such outlandish creatures.

Pitiful is a better way to describe them. The snowbanks around their barn had gotten so high that the "farmer" had simply stopped caring for them. They hadn't had food or water in days. We formed a bucket line to get water to them. There was pandemonium, especially among the dozen cows and calves, who bellowed and crowded, trying to get at the pails.

When everyone had gotten some water and things calmed down, we started getting the sheep, goats, and calves into pens. The cows would have to remain loose in the arena. Nancy and I set about catching the two young pigs.

Talk about greased pigs. Pigs don't have to be greased.

When finally we did catch them, they squealed so shrilly that we nearly dropped them again. Only when we got them into their pen and they discovered the food awaiting them did they stop screaming.

One of the calves was in bad shape. She collapsed. We made her a bed, pulled her onto it, and covered her with blankets. When all the animals had been squared away and Nancy and her crew departed, Dawn and I sat with the calf, trying to get her to drink something.

Two of the ducks favored us with aquatic entertainment as we sat there. They were Muskovys, white with red masks around their eyes and over their beaks. We had both hot and cold running water in the stable, so a horse-watering tub filled with warm water had been set out for the cows. The Muskovys found it. It was fifteen below zero outside and five above zero in the arena, but the Muskovys went swimming.

What splashing, what diving, what preening.

I christened them Esther Billiams and Ricardo Duckalban.

They played in the tub for hours, in five degrees of temperature. Silly ducks. We thought they had a clean fetish.

We subsequently learned that if ducks can't immerse their bodies in water frequently, they can freeze to death, or at least be as cold as we would be if turned out naked into frigid weather. Swimming, then preening, releases oil from glands at the base of their feathers. The oil keeps them warm and buoyant. So what appeared to us as insanity was the ducks' deliriously happy way of warming themselves up.

At about four in the morning, the calf went into convulsions.

We called Leigh Lain, who came right over and put the poor little thing to sleep.

A reporter and photographer from the Utica *Observer-Dispatch* arrived the next morning. The morning after that, the paper carried a story with a large picture of Dr. Leigh Lain standing beside the calf that she'd had to euthanize during the night.

Unfortunately, the caption beside the photograph said that the animals had been taken *from* Spring Farm CARES rather than *to* Spring Farm CARES.

Those who bothered to read the article would understand the error, but many people only skim. Our phone started ringing.

"What's going on?" "We thought you were good people." "I'll never donate to you again!"

I called the news editor.

"Oh, yeah," he said. "It does say 'from.' Sorry. We'll print a correction tomorrow."

"In that little 'Corrections' box that no one ever reads?" I said. "No. *One word* trashed us in the minds of thousands of your readers. I want a very *prominent* correction in the morning. And to repair the damage, I think you should do a feature article on Spring Farm CARES. Within the week."

It was a lovely feature article, with photographs and all.

Most of the animals were with us only a few weeks before being transferred elsewhere, but while they were with us, we learned to love pigs.

What wonderful animals, affectionate, with a great sense of humor—and so clean.

We kid you not. Left to their druthers, pigs are immaculate. When left outdoors, they roll in mud only to keep from sunburning. In their pen they were perfect houseguests, carefully depositing their evacuations in one corner, keeping the rest of their pen tidy.

To our delight, the four ducks were left with us—the Muskovys, Esther and Ricardo; Emerald, black with emerald head; and his mate, Pearl, guess what color. Pearl was an opinionated quacker who kept Emerald in line. And just let him wander away, out of her sight. The whole world heard about it.

But Emerald and Pearl were just ducks. Muskovys are from another planet. Well, not another planet, but they're native to Latin America.

Only as I write that do I realize how appropriate it was to name the male Ricardo Duckalban, since his movie star namesake is Mexican. Having personal acquaintance with both the movie star and the duck, I can testify to the great charm possessed by both. Whoever first said "Lord, love a duck" had obviously just met a Muskovy.

Muskovys don't quack. They hiss, mutter, splutter, squeak, squeal, and squawk. Actually, they almost talk. Muskovys are set apart by their intelligence, character, personality, sympathy, empathy, sense of humor, and, in the females, extreme nurturing tendencies.

Ricardo made himself the center of attention some days after his arrival by helping our chiropractic vet, Sue Ann Lesser, treat her canine clients. Sue Ann and her assistant came to Spring Farm once a month, sleeping over for a couple of nights and adjusting both Spring Farm animals and outside clients that we'd booked for them.

That day, Sue Ann set up her table next to one of the stock gate pens in the arena. Ricardo promptly flew up—Muskovys, also known as Tree Ducks, are great flyers—and perched on the gate, watching with interest. Jokingly, Sue Ann began to talk to him as she worked on her first client dog, explaining to Ricardo what she was doing. She noted that, as Ricardo tightrope-walked along the top of the stock gate behind her, the dog's head would turn, watching the bird. In jest the first few times, then in earnest, whenever she needed a dog's head turned just so, Sue Ann would say, for instance, "Ricardo, please move down the gate to my right." Ricardo would oblige, and the dog's head would follow. "Stop right there, Ricardo. Perfect." (Crack.) "Got it. Thank you, Ricardo."

What seemed like a fluke the first couple of times turned into a real partnership. Ricardo remained beside Sue Ann till the very last client, moving as directed.

We began to watch our Muskovys with new respect.

Some days later, tragedy struck. Esther and Ricardo had begun to fly back and forth between the arena and the fence of our outdoor ring. Even after a second blizzard dumped another couple of feet of snow, we didn't worry about letting them fly up to the fence. They knew where to find their food, shelter, and swimming pool. They wouldn't go flying off into that snow-drowned world.

As I said, Muskovys are great flyers. One day Esther flew back into the arena alone. Ricardo was gone.

We initiated a search, floundering through snow that was often up to our chests. Surely he hadn't purposefully left home and mate. Surely a snow flurry had confused him and he'd gotten lost.

We searched, then watched, waited, and despaired.

The next morning Les Lebrecque, who lives a quarter of a mile away, called.

"Are you by any chance missing a duck?"

"Yes!" I cried. "Did you catch him?"

"No. But I wish *you* would. He's nesting on our chimney flue."

How clever of Ricardo to find such a warm, cozy place.

"He's blocking the flue and filling our house with carbon monoxide. I'm going to have to shoot at him if he doesn't leave soon."

"I'll be right down."

Being right down was easier said than done. Dawn was in the middle of her scheduled consultations for the day, so I went alone. Our driveway hadn't been plowed since the second blizzard. Route 12 was closed to any but emergency traffic, but town plows were keeping it clear. The snowbank they'd created at the edge of the road was up to my shoulders. I swam through, towing my bag of duck food, a sheet to, I hoped, throw over Ricardo, a dish, and a thermos of water.

As I reached the plowed, deserted road and started walking, I could see the white speck, smug and snug, atop the Labrecques' chimney. Theirs is a high, three-story house. How could I entice him down from there?

The next hour was spent standing looking up, plaintively calling, "Please come down, Ricardo. Look at the nice food, Ricardo. And water."

"I'm comfortable," said Ricardo whenever he deigned to respond. "Go away."

"Ricardo, you've got to leave that spot. Les says he'll shoot you. He says he's partial to duck. I think he's kidding, Ricardo, but I'm not sure. And Ricardo, there's no way for you to get food and water except to come to me or fly back home."

"There's plenty of food across the road."

He was right. Across the road is a large, flat cornfield where the wind whistles in winter to such an extent that it keeps most of the snow moving, off the field and into the road. A hungry bird could find lots of stray corn on the cornstalk skeletons.

I finally secured a promise from Les not to shoot at Ricardo just yet and ran back home. I intended to haul Esther and a small coop down there, hoping that the sight of her would lure Ricardo down. Dawn had finished her consultations, and as we floundered around the place, gathering supplies, she began broadcasting to Ricardo, mentally showing him the way home—he might not know, he'd been with us such a short time. We also called other neighbors, asking that they be on the lookout for him.

In the middle of preparations, John Williams, from the next house down from Les's, called.

"Your duck's in our yard. I've got food. I'll try to get him."

Minutes later came another call.

"He's flying back in your direction. But right now he's across the road in the cornfield."

We ran out and waded toward the road, hoping to get down below Ricardo and, with a combined presence, keep him flying back in the right direction.

We were too late.

All day long, aside from snowplows, there'd been no more than three vehicles an hour on that road. Ricardo flew right in front of one of those few vehicles. He was flying toward the arena when he was hit. Coming home.

We were devastated.

Esther, however, just shrugged.

"Boys are silly. I don't like boys."

And as we wondered whether we should clip her wings, and those of Pearl and Emerald, so that they wouldn't fly away as well, she said, "Unlike Ricardo, I know a good home when I see it. You'll notice that I came back when he flew away. I won't leave you. As for Pearl and Emerald, they're too busy eating and quarreling to even think of flying. They're so boring."

So no wings were clipped. Esther's promises aside, there were foxes around, and about once a month a pack of coyotes came through. We couldn't deprive the ducks of their only defense.

Upon consulting a book on ducks we began to understand Esther's attitude—and Ricardo's. Although Ricardo had been aptly named Duckalban on account of his synchronized swimming with Esther, temperamentally he was nothing like his namesake, the devoted family man Ricardo Montalban. Muskovys don't form mate bonds. Males show no inclination to stay with females, and, as for the females, unlike Pearl, they just don't seem to give a damn.

Esther gave so little of a damn that we began to wonder how Muskovys ever even get born.

Breeders consider Muskovy females the best egg setters in duckdom. There's a film called *The Pumpkin Eater*, about a woman who's a compulsive baby factory, depressed and unfulfilled without a bun baking in her oven. That's the way it is with Muscovy females. And with Esther.

There was just one problem. Esther didn't like boys. She especially didn't like Emerald.

Poor Emerald, how he tried. But he couldn't fly well—while with just one flap, Esther would be up on a stock gate, so near and yet so far. No matter how hard Emerald flapped, Esther was always one flap ahead of him.

But then she began nesting. She chose a hideaway, imported hay, plucked her down for a lining, laid eggs, and, in March 1993, commenced setting. She must, we reasoned, know what she was doing. It must be that Emerald had finally gotten the flap on her. At the proper time, we'd see ducklings.

The proper time came and went. Esther began rolling eggs out of the nest. Then, egg by egg, she carried them down the driveway and threw them onto the stones. *Smash!*

"Yuck!" she'd say and waddle back for another of the offending orbs.

She then replaced the bedding, plucked herself nearly naked again, laid another clutch of eggs, and resumed setting.

Talk as we would, we couldn't convince her that if she continually rejected the boring Emerald's advances, her eggs would come to naught. Dedicated and determined, she ignored us.

To say that Esther was job-oriented is an understatement. She almost never came out from the nest except to dispose of old eggs, replace the bedding, pluck out more of her down, and start again. She sat straight through our celebrity auction, with a hundred people milling around the piece of furniture under which she had her nest. And she sat straight through the chaos of the fire.

We made sure there was always food and a tub of water right beside her, but whenever she did put in an appearance, we despaired. She was so ragged, so sickly-looking from the continuous plucking of her plumage and the continuous setting. When she continued to set right through the winter, in freezing temperatures, with most of her warming down and feathers sacrificed to the babies that she insisted would soon be there, we wanted to cry.

Fourteen months after she first commenced setting, she emerged from the nest followed by one lone duckling. We exploded with shouts of joy and congratulations as she paraded him for all to admire. Once, just once, Emerald *had* flapped hard enough.

We treasured that duckling as we'd treasure a long-awaited grandson. Tyrone Shower.

Esther enjoyed him for about six weeks after his birth, encouraging him to swim in the tiny pool we made just for him, showing him how to catch insects and find grubs, select plants and grasses, and, finally, climb into the adult duck pool. With each passing day he looked more and more like Emerald. He'd inherited no Muskovy characteristics.

Then one day Esther led Tyrone over to Pearl and Emerald, turned, and walked away. By means of a language which we humans will never understand, a peaceful and quite lovely adoption was accomplished, with no paperwork and no social workers. Pearl and Papa Emerald accepted Tyrone as though he'd always been theirs, while Tyrone acted as though he'd never been parented by any other than those two. He adapted immediately to their boring, vociferous little world, while Esther flew off to the other side of the arena to pursue her strange, lone, Muskovy ways and purposes.

Tyrone would never have fitted into her hippie world, would never have been happy trying to be like her. How easily they all recognized this, how sensibly they dealt with it.

What a great world this would be if we humans would deal with matters of heart, soul, and spirit as gracefully as do ducks.

*   *   *

Nancy McElwain had reasons other than Sugar and business for visiting us so often. Spring Farm became her R and R. She often drove out of her way after work to be here. Dawn and I would drop whatever we were doing, and we'd all go sit in the haymow, put our feet up, relax, and chat.

The haymow was a spectacular but comforting place in which to unwind. Its furnishings were antique, for the most part. The wall space was decorated with family quilts, marvelous paintings, prints, and photos, while tabletops were decorated with precious items such as my Ch'ing Dynasty vase. The north end was magnificent with its spiral staircase, our two-level library, and the Romanesque archway into our apartment. About half of the floor space was occupied by the apartment and by the granary, but the barn was thirty-five by seventy feet, and the vaulted ceiling soared to forty feet, flying free of those enclosures. Sometimes it felt as though we were in the banqueting hall of some old castle. At other times, after sunset, with dim lights casting soft shadows onto that vaulted roof, it felt like a cathedral. At such times, the haymow seemed sacred.

In spring, summer, and fall, the haymow door, twelve by twelve feet, was left open but screened in, as was the large door downstairs. One could sit in that wonderful room, appreciating its ambiance, and, at the same time, be part of the outdoors, watch the horses in the hill paddocks, see the trees and sky beyond. It was to this place of peace that we, and friends like Nancy, retreated when we needed to refresh our souls.

It was also used for lectures and workshops and to serve large buffets. On occasion it came to the rescue when neighborhood and family picnics were rained out. We held garage sales there. And our thrift shop was, of course, in the granary.

One of our most enduring memories of the haymow will always be the night that Oliver Augustus got up into the rafters.

Oliver Augustus was a feline Dennis the Menace, long-haired, white with black spots, with a face that shouted mischief. He was my cat, gotten from the Rome Humane Society shortly after I returned home from Hollywood.

On the night in question, the door from the downstairs of the barn was somehow left open. We found Oliver Augustus missing, went to the haymow, and called him.

He answered from way over our heads. He was perched in one of the roof braces, thirty-five feet above us.

"Oh, my God," we both said.

"How'd he get up there? How will we get him down?"

"If he tries to jump down . . . or if he falls . . ."

At which point he started leaping from brace to brace.

"Be careful!" we both cried.

"Stay where you are till we figure this thing out!"

He was in the braces just over halfway toward the south end of the barn. If he continued jumping along the braces toward that end, he'd come to a wide plank that acted as another brace. It ran from one of the braces in his path over to the middle of the south wall, ending at a ladder of boards which had been nailed, from the floor to the window in the peak, onto the barn's vertical ribbing.

"I'll climb up and try to get him to come to me over that plank," I told Dawn.

"Oh, Bonnie!" said Dawn, who has vertigo.

"The ladder's safe. But I won't be able to climb back down and carry him at the same time, especially if he gets scared and starts to scratch. Go call the fire department, they must have a long ladder they can set up to help us."

As Dawn ran to the phone, I climbed to the peak. Just below the window I got up onto the plank, which was nailed to a ledge of two-by-sixes running along the south end of the building just under the window. I wedged one leg down in between a couple of the ladder rungs and the wall of the building and looped an arm around another rung. Thus secured, even though sitting thirty-five feet above the floor, I couldn't fall.

Oliver Augustus and I were now on exactly the same level.

"Come on, Augustus," I wheedled, patting the plank. "Just jump down along a couple more braces and come to me."

The plank was two by twelve inches and about fifteen feet long, No problem for a cat to cross. Augustus started jumping.

"That's a good boy."

He got right to the plank and stood looking at me. Only fifteen feet across that plank, and he'd be in my arms.

"Noooo!!!"

Instead of coming across the plank, he kept jumping along the braces.

Dawn had just returned. "The fire department's on its way. What's the matter? Oh! No, Augustus! Go back to the plank!"

Augustus had other ideas. He continued down the braces to the wall and jumped onto the ledge of two-by-sixes.

"Oh God! He can't go that way. He'll fall."

For the ledge was exactly flush with the vertical two-by-six-inch ribs of the barn. There was no way to walk across the ledge, blocked as it was every couple of feet by those ribs.

Yet Oliver Augustus did walk across the ledge. With Dawn and I cringing, expecting to see him hurtle to the floor, he negotiated the ribs with the fluidity of a serpent, his body arching in and out in a continuous "S" motion.

"Hi!" he said as he climbed into my arms. "This is neat, huh? I didn't know that you like to climb, too."

By then we heard the fire department driving in. No sirens. Not for a stuck cat. Soon Dawn was joined by a dozen of Clinton's volunteer firemen, who stood gaping up at me.

"I thought we were supposed to rescue a cat. Bonnie, what the hell are *you* doing up there?"

The speaker was Marty Crouch, with whom I'd graduated from high school.

"Did you bring your ladder?" I asked.

"What ladder?"

"Don't you have a long ladder?"

"No."

"How are we going to get her down?" asked another fireman.

"I can get down. It's the cat that we have to get down."

They paid no attention, discussing among themselves how to rescue me with some sort of net.

Mother came in, alarmed by the arrival of the fire department. She was relieved to find no fire and not at all perturbed to find me and Oliver Augustus looking down at her from the peak. Over the years she and Daddy and I had been up and down that ladder hundreds of times.

"Oh, that Oliver Augustus," she said when Dawn told her what had happened. "He's such a scamp."

She solved the problem immediately, putting Dawn and me to shame.

"All you need is a pillowcase. Put Augustus in a pillowcase, and you can climb down with him."

"Right!" I said. "*Great* thinking, Mommy. Dawn, run and get a pillowcase."

"I'll get a hay net, too," said Dawn. "If you put the cat into the pillowcase and then the pillow case into the hay net, climbing down will be even easier."

So as the firemen continued to discuss the means of my rescue, Dawn ran into the bedroom for a pillowcase and out to the stable for a hay net. She was back in a couple of minutes and handed them to Marty.

"Just take these up to Bonnie."

Marty looked at the rungs nailed to the barn ribs.

"I'm not going up that thing. Don't worry. We'll find a way to get Bonnie down."

"Oh, for Pete's sake," said my mother, who, at that point, was eighty-four years old. "Give them to me, Dawn."

Before the firemen could protest, she was up the ladder, hand-
ing me the pillowcase and the hay net.

I opened the pillowcase invitingly, and Oliver Augustus walked
in to investigate. Within seconds the pillowcase was in the hay net,
and we both climbed down.

The next day it was all over town how the fire department had
had to rescue Bonnie Reynolds from a ladder at the top of her barn.
Some people might still believe that old firemen's tale.

Tragedy, in the form of an automobile, struck Oliver Augustus
shortly thereafter. He loved to hide, then dash out the door whenever we entered or left the barn. He dashed out once too often. We
found him dead beside the road a couple of hours later.

He'd been named for a cat named Oliver, a beautiful blue-gray
tiger stray who I'd had in my Hollywood home. At that time, I ran a
cat rescue and spay/neuter/adoption operation that our vet, Edd
Jordan, called, "Reynolds Unlimited." It wasn't incorporated; I just
did it, with the long-suffering cooperation of my husband, Gene.

Oliver was a wonderful cat. His most memorable trait was his
eagerness to play with water. Let a tap be opened anywhere in the
house, Oliver would come running.

Which is why Oliver Augustus became his namesake. But not
only did Oliver Augustus love to play with water from the tap, he
loved toilet bowls better than most dogs and spent long, happy
hours hanging over toilet bowls, energetically agitating the water.

Almost a year after the demise of Oliver Augustus, a friend of
ours, Bob Jones, was turning into our driveway and spotted a long-
haired orange cat sitting at the side of the road just where Oliver
Augustus had been killed. Bob jumped out of his car, ran over, and
scooped it up.

"Sonya Pia," he scolded, assuming that it was she. "You
promised never to go near the road."

And he brought us the cat.

Of course it wasn't Sonya Pia. It was a male, perhaps six months old at the time.

We gave him some name that I can't even remember at this point. It was weeks later when Dawn went into the bathroom and found that cat hanging over the toilet bowl. He'd done a job on it, splashing water everywhere.

"Oh you!" cried Dawn. "You're just like Oliver Augustus!"

A chill ran down her spine as the cat turned and looked her straight in the eye.

"I thought you'd never recognize me," he said.

And so he became Oliver Augustus Perrier, a third regeneration of a water-loving cat spirit and a scamp as mischievous as Oliver Augustus had ever been.

In the summer of 1992, Bonniecat Endore, the cat I'd brought from California, died. She'd had a long and good life, considering her precarious beginning. In 1975, a friend, Gita Endore, had found her starving on the Santa Monica beach outside the Synanon facility. Gita took the cat to her mother, Henrietta Endore, who took her in and named her after me. In 1979, as she was dying of cancer, Henrietta gave me my namesake. To avoid confusion, I called her Bonniecat.

Since my return from California, though my dogs had come out to the barn with me, Bonniecat had stayed in the house with Mother, as her cat.

It was a summer's day when Bonniecat died. She'd been going downhill for weeks. Now the end was obviously near. We carried her out and sat on the patio behind the house, Mother, Andy, Dawn, and myself. Bonniecat laid on Mother's lap, and we just talked, frequently stroking Bonniecat, giving her company as she made her transition.

After that, Mother said, "No more animals for me."

We'd lost Foxie and Mr. Fraser a couple of years before. Of the animals who had come from California with me and brought so much love and laughter to my parents, only old Daffy was left, living out in the barn with Dawn and me.

"I don't want to get attached to an animal ever again," said Mother. "I can't bear to lose them."

The angels had other plans.

One day a lady arrived with a carful of donations. After we'd helped to unload them, she said, "Oh, and yes, I've got this cat."

Unseen until then, in a carrier on her front seat, was a big black cat.

"He was a stray. The only place I could put him was in my cellar, and he can't stay down there forever. Please take him. I call him Spook."

The only place where we could keep him was in the haymow.

Which proved to be a problem, because Spook attacked all of the other cats there—UPD and Marsha Mellow, plus Thistle, brought to us by another rescue group, and Tessie, a cat that we had taken in just before she was to be euthanized because of "pee problems."

Those cats all began living under furniture, hiding from Spook. What to do?

We had two events coming up. One was a Penelope Smith workshop, the other a garage sale. For weeks we'd been arranging donated sale goods there in the haymow. Mother made it her business to come out every day and clean things.

"They sell better if they look nice," she told us.

Now, whenever Mother entered the haymow, the black cat ran to her, stood on his hind legs, and stretched his front paws up to her.

"What a nice cat," she said the first time he did that. "What's his name?"

"Spook."

"Oh, I don't like that name. I'll call him Pookie."

Pookie became her constant companion whenever she was in the haymow, walking beside her, sitting beside her, and talking to her constantly, though she didn't hear him.

"Take me home with you. You need me," he kept telling her.

And to Dawn he said, "I'll guard her and keep her safe. Tell her."

"Gosh, Gramma Dean, that cat sure likes you. Wouldn't you like to have him?"

"No, I don't want any more animals. He is nice, though, aren't you, Pookie? Yes."

And she'd take his face between her hands.

"You're the best boy in the world, aren't you?"

"I really think you should take him, Mother."

"No. I don't want another animal."

When Penelope arrived, she immediately picked up on the situation.

"That cat *loves* Bonnie's mother," she told Dawn. "He says he came here just to be with her."

"We've tried to tell her that. She doesn't want another animal."

"He's supposed to be with her. He's attacking the other cats, isn't he? He says he'll keep doing that until you arrange things. Do you think it would help if I said something to her?"

"I don't think it will do any good," said Dawn. "But go ahead and try."

Penelope marched right into the house and confronted Mother. Some minutes later, Mother appeared in the haymow.

"I've come for my cat."

Pookie ran to her, stood on his back legs, and reached up to her. Mother gathered him into her arms.

"Penelope says I'm supposed to have him."

And she left.

Oh, well. As long as *Penelope* had said it.

So Pookie had a home. And as he'd promised, Mother was his life. When she washed dishes, he sat on the sink beside her. When she went from room to room, he was right behind her. When she watched television, he sat on the table beside her chair. When she went to bed, he slept at her feet. He never asked to be cuddled. He asked only to be allowed to guard her.

A dozen times a day, Mother would stop, take his face between her hands, and say, "Pookie, you're the best boy in the world. Just the very best boy."

Those words meant more to Pookie than any cuddling ever could.

14

Miracle Recoveries and the Origin of the Ghost Brigade

Spring Farm began to get a reputation among the vets at Cornell, a reputation thrust upon us by extraordinary circumstances.

One summer morning back in 1989, Babe had come up missing. At that time the Thoroughbreds stayed out in the pasture overnight, then came inside during the heat of the day.

On this particular day it was brutally hot by ten, and we went out to bring them in. They were all waiting at the gate.

All except Babe.

"Bo and Four Bales and Gypsy and Babe always stick together," said Dawn in alarm. "They wouldn't have left her up there alone. Not all of them."

She listened for a moment.

"Yes. Four Bales says Bo and Gypsy wanted to stay with Babe, but Four Bales made them all come to the gate so we'd know that something's wrong."

"It must be bad," I said. "Can she tell us where Babe is?"

"She just says 'up on the hill.'"

That narrowed the area in which to search an eighteen-acre pasture. Hastily we let the horses into the arena and, grabbing a halter and lead, took off running through the little valley along the creek and up onto the hill, to a flat area of some seven acres. We separated, Dawn left, I right.

I finally spotted Babe. She was down, surrounded by flattened vegetation, which indicated that she'd been struggling for hours. She was covered in a froth of sweat, delirious, and seemingly near death.

Dawn came running to my frantic call. We tried to get her up. She didn't even seem to know that we were there.

"The heat alone will kill her!" I cried. "Go call Leigh Lain. Please God she's home."

Dawn took off, leaping like a gazelle over rocks, shrubs, and hillocks, while I started pulling Babe's ears. Ear pulling, or "sliding," is a TTouch that affects the many dozens of acupressure points in the ears and brings animals, and people, out of shock.

It seemed to be working. Babe was becoming aware of me.

I ran to bushes and broke off leafy branches, gathering them together into a bunch with which I alternately shielded her head from the sun and fanned her.

It seemed forever, but Dawn was back in less than fifteen minutes.

"Leigh's coming."

"But what can she do when she gets here? We've got to get her out of this sun. We've got to get her up."

My thought was to at least get her over into the shade of one of the larger bushes.

We got the halter and lead onto Babe and commenced to shout at her, to slap and whip her with whatever we could find.

And she tried. She came to and tried to get up.

"Pull! Pull on the lead!" I cried.

Dawn pulled. I got behind Babe and whipped and rocked and pushed.

She struggled and struggled.

Then suddenly she was halfway up!

I threw my shoulder against her butt, pushing and lifting with all my strength while Dawn pulled with all of hers.

"She's up!"

We began shouting to each other.

"Don't let her go back down!" "Get her moving forward!" "Brace her on that side!" "Keep her going!" "Maybe we can get her back to the stable!"

She was weaving drunkenly. Dawn and I put our bodies on the line, bracing her as she'd start to tumble this way or that. We kept her moving forward, toward the path down the side of the hill. As she went, she gained momentum.

And then she began to whinny.

"She knows!" Dawn called. "She's with it now, she knows where she's going."

We were soon left behind, huffing and puffing, as Babe trotted incoherently, but purposefully, back toward the stable.

Leigh was just walking into the arena as we got Babe into the welcome shade and relative cool of that place.

Bless Dr. Leigh Lain. She's become one of the rocks upon which Spring Farm stands. She lives just four miles from us and has been known, in an emergency, to be here in less than four minutes. She's forthright, uncomplicated, and totally honest. She'll tell it like it is whether you want to hear it or not.

One wonderful part of her honesty is in regard to her own areas of expertise or limitation. Though her practice now is essentially equine, in those early years it was essentially bovine, and she was very careful with diagnosis and treatment.

"I dunno," she'd sometimes say. "I may be in over my head here. Let's call Caz for a second opinion"—Dr. Koenneke and Cazenovia Animal Hospital being another one of our rocks.

We've trusted Leigh completely, and our trust has never been misplaced; while with her "hunches" and "feelings," she's saved the lives of many Spring Farm animals.

She was about to do so again, though she was stumped by Babe's condition.

"Do you get anything from her, Dawn?"

That's another reason why we love Leigh Lain: she's completely open to both animal communication and homeopathic alternatives.

"No. Except—I get the feeling *she* feels like she's in a sort of green fuzz."

"I've got a hunch," said Leigh. "Get a pail. I'm going to siphon her stomach contents."

A long, flexible hose was inserted into one of Babe's nostrils, down her throat, and into her stomach. Leigh then put her mouth to the end of the hose and sucked, quickly putting the hose into the pail as green swill came pouring up and out.

It poured and poured. Dawn had brought a five-gallon utility pail. One gallon of green swill, two, three—

"This isn't right," said Leigh.

—four, five . . . Dawn was just about to run for another pail when it stopped.

"Five gallons is about everything she's eaten in almost the last day," said Leigh. "The digestive juices have turned it to liquid, but none of it's gone into her intestines. We've got to call Cornell."

Cornell urged us to get Babe there with all dispatch and to ship her with the stomach tube still in, so that anything going into the stomach would keep coming back out.

Dennis came running when we called. He drove Tiger Lil and Dawn navigated while I rode in back with Babe, standing at her head and offering her water as we went. Everything she drank came right back out the tube, but she was grateful to wet her whistle.

She had anterior gastroenteritis, common in southern states, seldom seen in the North. Yet Babe's was the third case that Cornell had seen in two weeks.

The first two horses had died.

Babe was given a zero chance of survival.

Anterior gastroenteritis, akin to chicken pox, shuts down the passage from the stomach to the intestines. Everything eaten or drunk stays in the stomach—until, since horses can't throw up, the stomach bursts. Leigh's tubing had forestalled that unspeakable event, but still the prognosis was zilch.

Ten days later, we brought Babe home, eating, drinking, and defecating normally.

Why?

No one really knows. For our part, we went to see her every day and, to the amusement of vets and students, did TTouch on her, taking special care to pull the ears a lot.

Leigh Lain, TTouch, whatever they did at Cornell, and love. That's about it.

Yet something else shares credit for saving Babe: the wisdom of Four Bales.

Had she not made all the horses come to the gate, Lamoka Babe would have died.

Our next Cornell miracle, in late spring of 1990, was Buckwheat.

It was a shock to all of us when Buck got sick. He was so big, strong, healthy—eternal.

At first we thought he had strangles. He didn't, though whatever he did have eluded diagnosis. We kept him in his stall for a couple of weeks, but one day he seemed much better, so we turned him out with his girls.

When we brought them in, Buckwheat was hardly able to drag himself.

"There's something really wrong," said Dawn. "He's not in any pain, he just says he's never felt so tired."

Jackie and Dennis were away on business, so Dawn was making the decisions. She called the equine vet whom Dennis and Jackie had been using for Buck. He refused to come and see him.

"Awww, he's just tired after his first day out," he said.

But Dawn wouldn't let it go, and, over the next couple of hours, we watched Buck sink even lower. Dawn called Leigh.

Leigh was in bed with the flu. "But if you really feel that it warrants it, Dawn, I'll come."

Besides, this was Buckwheat.

Not only did Leigh come over, she returned twice during the wee hours. By sunup, Buck was standing in a corner of his stall, pressing his head against the wall—pressing, pressing, very hard, as though trying to drive a demon out of his skull.

"Head pressing," said Leigh. "That's not good."

Dawn had talked with Dennis and Jackie. Their orders were "Never mind the cost. Do whatever needs to be done." So we loaded Buck and headed for Cornell.

At first the vets gave him a 40 percent chance of survival. After a sonogram, however, they lowered his chances to 10 percent. Because the sonogram could find no liver.

The next day they did a biopsy. The biopsy also found no liver; the probe came back out with only muscle tissue. Of course, they said, maybe the probe had simply missed the liver.

Still, they lowered his chances to 3 percent.

Maybe we were growing cocky, but we wouldn't accept that.

No; we weren't going to lose our Buckwheat. And weekdays, Dawn and I went to Cornell, while on weekends, Dennis and Jackie went down.

After the first couple of days we'd arrive with buckets of dandelion greens. Because on the second evening, Dawn suddenly stopped what she was doing and said, "I just got a message. I don't know where from, but Buckwheat needs to eat dandelion greens, and he needs burdock leaves and spearmint wrapped around the bottoms of his feet. And I'm seeing . . . a Buddha."

The following morning she went to Park Row Booksellers in Clinton and got directions to the herb section. Halfway down the aisle she saw the book that she needed, sitting face out on the shelf.

On the cover was the exact Buddha that she'd seen in her "message."

According to that book, dandelion greens, burdock leaves, and spearmint are specific remedies for liver detoxification.

We weren't brazen enough to go to Cornell and do poultices of burdock leaves and spearmint on the bottoms of Buck's feet, but dandelion greens we could do. And we mentioned to the head vet that dandelion greens are good for liver detoxification. He must have looked it up, because the following day there was a sign on Buckwheat's door: FEED DANDELION GREENS AT WILL.

Of course, each time we visited we gave him TTouch. As with Babe, passing vets and students watched curiously, sometimes surreptitiously. Some seemed amused; others began to ask questions. Mostly they just watched and said nothing.

There was yet another remedy that we used on Buck: quartz crystals. His reaction to those treatments was very strong and very positive.

After a week, he'd improved to the point that we were allowed to lead him out to the lawn. The chief vet sometimes wandered by as Buck grazed.

"He's coming along," we'd say cheerfully.

This same head vet had witnessed Babe's "miraculous" recovery. And he knew about Kazinka. He never showed any expression. He'd just watch and nod.

Each day Buck became more and more his old self.

After two weeks, they sent him home. They did a second sonogram before he left. It, too, could find no liver. Yet now the horse seemed perfectly fine.

We did have one puzzling exchange with the head vet. That was when we described the way that Buck had pressed his head to the wall that first morning.

"He can't have been head pressing."

"He kept going into the corner of his stall and pressing his head very hard against the wall. What is head pressing?"

"Head pressing is pressing the head very hard against the wall."

"That's what he was doing."

"You have to be mistaken. Horses who head press do not recover."

"Even though he kept pressing his head against the wall, that wasn't head pressing."

"Correct. Horses who head press do not recover."

Who's on first?

Whatever. We brought Buck home to a liverless life and poultices of burdock and spearmint. But the lack of a liver seemingly made up for the lack of something else. The gentlemanly Buckwheat turned stud, the object of his exuberant new affection being Dulcie. Every time we turned around, he was mounting her.

"Buckwheat! She's a pony! You're too heavy for her."

"But I like her."

"Buckwheat, you can't do anything. You're a gelding."

"Who cares. It's fun."

Dulcie seemed to agree. Throughout the summer, Buckwheat continued to play massive Romeo to Dulcie's diminutive Juliet, while Deeteza and Scherry looked on, yawning.

That summer Dawn and I were hit by lightning. Looking up from our work one afternoon, we realized that Buck and the girls were agitated, racing back and forth in their pasture, watching the sky. We went out to bring them in.

A thunderstorm was approaching, a long way off, over toward Syracuse. But the sun was gone, the atmosphere had taken on a sulfurous glow, and there was an unaccustomed hush, as though the world were listening to something. It was that eerie glow and strange silence that was disturbing the horses.

Dawn waited at the gate to the run-in shed while I ran down to the creek and shinnied across on the wooden fence.

"Come on, guys, let's go in."

The horses resisted my attempts to herd them, running this way and that, still watching the sky.

"Come on! What's the matter with you?"

I finally got them down to the creek, but at its edge they balked, refusing to put so much as a hoof into the water. Instead they milled, becoming ever more agitated.

Then the mallet hit me over the head. A hard rubber mallet, swung by a giant.

Thought and action were split second. I dropped to my knees and curled into a ball, as I'd read one should do when hit by lightning. Even as I did that, I assumed that I'd bought it.

I remained curled until I realized that (a) I was alive and (b) four frenzied horses were galloping in circles around me and if I didn't do something about that situation I *might* die. I rose and shooed them. Now they dashed across the creek, up the hill, and into the stable.

They'd known that lightning was coming. They'd refused to set foot into the water until the charge had come and was dissipated.

It was then that I heard Dawn calling.

"Bonnie! Bonnie!" Her voice was desperate.

I couldn't see her. She was out of sight over the little hill.

"I'm here."

"Thank God."

"I was just hit by lightning."

"So was I."

"What?"

Dawn had been standing holding the iron gate of the run-in shed. She hadn't consciously dropped to the ground, she'd been knocked flat.

Reading the obituaries the next morning was Life Appreciation 101. Two people living nearby had been hit and killed at about the same time that we'd been hit. Our obituaries could have been in that morning's paper.

What sort of lightning had this been, to tell the horses it was coming, to hit us both while separated by about seventy feet, knock Dawn to the ground, hit me over the head, and, I discovered, burn the right side of my face—but not kill?

Andy, of course, insisted that it hadn't been lightning.

"If it had been lightning, you'd be dead."

"Do you see this burn on the side of my face?"

"It wasn't lightning."

"Then what was it?"

"I don't know, but it wasn't lightning."

"Okay," I said, and aimed the next one at his atheist heart. "It wasn't lightning. It was the finger of God."

"Humph!" said Andy and went upstairs.

The finger of God. Well, maybe it was.

Buck remained happy and healthy through the next winter, summer, and fall.

Then he got shot.

It was hunting season. We heard the shot and looked out, muttering angrily. It had sounded really close. Our property was lavishly posted, but hunters are generally illiterate.

No hunter was visible, however, and the sound of gunshots can be deceiving. The Savickis allow hunters on their property, and we're forever thinking that hunters shooting on their land are shooting on ours.

Deeteza, Scherry, and Dulcie had heard the shot and were running to the stable. Buckwheat followed—not running, walking. He stopped at the creek as though to drink.

We went back to work, thinking no more about it. Until we went to the stable to do the chores and discovered that Buckwheat was still standing on the other side of the creek. I went to get him and found him almost unable to walk. With difficulty we got him to his stall. We didn't think of the gunshot; we thought he had a sudden lameness, as did the vets who looked at him.

He improved a bit over the next days. Then, suddenly, he was down on the pasterns. That's like a human being suddenly starting to walk on the backs of the ankles, with the feet pointing forward—an impossibility with a human, but not with the articulated bone structure of a horse.

Buckwheat needed desperately to go down. We got him out into the arena, where he could lie down without fear of getting cast against a wall so that he couldn't get up again.

And down he went.

We made him comfortable with a blanket and a blanket-covered pillow of hay. Leigh was called. We were all working from a false premise. Buck was at least thirty years old. The Haymans had had him for eighteen years, and they'd been told when they purchased him that he was at least twelve, probably much older. Thirty is a champion age for a horse, especially one as large as Buck.

Buck took great delight in teasing us about his age. He'd never give Dawn a straight answer, and as she began to teach workshops in animal communication, he played the same game with students.

"Twelve." "Twenty-seven." "Thirty-eight." "Two."

Even Penelope Smith was teased. One evening while at Spring Farm for one of her clinics, she walked into the arena to visit the animals.

"Hey!" she heard. "Would you believe fifty?"

"That big buckskin," she said when she returned to the barn. "He wanted to know if I'd believe fifty. What's he talking about?"

We laughed and told her of Buckwheat's teasing.

"You'll probably never get the truth out of him," said Penelope. "It's become too much of a game."

Now, with Buck down on the pasterns, we all assumed that age and that missing liver had finally caught up with him.

At some point some vet had told us that if a horse lies down for much more than ten hours it won't be getting up again. It's a belief held by many vets and horse people.

It's incorrect.

Our horses have taught us that, as with us when we're sick or old, sometimes they just have to lie down, sometimes for a lot longer than ten hours.

We've also learned that horses are *afraid* to lie down! The fear is virtually fed to foals with mothers' milk.

"You must never lie down for a long time when there are humans around. They'll think you're too sick to get up again and they'll kill you, thinking they're being kind."

At Spring Farm we've learned the difference between lying down and being down.

Buck was lying down. That first time he remained lying down for close to twenty hours.

How we fussed over him. How we catered to him. He ate it up, along with the delectable goodies we served him. The best hay, carrots, apples, and, when Dennis and Jackie came, his absolute favorite, pizza.

Mostly, though, he just lay flat out, sleeping soundly. We interrupted his sleep only to roll him over several times, so that his blood wouldn't pool. Does anyone want to know how to roll a horse or get it to its feet? Just call us. By force of circumstance we've learned all the tricks.

Why don't we simply put elderly horses down? many people ask.

First, we feel that animals have as much right to loving care in old age as do we. You don't euthanize, say, your father because he has difficulty getting out of bed. At least, we hope not. Neither do we do that to animals.

Second, the study and improvement of geriatric care of horses and other animals are part of the intentions that we proclaimed when we became a 501c3 charity, explicitly stated in our Articles of Incorporation.

Last, but far from least, just as sharing their last years with my parents, caring for them, loving, and understanding them more intensely than ever before was a privilege and food for the soul, so it has been with our elderly animals here at Spring Farm.

We were, however, that first time with Buck, misled by the "not much more than ten hours" old vets' tale. The horses in the stalls near where he lay shared our concern. Whenever we went to do anything with him, they'd all watch, nickering encouragement. So it was that when we decided after nearly twenty hours to get tough with him and get him up or else, they were all watching.

Jackie and Dennis were there, Leigh, Dawn, and I. We got a halter and lead onto him and commenced, with shouts, slaps, rocking, and pushing, to demand that he rise.

And he did!

The watching horses squealed, whinnied, and pranced around their stalls, celebrating for good old Buckwheat—and for themselves. Celebrating the right of Spring Farm horses to rest when they needed to, and to heck with old vets' tales.

The Unsinkable Buckwheat Hayman.

But he wasn't out of the woods. Strength had returned to his pasterns, yet he could hardly walk and spent most of his time lying down.

Then one day what we thought was an abscess burst open at the back of his right front leg, where it attached to the body, in what we'd call the back of the armpit. With each passing day that area became more of a disaster.

Jackie opted to treat it homeopathically, with a mixture of myrrh, goldenseal root powder, and boric acid. She came each day to clean the wound and apply the concoction. It was a long time a-healing, at one point larger than a salad plate.

Only then could we see the corkscrew pattern to the wound and an entry hole, and only then did we remember the gunshot.

We all, including Buck and the vets, agreed that surgery to try to find the bullet would do more harm than good. So Jackie kept on, day after day, cleaning the wound and applying her concoction. After many weeks the wound closed and Buck seemed comfortable again.

Then one winter's morning we found him down in his stall—not lying down, down. Thus began a siege that lasted for a year and a half, during which time Buck lived either loose in the arena or in a large arena enclosure made from stock gates.

We never did know exactly what was wrong with him—liver problems, stress from the bullet, old age, or a combination of all three. He'd be fine for weeks. Then suddenly he'd lie down and stay down for increasingly long periods. Or he'd be in a transitional state, lying down for an hour or so, then getting up and lying back down almost immediately.

He was perfectly comfortable about lying down. He knew that he'd have a soft bed of straw, that his pillows would be fluffed, that hay bales would be placed behind him to help prop him up-right, that he'd be snugly blanketed. He knew that his slaves would provide endless hay, water, and treats, that he'd be rolled periodically, and that, if he needed help, we'd help him to his feet. He knew that he'd have regular chiropractic care, lots of massage, and TTouch.

The horse had it made!

I slept on an air mattress in the arena with him most nights that winter, making sure that he stayed comfortable and didn't get into trouble. As when I'd slept beside Kazinka, some nights were way below zero. Jackie and Dennis, stopping in at 5:30 each morning on their way to work, got used to seeing no Bonnie, only a pile of frost-covered quilts that snored.

It was during Buck's last year and a half that Kazinka became his devoted companion. For some weeks she watched us fuss with him. Then one day she told Dawn, "I've decided to help you with Buckwheat. Let me come out with him. I'll take care of him."

She was true to her word. When he was lying down, she stood over him, nose touching him solicitously. If she lay down herself, she positioned herself so that she could reach out and touch him. When he was up, she stood or walked beside him. Far be it from us to suggest that her dedication was other than selfless. But as Buck's Siamese twin, she now shared his treats, including frequent pizza and the glazed doughnuts that Jackie and Dennis brought each Saturday morning.

Kazinka wasn't in the best of condition herself. She was only twenty-two, but she had emphysema. Azium usually controlled it, but one day, when we'd called Leigh during a particularly bad spell, Leigh made so bold as to offer an unpopular opinion. She uttered the words while standing just at Kazinka's left shoulder.

"If this gets any worse, you're going to have to think about putting this horse down."

Then the strangest expression came over Leigh's face—wide-eyed horror, culminating in a cry of pain.

Very carefully, Kazinka had lifted her left front foot, placed it onto Leigh's left foot, and transferred all her weight onto that foot.

"No pun intended," said Leigh ruefully when we got her out from under, "but she told me in no uncertain terms where *she* stands. Sorry, Kazinka. I keep forgetting that you guys understand everything we say."

No, neither Buckwheat nor Kazinka was ready to go just yet. That spring, summer, and fall they enjoyed each other's company and the private paddock just outside their pipe corral enclosure.

Come winter, Buck went downhill again. In February he lay down and didn't get up. Eighteen days passed. On the nineteenth day we determined to go for broke. If he could get up, we were going to get him up. If he couldn't get up, well . . .

We had a dozen people there, pulling, pushing, lifting, shouting. As we shouted, the horses whinnied. The arena was a bedlam of shrill encouragement.

Once again, the Unsinkable Buckwheat Hayman got to his feet.

What cheers. What equine squeals.

What relief! None of us would have had the courage to put him to sleep.

Happiest of all was Buckwheat. He declared to Dawn that he was going to see another spring, that he was going to taste fresh green grass again, out in his private paddock.

But the day that the grass was long enough and we opened the sliding door into the paddock so that he and Kazinka could go out, he found that he was too stiff and fragile to hobble out the door and down the slight slope to the grass.

He hung his head and went into a depression. Kazinka stayed by his side.

Comparing notes later, we realized that all his loved ones had received a message from him that day. A farewell. And that afternoon, I heard Dawn screaming for me. I ran to the arena. Buck was down, dying. I ran back to the barn and called Dennis at work. He wasn't in his office, and I left a message. I called Leigh. She wasn't home; I left a message. I ran back to the arena.

Dawn was at Buck's head, sobbing, trying to talk to him, trying to calm him. It wasn't a quiet death. He was out of his head, clawing and flailing with his legs, as though trying to get to his feet just one more time.

Then, just at the last, he grew quiet. His eyes refocused, and he looked up at us. For brief moments, Buckwheat was back.

It was like one of those old movies. The detective leans over the only witness to a murder, who's just been shot, obviously by the murderer. "Quick, Charlie," says the detective. "Who did this to you?" Charlie says, "It was—it was—" Then his head flops sideways and he's dead. I leaned over Buckwheat and said, "Tell us, Buckwheat. Now or never. How old are you?"

He looked right at me, and Dawn heard him say, "I'm thirty-seven, Aunt Bonnie. And that's the truth."

Then his eyes glazed and he was gone.

Kazinka took his death hard. When Bob came with his backhoe, we tried to take her to a stall. She refused to go.

"I want to watch," she said.

We'd decided to bury Buck in their own little paddock, just at the base of the slope that he hadn't been able to maneuver that morning. We slid the door open, and Kazinka watched as Bob dug the grave, then returned for Buck.

Our method of carrying horses to their graves wasn't wonderfully dignified. Bob had stout canvas straps that we put around Buck's feet, front and back. These Bob attached to the bucket of the backhoe. Then he raised the bucket high. Buck was thus carried, hanging upside down, out the front door, around the barn, and into the paddock through the lower gate. That awkward trip was compensated for by the fact that Bob was thus able to lower Buck gently down into the grave, positioning him in peaceful repose, rather than dumping him in as would be the case if he'd been carried in the bucket.

Kazinka watched it all. She never moved as Buck was lowered in, as we jumped down in with him to further arrange the body, or as we scattered daffodils from the garden onto our dear, golden friend. Only when the backhoe began to shovel the dirt over him did Kazinka turn and walk away.

She virtually stopped eating. Over a period of weeks she became skeletal. We tried giving her a new friend. We put an Arab mare named Tara into the pipe corral enclosure with her. But then thirty-year-old Tara up and died as well.

Yet Kazinka faked us out at the end. We thought that she'd decided to live. Tara had been a pampered pet, rarely confined, roaming the arena and stable. And one night I got a very clear communication from Kazinka.

"I want to be the new Tara. I want to be with you."

So we opened her gate and left her free to roam arena, enclosure, and paddock at will. She never did go back out into the paddock again, but she loved the freedom of the arena and her appetite returned. She followed us as we did our feeding chores, even into the stable proper, stealing hay and grain from us and teasing the other horses with her freedom and favored status. Impishly, she accosted everyone who entered the arena, hugging them to herself and shamelessly demanding attention. It was her babyhood all over again, she was the coddled and spoiled twin, just a big pet pooch. She regained some of her lost weight, and for weeks she thrived.

Then one morning Dawn came into the office of the barn looking worried.

"Kazinka just told me that she's going to go."

That afternoon, as Dawn was walking past the door of the arena, the horses inside let out a scream. Dawn ran in and found that Kazinka had quite simply keeled over, dead.

She'd done so right where she'd stood watching Buck being buried, in the doorway to the paddock, not thirty feet from his grave. And she'd managed to fall out the doorway into the paddock, reducing the distance to the grave.

"I want to be buried beside Buckwheat," she told Dawn. "But I'll be darned if you're going to carry me dangling upside down like you did with him, parading around for all the neighbors to see. So undignified! I've put myself where you only have to take me a few feet."

As always, Kazinka had her way.

But then she told us why she'd departed so quickly.

"Buck is coming back, and I have to be with him. We're going to be twins. Llamas. And we're coming to Spring Farm."

Llamas? Pretty expensive creatures. We couldn't feature anyone wanting to give us twin llamas.

To confuse the issue, the night of the day that Buck had died, he'd dictated a four-page letter to me, with personal messages for his various loved ones. (Somehow my chief communication skill has been getting posthumous messages from our animals.) His letter announced his plans to organize the spirits of the animals who'd lived and died here into the Spring Farm Ghost Brigade, to patrol and to guard us from intruders. Especially, he said with emphasis, from hunters.

Wow. Pity the poor hunter who met up with Buckwheat and his crew.

The idea of the Ghost Brigade was comforting to us. When things got tough, we could just raise our eyes to the sky and cry out, "Buckwheat!"

And we'd hear that John Wayne drawl: "Don't fret, little ladies. I'll fix things for ya."

Then, "Yooh-oohh! Move out!"

And hoofbeats and the patter of paws as the brigade trotted smartly off to set things right.

Interestingly, in the hunting seasons since the death of Buckwheat, incursions by hunters onto our land have almost ceased. According to Deeteza, there've been quite a few would-be trespassers. But the Ghost Brigade has dealt with them.

"And I don't think they'll ever be back," she said.

Oh, by the way, Buck and Kazinka died in April and July 1993, respectively. In December 1993, we learned that we were to be given two baby llamas.

15

New Hooves and a Taste for Glazed Doughnuts

Most people have heard of horses foundering but don't know what founder, also called laminitis, is. In *Black Beauty*, Beauty foundered when a stable boy gave her cold water after a hard gallop. Horses can founder from things such as rich hay, excessive spring grazing, and too much grain. Pony breeds developed in and for arid regions are exceptionally prone to founder when allowed rich forage. Founder can be mild, producing feet that are slightly to very sore, or catastrophic. A horse can lose its hooves.

The sad thing is that horses and ponies are most often "killed by the kindness" of well-meaning owners. So it was with a Quarter Horse named Chubby. Chubby's owner gave her free-choice second-cutting alfalfa hay and grain during her last month of pregnancy. With a two-week-old foal at side, Chubby was losing her front hooves.

Ordinarily that would be a death sentence. But Leigh Lain suggested to her owner that perhaps Dawn and I could save the horse. Leigh meant save the hooves and save her life. The owner's concern was more pragmatic: if Chubby were put down, the foal, Penny, would have to be bottle-fed. He was going through a divorce and no longer lived on the premises. Bottle-feeding was impossible. Could we, he wanted to know, keep Chubby comfortable and functioning until Penny could be weaned?

He wanted a milk spigot for the duration.

Dawn and I had never dealt with such disastrous founder. TTouch might be able to keep her comfortable enough. And extraordinary nursing care was part of our stated intent.

But save her life? Leigh had more faith in us than we did.

We went to Chubby's barn, six miles away, to analyze the situation and meet our patient. She was lying in a twelve-by-twelve-foot box stall, heavily bedded for her comfort.

"Can she get up at all?" I asked the owner.

"Only to change sides. She goes right back down."

"Hello, Chubby."

The gaze that greeted us was one of calm dignity.

There was no dignity in Penny, who was bouncing around the stall as though on pogo sticks. Poor baby, she'd been locked in that tiny space with her mother since birth, having to nurse by getting down onto her belly.

We went in to look at Chubby's hooves.

"Wow," breathed Dawn.

Each front hoof was beginning to separate from its coronal band, the place where the hoof ends and the flesh and hair of the leg begin. Ugly abscesses bubbled all along the bands.

I looked into Chubby's soft eyes, reached down, and stroked her.

"We'll help you, girl. Some way."

We started on TTouch there and then. Chubby lay back, sighing with pleasure, while Penny crowded in, aggressively curious. It wasn't going to be easy with that little one around.

We contracted with Chubby's owner for ten dollars a day, plus all expenses.

"Bedsores will be a big problem," said Dawn as we drove home.

"I think we're going to have to go over there more than once a day."

"I do, too," said Dawn. "Two—maybe even three times. *Someone* has to keep checking on the two of them. I guess any extra visits will be on us."

"Yeah. She's a special soul. What did you get from her?"

"Peace. Serenity. She's grateful for the help and sorry for Penny. I wonder if we *can* save her."

We called George Buell and described the situation.

"Any way to help her keep the hooves that she's got now?" we asked.

"Not if they're that abscessed. But we can help her grow new ones. It can de done when people take the time and trouble. I'll dig some information out of my farrier journals."

The next day he arrived with some journals.

"You girls are letting yourselves in for a lot of work. It'll take months. And she might still have to be put down in the end."

"You have to meet this horse," I said. "She's worth the effort."

"Oh, I'll meet her. I'm going to shoe her."

"*Shoe* her?"

We were aghast.

"Yep. I've been reading. Best thing is to get shoes onto her, with frog pads. The shoes will give her something firm to stand on and the pads will put pressure on the frogs to get blood pumping down into those feet."

We called Chubby's owner.

"What if we could save Chubby? What if we can help her grow new hooves? Would you go for it? Even if it's expensive?"

"If we can save her, sure," he said.

We bought our supplies and started that very day. We made sugar and Betadine—"sugar-dine"—into a paste the consistency of peanut butter. This was liberally smeared onto two long strips—we used cheap, gauzy leg wraps, cutting them into strips the proper width and length. The sugar-dine-laden strips got wrapped around each coronal band and then secured in place with elasticized bandage wrap, which enclosed the coronal band and the entire foot.

We would never have gotten past even the first day without the cooperation of our patient.

"Lie back now, Chubby."

Chubby lay back.

"Now hold still while we wrap your feet."

Chubby held still.

Throughout a process that took more than half a year, she remained a full partner in her own rehabilitation. Oh, once in a while she grew impatient. Once in a while she was short-tempered. Those exceptions proved the rule.

It was hard for us to visualize what was going to happen with her hooves. When one is told, "The horse will lose its hoof," one imagines the whole thing just falling off in a chunk!

A horse's hoof is not some clunky block. It's an intricate, delicate apparatus. Actually, the hard outer hoof is composed of densely packed *hair*. The hair grows out of the coronal band, down around the articulated bones, veins, tissue, and components of the inner foot, somewhat as our fingernails and toenails grow out of our cuticles. If the sugar-dine did its job of promoting granulation tissue, a new hoof would begin to grow out of the coronal band, pushing the old hoof ahead of it. The old hoof would be kept on as long as possible, to act as a bandage, protecting the bones, tissue, and blood vessels of the inner foot. If all went well, somewhere in the future, Chubby would have brand-new hooves on which to stand.

Three days after we started the sugar-dine, George shoed her front feet. It took four hours and was agony for Chubby, excruciating for us. Leigh was there, to administer painkillers. We'd have preferred to put Chubby under, but her heart rate was so high that tranquilization might have killed her. As it was, each tap of George's hammer sent her heart rate soaring to 120. He had to wait after each tap, until the heart rate dropped.

Were we doing the right thing?

The next morning when we entered Chubby's barn we found her owner in her stall, wearing a broad grin.

Chubby was standing! Eating hay from her rack!

Good old George. She could now stand for many minutes at a time.

We continued with the sugar-dine, changing the dressings daily. It was another couple of weeks before—

"Bonnie! Look!"

Dawn had been removing the old dressings as I prepared the new ones.

I ran into the stall and knelt beside her.

"Ohmygawd, there's something there. Chubby, your new hooves are *growing!*"

What joy. Chubby seemed to smile, and Penny commenced bucking around the stall.

And so we went, day after day, week after week, with sugar-dine and TTouch. Plus which we gave her a total body rub each day, with a mixture of eight drops of arnica to a quart of witch hazel. To spots where bedsores threatened, we applied Bach Flower Rescue Remedy Cream in lavish amounts, ordering it by the case. Chubby stayed comfortable. Any bedsores that did appear remained under control and uninfected.

Her shoes had to come off after a month or so, for the old hooves had to be trimmed off apace with the growth of the new hooves pushing them downward. George ordered special plastic shoes that he glued on, but they didn't stay on well. It didn't matter. By that time, the abscessing of the coronal bands had cleared up and the fresh hooves were coming along so nicely that Chubby was able to stand comfortably for minutes at a time without shoes!

We nursed her in that barn for five months. Came the time that sugar-dine wraps were no longer needed. The new hoof was growing all on its own, and the coronal bands were healthy.

The decision was made to truck her and little Penny to Spring Farm.

That decision was made by Chubby herself. Whenever we'd talked to her before about moving, she'd said no. Then suddenly one day she told Dawn that she felt she could do it.

We hoped we weren't pushing things. But she'd have to walk only about twelve feet to the trailer. She could lie down during the ride. There'd be a much longer walk through our arena, to the nursery stall, where we'd be putting her and Penny. But she could take all day to travel that distance, lying down as long as she needed to between steps.

And it was time for the move. The owner's enthusiasm for the project had evaporated. We hadn't been paid, or reimbursed for supplies, after the first couple of months. We might as well have Chubby at home and not have to keep driving back and forth.

The day of the move, our hearts were in our throats. We'd prepared her exit route with care, creating a deep path of sawdust to keep her feet clean, and we'd constructed a ledge of soil so that the stock trailer could back right up to it and Chubby could walk straight in without having to step up.

Everything went splendidly. She didn't hesitate for a moment, and Penny stuck right by her side. Before we knew it, we were in the stock trailer, the driver was closing us in, and we were off. We'd bedded the floor deeply, but a proud Chubby rode the six miles standing. At the door to the arena, she stepped down out of the trailer just as proudly. Then—slowly, "ouchily," yes, but with great dignity and without stopping—she lead her foal past welcoming nickers to her nursery stall.

Then she lay down.

For days, little Penny made the most of that stall. Its Dutch door opened onto a small paddock. For the first time, she was able to run, out and around the paddock, into the stall, out and around the paddock, into the stall. Chubby was happy, watching her foal at play.

Her happiness was short-lived. Less than a week after the move, Chubby's owner informed us that he'd sold Penny. We begged him to wait another month or so before separating them, but he'd hear none of it. The new owners came for Penny that very day. They had a heck of a time loading her. She shrieked as they separated her from Chubby, broke away from them repeatedly, running back to Chubby, fighting them, kicking them. They had virtually to hog-tie her and drag her out.

Poor little Penny. She'd been as brave in her own way as had Chubby, enduring confinement that a foal should never have had to endure. Oh yes, again and again she'd made life difficult for us as we worked with Chubby, sticking her nose in where it wasn't needed, erupting into sudden playful—and potentially lethal—bucks and kicks. All in all, though, she'd been a great kid. Now, suddenly, she was gone. Our hearts broke for her. And for Chubby.

More heartbreak awaited Chubby. Her owner abandoned her. It had been agreed that he'd supply Chubby and Penny with hay. He delivered one pickup-load full. Then, with Penny sold, he stopped coming. We never saw or heard from him again, and he never paid what he owed us.

Chubby was devastated. She loved him dearly. And she'd say nothing against him. We ourselves had to be careful what we said about him within her hearing, for she couldn't bear to hear negative comments.

She was, however, full of apologies for herself. For her very existence.

"I'm so sorry. So sorry," she kept telling us. "Now you're stuck with me."

"Chubby, we're not sorry. We'd have taken care of you with or without money. We *did* take care of you without money. And we're not stuck. We love you. You're ours now, and we're yours. We're a family here."

Came the day when George removed the last of her old hooves and left Chubby standing on her new hooves. They were lumpy and uneven, far from pretty. But they were there. We'd done it, Chubby, Penny, George, Leigh, Dawn, and I. Precious few horses in this world have been nursed through a change of hooves, and Chubby was one of them. She'd never be able to frisk around again. When she walked, it would be slowly, carefully. And she'd spend as much time lying down as standing up. But she was alive, living with people who cherished her and who recognized a great spirit when they saw one.

Unfortunately, the loss of Penny, and then of her owner, robbed Chubby of any joy in her accomplishment or circumstances. She went into a deep depression.

Our friend Sugar was also laid low by a loss. People had told us of the herd of ponies to which Sugar had belonged being sold away, of dying, one by one, until only Sugar was left, so alone in that field. Shortly after she came to Spring Farm, Sugar dictated a poem to Dawn:

> *In a field—a princess made*
> *Proclaimed by time—alone*
> *With feet of clay—immovable*
> *She dreamed of becoming free—soon*

But time dragged on—slowly
and adornments plagued her—abundantly

For thorns and burrs clung to her hair—and grew
The sun no longer reached her skin—so pale

She grew tired—so weary of captivity
Tied to the land
free to move
but unable

Silence was so frequent to ears
now deaf
Ne'er a touch was to her skin—so old
Skin grew less to cling to bones—aching
Teeth grew tired of nothing—bored

The princess proclaimed by time—forgotten
But for some souls who cared—
and visited

Shocked by the invisible chains—
so strong
They vowed to set her free—at last

A tear streamed down the princess—fair
"At last!" she cried—
"Someone to care."

Without adornments in her hair
so light now
time indeed proved a princess—invincible

And touch to skin so aching—starved
is what broke the chains—
freeing her heart

A soul to wander free and clear—forever
A kingdom befitting a princess—Heaven.

As happy as she'd been to arrive at the heaven of Spring Farm, Sugar had been doubly happy at the arrival of her friend Bubbles.

Bubbles was a ham. Her first exposure to celebrity was during a Penelope Smith workshop, when Susan Nackley Mojave, from local TV news, asked us to bring out an animal for Penelope to talk with on camera. Bubbles supplied a most entertaining interview and thereafter was wont to tell any animal or person who cared to listen, "I'm a star, you know. I was on TV."

She also loved to dress up, a predilection ferreted out by Dawn. Certain animals love to be dressed up as much as Dawn loves dressing them up. For years, on Halloween, Dawn had taken Spangles, prancing proudly, in costume, down to the house to trick-or-treat for Gramma Dean. After Bubbles's arrival, there were two animal trick-or-treaters. To Mother's delight, Dawn would lead Bubbles right into the kitchen, to show off her costume and collect her treat.

Bubbles also willingly loaded into Vanessa, to appear at various events in inner-city Utica. She'd wear a party hat and, on her back, a colorful patchwork afghan. Kids loved her. Most of them had never seen an animal other than a dog or cat and guessed that Bubbles must be a goat, giving us the opportunity to expand their knowledge of the animal world.

Sugar had no resentment of Bubbles's celebrity. Sugar had her own celebrity.

In the back of her stall was a long set of shelves containing her music box collection. We discovered her love of music one day when we wound up a donated plush toy music box while standing near her. Sugar came over and listened so intently that we wound it up for her again and again.

"May I have it?" she finally asked.

So we put the musical toy on a shelf in her stall. Each night, as we left the stable, we'd wind it up and leave it playing for her and all the other horses.

We also then put a radio onto her shelves. After sampling various kinds of music, she settled on soft rock as her favorite.

And she had a favorite song, Bette Midler's "From a Distance." Because, as it turned out, Spring Farm was visible, across the valley, from the field where Sugar had been imprisoned. She told us that she'd used to gaze over at our far hill and dream that someday someone would come from that hill and rescue her. From a distance.

One might ask why there were shelves in a pony's stall. They were there to display the gifts given to Sugar by her many fans— cards, poems, toys, pictures, an Indian drum, fetishes, crystals— Manci Ohrstrom from Virginia once had a florist deliver a bouquet to Sugar.

When word got out that Sugar liked music boxes, the shelves filled rapidly.

We have sweet memories of those music boxes. Each night, as we closed the barn, we'd ask Sugar and Bubbles which one they wanted to hear. They took turns choosing. We'd leave the darkened barn with just one dim night-light, with the comforting sound of the horses munching on their hay and the tune from the selected music box floating over all.

It doesn't get much better than that.

Bubbles's death hit all of us hard. One day she was simply unable to swallow. She didn't lack for veterinary attention. Sue Ann Lesser was staying with us at the time, and Leigh Lain came several times a day. Neither of them could figure out what was happening.

Was there a plug of hay lodged in her throat? We considered tubing her, to push whatever it was down the throat and into the stomach. But Leigh was loath to attempt that procedure on such a frail and elderly pony.

"If I poke a hole in her larynx, she's a goner."

So we kept massaging her throat and syringing tiny bits of liquid sustenance into her mouth, hoping that the blockage would break up or make its way into the stomach.

Dawn was distraught, as she was scheduled to leave for California to attend Penelope Smith's teaching workshop. Indeed, Bubbles died on February 5, 1993, just hours after Dawn left.

Alone, with Dawn in midair somewhere between New York and California, I received a long message from the departed Bubbles. Among other things, she said that nothing could have saved her. Her thymus had shut down. Knowing little about the thymus, I checked the *Encyclopaedia Britannica*.

Medical science also knows little about the thymus. It's thought mainly to affect youthful development, then to be of little importance in adults or the elderly.

But one thing leaped out at me: disease of the thymus often produces muscular weakness. Could this include weakness of the muscles that allow one to swallow? Perhaps the thymus is more important in adulthood and old age than suspected—a tip to researchers from a "dead" Shetland pony.

Sugar asked that Bubbles's body not be removed for burial immediately. That was no problem, as temperatures were hovering around zero. I covered Bubbles's body with a blanket, her head visible, as though she were sleeping. For the entire weekend and through Monday, Sugar stood over the body of her friend.

Dawn returned from California Monday night to an emergency with Toby, a thirty-year-old, fourteen-hand, black-and-white pinto pony whom Dawn had adopted as her own "riding horse." Ever the reluctant rider, she rode him secretly, when there was no one around, up in the outdoor arena, bareback, even cantering when Toby offered it.

In kindness, one *had* to ride Toby bareback. He had the worst scarring from saddle sores that we'd ever encountered. Toby had seen so much use that it had become ab-use.

Toby was a special pony. His gaits were so smooth that children fought to be the lucky one to ride him in "fun" classes, where a glass of water had to be carried through walk, trot, and canter without spilling. Toby's rider always won, for Toby fairly glided along.

It was that popularity with children, and the resulting overuse, that had gotten Toby retired to Spring Farm. Because one day he'd had it; he began attacking children.

He was a maudlin little fellow. One Thanksgiving, when we asked all the horses to tell us what they were thankful for, two of his horse friends, Topaz and Amber, said that they were thankful that Toby finally knew that he wouldn't be forgotten. He'd thought, before coming to Spring Farm, that though he'd lived his life painfully serving children, none would remember him. Now he knew that his Spring Farm friends wouldn't forget.

He was colicking when Dawn got home that Monday night. He colicked frequently, probably a result of his painful life and un-happy thoughts. We worked with him until after midnight, at which point he seemed recovered. We left him with the run of the arena and went to bed.

The next morning we found him dead, sitting upright, his legs tucked beneath himself in an amazingly natural position. He was right beside the stall of Sugar and Bubbles, his head turned toward the body of Bubbles, there on the other side of the stock gate.

Once we got over our shock and tears, Dawn connected with Bubbles.

"He'd been wanting to go for some time, but he was afraid to do it alone. So he came with me. I helped him make the transition."

The position of his body would certainly support the truth of that statement.

Now Sugar asked that the body of Bubbles be removed. She abandoned her vigil, went to the back of the stall, and didn't look at Bubbles again.

We buried Bubbles and Toby in the same grave. It seemed fitting. It seemed that Bubbles's body had waited for Toby's, to help him through even that part of it.

For this burial, though, because of bad weather and slippery conditions, Bob opted not to use his straps but to carry the ponies in the bucket and slide them into the grave.

There were two trips. Toby went first. He settled onto his back in the grave, leaning against one wall, his legs curled up and his head toward that wall. He looked like a sleeping kitten. We decided that position was just fine. When Bubbles went in, she landed standing against Toby's right side, her head draped protectively over his chest. In that touching embrace, we left them.

We do memorial stones for each of our animals. Bubbles's stone says, "Bubbles—TV Star." Toby's says, "Toby—We Remember."

Sugar went into a depression so deep that she informed both Dawn and Penelope Smith that she wished to die as well. To prove it, she started going downhill.

So now we had two depressed horses, Sugar and Chubby. Hoping they'd cheer each other up, we built a new pipe corral enclosure and moved the two of them into it together.

They hit it off. Indeed, they had Indian past lives in common, Sugar as the Indian medicine woman Nicohee, and Chubby, so she told us, as the Indian woman Sacajawea.

They did seem a tad more cheerful. Yet the undercurrent of depression remained.

Then, on the morning of April 9, Dawn found Sugar dancing around the stall. Crippled as she was, the fact that she was dancing could hardly be missed.

"Bubbles is coming back! You've got to find her, quick!"

Bubbles, she explained, was in utero in a Shetland mare and would be back at Spring Farm by April 23, still in utero. Then she'd be born in the very stall where she'd "died" less than three months earlier.

The idea that Bubbles could be reborn in such a short time—since the gestation period of horses and ponies is eleven months—didn't disturb us any more than had Prinnie's quick return. Those who've read the works of Jane Roberts and Seth will remember that Seth says there's no set time for a soul to enter into, or "take possession" of, a fetus. Some, he explains, do it at the point of conception in order to reexperience the entire, very pleasant womb experience, while some take conception for the womb experience alone, checking out before, or shortly after, the birth. Others enter at various points in the gestation. Some come and go, sometimes deciding to vacate altogether. Sometimes one soul will vacate to let another soul take over. Some enter just at the moment of birth, and interestingly, Seth says, some enter only after the birth, sometimes days or even weeks after the birth! The heartbreaking crib death syndrome is sometimes a situation where a soul not really committed to living that particular life simply leaves.

The various entrances into fetuses that have been described to us by our animals seem to bear out this "optional entrance and exit" theory.

We've also experienced situations where a sick animal, which really should die, recovers—but with such a different personality that it's obviously not the same soul in that body! Or where a perfectly healthy animal changes personality so suddenly that it's not the same animal. We call this switch of souls in a living animal a "walk-in."

So the mechanics by which Bubbles intended to get reborn were unimportant to us. Our problem was that there aren't that many Shetland mares around, much less a pregnant Shetland mare whose owner would be eager to give her to Spring Farm CARES.

And we certainly couldn't pay for her.

Besides, even if we found a mare, how would we know she was the right one?

Our arguments cut no ice with Sugar.

"Get busy! Find her!"

We started calling around. Two weeks passed with no luck. Oh, we heard of a couple of mares, each more than a hundred miles away, each costing more than a thousand dollars. No way.

Then, on the evening of April 22, we received a call. An elderly woman living ten miles away had a whole herd of Shetlands and a pregnant mare that she'd sell for $350.

We gritted our teeth and came up with the money. This had to be Bubbles.

The next day, D-Day, or rather B-Day, April 23, we trucked Missy and her precious cargo to Spring Farm. We put her into the stall that had belonged to Sugar and Bubbles. It was next to the stall now occupied by Sugar and Chubby. The two Shetlands touched noses through the stock gate, and Sugar was content.

Mr. Bubbles was born on the morning of May the fourteenth. One of the great losses in our fire was that of all the videos that we'd shot over the years. On the tape of Mr. Bubbles's birth were clearly recorded the next two incidents.

Present that morning was one of our volunteers, along with her daughter, Mindy, at that point two years old. The woman had been bringing Mindy along with her since the girl was a tiny baby. The warm tack room had served as Mindy's nursery, but on nice days, the mother often put the baby into a rocking cradle-chair in front of Sugar and Bubbles's stall. Bubbles would reach her head through the pipe gate and actually rock the cradle. She'd babysit that way for hours.

The word "Bubbles," which Mindy rendered as "Bubba," was

one of the first words Mindy ever spoke. Mindy had a little wheeled horsie that she rode around the barn, but it couldn't compare to her Bubba. She and that pony loved each other, and her little life was saddened by Bubbles's death. She'd seen the body, and it had been explained to her.

The bond between Mindy and Bubbles was far from our minds as we assisted in the delivery, but, held up by her mother so that she could see, Mindy watched with rapt attention. At 10:15, I tore open the sac. The tiny new creature, not much bigger than Mindy's wheeled horsie, took his first breath.

"Look," the mother said to the child. "What is that?"

"Bubba!" said Mindy. "Bubba!"

Throughout the process, Sugar had been glued to the pipe corral separating the two pens. "Bubba" was delivered just six or seven feet from where Sugar waited. He got to his feet after only fifteen minutes. At which point, ignoring his mother, he responded to Sugar's nickers, tottered over to the gate, put his head through, and he and Sugar kissed.

To further convince us that this was, indeed, Bubbles returned . . . Sugar and Bubbles's pipe corral enclosure had adjoined that of Buck and Kazinka. On Saturday mornings, when Dennis and Jackie brought glazed doughnuts, the two ponies had always mooched their way into the act. Indeed, Bubbles had only to see the Haymans coming and she'd begin whinnying, stomping in circles until she got her doughnut bits.

Remember that Mr. Bubbles was born at 10:15 on a Friday morning. As it happened, we were having a garage sale/open house the next morning. The Haymans arrived at eight to help us prepare, bringing a bag of glazed doughnuts for Kazinka and the other horses. They put the bag on a table sitting in front of the stall where Mr. Bubbles, less than twenty-four hours old, lay sleeping. As we all stood ohhing and ahhing over him, he woke up. He got to his feet, looked around—

—and his eyes went BOINGGG!

He saw that bag of glazed doughnuts. Like a shot, he was over to the gate, sticking his head through, trying desperately to reach the bag. When offered tiny bits, he wolfed them down.

Scientists demand measurements. Well, we can give them one measurement: the taste for glazed doughnuts stretches further than the grave.

A great peace descended onto that end of the arena. Not only did Sugar have her Bubbles back, but a month later Dream and her blind foal, Corri, joined our Shetland herd. Again, we had to dig into our meager funds and pay a few hundred dollars. But they needed to be gotten out of the place where they were living. With their arrival, Sugar ascended from Heaven to Seventh Heaven.

As for Chubby, the frolicking of the pony foals was exactly the tonic she needed. Soon she was joining Sugar in greeting visitors, developing a following all her own—and also, naturally, developing a taste for glazed doughnuts.

16

George Kigercat Finishes
the New Barn

S tealthily, on little cat feet, Halloween 1993 was approaching. Behind the cosmic scenery, the future of Spring Farm CARES was being arranged.

We'd never stopped worrying about George's safaris. Our anxiety increased as it became obvious that he *was* crossing the road.

"I never said I wouldn't cross the road," he said when confronted. "I only promised not to get killed in the road. I know what I'm doing."

One day, while gardening, Dawn looked up and saw George walking down the center line of Route 12.

"George! Get out of the road!"

"It's okay. There's nothing coming." For emphasis, he lay down, rolled, and stretched.

"George!" Dawn ran toward him.

He leaped to his feet and scampered to the door of the barn.

"Don't ever do a thing like that again."

"I know what I'm doing. I won't get myself killed."

So darned cocky. George just "silked" around the place, sure of our adoration and his ability to wrap us around his little claw. Yet years had passed since he'd become an indoor-outdoor cat, and he did keep coming home safely.

In 1992, he started talking about "the new barn I'm designing for you." After that, every time he went out, it was to "work on your new barn."

"We don't need a new barn. Even if we did, we've no money to build one," we told him.

"You never know when you'll need a new barn," he'd answer.

The winter of 1992–93 was a tough one, with deep snow that kept George inside. His urinary blockage reappeared, with a vengeance. This time it didn't respond to cantharis, so we opted for the "female urethra" operation. It was a bloody mess of postop home nursing during the first week, but then he healed quickly. Come spring, he started going out again, our usual, healthy, vibrant George.

One morning in late June as he went out, he turned and looked back at Dawn.

"I'll be finishing your new barn today."

He didn't return that day, nor that evening, nor the next morning. Worst of all, when Dawn called him, she sometimes got nothing at all. At other times she got "I'm lost. I don't know where I am. I can't find my way back to you."

Dawn went white the first time she got that message. "He's dead, Bonnie."

"No. Remember when he was gone for two days and kept saying he was lost? He'll be back."

She shook her head. "He's a different kind of lost now."

That afternoon, my niece Helen called from across the road. "Are you missing a cat?"

"Yes. Black and white."

"I'm sorry. He's in the field beside our house. He was hit by a car."

I went over for the body. There wasn't much left of him to recognize. But I'd have known that dear pink nose anywhere. I wrapped him in a blanket and put him in the garage, then went and confirmed the worst to Dawn.

George refused to accept what had happened. He wouldn't believe that he was dead.

"I'd never have done that!" he cried. "I promised I wouldn't be killed in the road. But I can't find anything familiar. Help me find my way back to you."

It was hours before he accepted the truth. No more the cocky cat.

"I'm sorry," he kept saying. "I'm sorry, I'm sorry. I don't know how it happened."

Then he said, "But I finished your barn."

As we sat there, two living people and a dead cat trying to console one another, we got a sign.

We always tell grieving clients to "watch for a sign." Dead loved ones always send one to let us know they're not really gone, that the bond is still there, that everything's okay. Dawn had mentioned only the day before that she'd never seen a live hummingbird, that she'd love to see one. I'd seen very few myself, and none at Spring Farm so we made plans to plant the kind of flowers that would attract them, right outside the big overhead door, so that, in summer, perhaps we could watch hummingbirds as we worked.

Now, suddenly, there was a hummingbird hovering just outside the screen of that very door, looking at us. It was gone in a twinkling. But we'd just been wondering about where to bury George. Now we knew: by that door, in the "Hummingbird Place."

Poor Mother. George's burial site turned out to be right in the middle of her secret patch of four-leaf clovers. I pretty much destroyed that patch while burying him.

On the other hand, perhaps burying George in a patch of four-leaf clovers was propitious.

Signs and communications continued in the days followed. He'd be back as soon as he could find a suitable body, he said.

Then one day he said, "You'll know me because I'll be with the bears."

We laughed, thinking he was joking, referring to his insistence upon hunting "big game."

In mid-September, we got a call from a student at Herkimer County Community College.

"I've got a three-day-old kitten that was abandoned on a golf course. Can you take it?" Then she added, "It's black and white."

Was it he?

We bustled around, preparing nursing equipment and formula, impatiently awaiting the kitten's arrival.

Eagerly we opened the cardboard box in which the girl brought him.

He was curled between two stuffed toys.

We burst into exultant laughter.

"With the bears." *Teddy* bears!

George, himself, was big game this time.

"This kitten is older than three days," I told the girl. "He's more like two weeks."

"No. I saw him being born. I think his mother's a Maine Coon cat, she's really big. She moved her other kittens yesterday, but she never came back for him."

Well, of course. He was taking the shortest route back to us.

"Just leave me here, Mom, right in the middle of the traffic on this golf course. Don't worry, I know what I'm doing."

Of course we named him George. We tacked on the surname "Belinda," in honor of a beloved cat who'd died at about the time that George Kigercat was killed. He'd retained George Kigercat's pink nose, plus George's smug self-assurance, poise, and savoir-faire—a little know-it-all, so sure of our love, so unafraid.

From the beginning, he seemed to be an adult trapped in a kitten's body, eager to get the kitten part over with. He didn't cry or fuss, he drank his formula without protest, urinated and defecated on cue, went back to sleep immediately (snoring lightly), opened his eyes fully exactly on his tenth day, grew at an alarming rate, and hopped into his litter box at the age of three weeks, using it with no coaching from us.

And at about that age, he gave me my very own personal sign.

He'd just reached the adorable stage of really seeing us, reacting to us, reaching out with tiny paws to explore and bat at us, his little eyes so sweet and innocent that it made us want to cry. One morning I held that adorable little creature up to my face, crooning and cooing. His innocent eyes returned the adoration. He stretched forward—and nipped the tip of my nose.

I heard George Kigercat shrieking with glee.

"*Gotcha!* You never saw *that* one coming."

It was the first and only time that the new George ever did such a thing or even tried to.

One special love nip. What a gift from beyond the grave.

On Halloween night 1993, Georgie was exactly six weeks old. He'd been living in a cat carrier with a heating pad and his teddy bears, and each night I'd carried him with me to Mother's house. In keeping with his adult attitude, however, he'd begun sleeping right through, requiring no middle-of-the-night feedings. So as we prepared to go to the house that night, I wavered. Perhaps I should admit that he was a big boy now and leave him in his carrier in the barn. I nearly did so. I started out the door without him. Then I couldn't bear it. Some other night, but not just yet.

We lost twenty-four animal friends that night and came close to losing George again. Thank God for tiny favors with pink noses;

that was not to be. I'm not sure that either of us could have been as brave about everything if even that kitten had died in the fire.

There's an exclusive club that everyone hopes never to join. It's members are those who've lost everything to fire. After a hurricane or flood, one might still be able to find some treasures in the ruins. Maybe even photographs, personal records, jewelry. Flames take everything, suddenly, irrevocably. Only fellow club members really know what they mean when they say, "I know how you feel."

Gail and Uncle Warren were club members. Their house got hit by lightning. It was all over in half an hour. We found a few little things in the rubble, but basically everything was gone.

In 1996, Penelope Smith would lose everything as a forest fire swept Point Reyes.

Years after a fire, one still wakes at night and thinks of things that were but aren't anymore. Years after a fire, one still finds oneself saying, "Oh yeah, we've got one of those out in the barn," before remembering that there's no barn for whatever it is to be in. One swims in a sort of surreal soup for weeks, months after a fire, as though flipped into an alien universe. And that fire continues to burn in the back of the mind for life.

One day, we overheard an employee, not a club member, saying to another employee, "For heaven's sake, they keep talking about that fire. Why don't they just get over it?"

The answer, of course, is that one never gets over it.

Unlike some victims, Dawn and I at least had Mother's house in which to live. Word of the fire had somehow made the late TV news, so reporters from the *Observer-Dispatch* and the TV stations were there first thing next morning. Nancy McElwain and the vet Judy Campbell were early to the scene, offering to help in any way they could. But the surviving animals were okay. It would be days before the stable and arena would be clear enough of smoke for them to return, but they seemed to be doing well in the pastures, even Chubby. Luckily, despite the previous night's snow, it wasn't terribly cold.

Another early-morning visitor was Mindy's mother. She arrived at Mother's back door carrying a kitten, a brown tiger with enormous green eyes, just about Georgie's age.

"You lost so many last night. This one rode over with me under the hood of my car. I didn't know she was there till I heard her crying when I turned off the motor. I guess she thinks you need her."

We didn't think we needed her, but she'd taken a very dangerous ride to get to Spring Farm, so we wouldn't say no. We named her Clarisse, and it turned out that we did need her. During the long, hard winter that lay ahead, the antics of Clarisse and George, along with a third kitten brought to us, a gray-and-white whom Mother named Elvis because he was a wiggler, filled us with delight and chased our blues.

Alan Lloyd came with his backhoe after breakfast and began to stir the rubble, to get it to finish burning so that the smoke would dissipate. Bob and Peg arrived with their backhoe and their entire family. They dug and laid a new water line from the well at the house to the stable, for the old line had passed through the barn and been destroyed. The stable was also without electricity, for that line, too, had passed through the barn on its way to the stable. We'd spend that entire winter without electricity in the stable, but thank God and the Miller family we had running water.

So much to think about! The phone company promised to come the next day to switch our service, and we needed a place to work and sleep. Our presence would be disruptive enough for Mother; we wanted to stay out of her hair, so we fixed up the attic.

What we call the attic is an unfinished, unheated room on the second floor. Andy occupied the finished rooms. The attic is U-shaped, wrapping around and enclosing the stairwell. At the bottom of the U, looking out the back of the house, we put up card tables for desks. On one side of the U we set up two box springs and mattresses. On the other side we placed a couple of easy chairs.

We brought Pink Flower up for company and moved into what would be our home and office for the next eight months.

One of our first calls was to Penelope, to inform her of our loss and have her talk with the animals who'd died, for we were still too emotionally shocked to even try. She verified the feeling of peace that Dawn had gotten as the barn burned. The animals were all okay. Then she laughed.

"One of them is still with you. A little brown dog. He's running up and down the driveway, jumping and cavorting, trying to make you laugh. He doesn't understand why you can't see him."

My fifteen-year-old Daffy Doggie. He'd been called Happy at first, because of his joyous antics. The previous afternoon, he'd started acting like that happy puppy again. He'd become stiff and infirm, but suddenly he'd started following me, rolling over, wriggling delightedly against the carpet, asking to have his belly rubbed. He hadn't done that in years.

On some subconscious level he knew and was impelled to tell me, "This is how I want you to remember me."

On some level they all knew what was going to happen. Comparing notes, Dawn and I realized that each of them had said goodbye in some special way. Zoe, who hadn't played ball for many months because of a sore ear, had played long and hard, eyes sparkling. Archibald Peabody III, that stoical character, had become pushy, demanding attention, showing affection in a way that he never had. Each of them had made him- or herself felt in special ways during the twenty-four to forty-eight hours before the fire.

On some level they had all been "in on it." They, along with massive spiritual forces that we were only just beginning to understand, conspired to zap the barn and its contents from the face of the earth. Animals, barn, and contents literally sacrificed themselves to launch us, and Spring Farm CARES, into new spiritual space.

And on some other wavelength, they all still existed, while, in our memories, they were all still with us.

Some even informed us, through Penelope, that they'd be returning.

"Not all at once!" I cried, trying to bring levity to the situation.

Penelope laughed. "They promise to stagger their appearances."

The barn would be back, too, in a different guise. For even that first day, I said to Dawn, "We're going to rebuild."

"Now we know why George Kigercat was so intent on designing a new barn," said Dawn.

Despite all our "spiritual understanding," we still sometimes lost it. When Dawn went to the Clinton post office a couple of days later, the clerk began to commiserate with her. Realizing who Dawn was, one of the customers, the mother of one of the firefighters, launched into a graphic description of the fire.

"—and the way that those trapped animals screamed! My son says he'll never forget the screams of those dying animals!"

Dawn came home sobbing.

"Doesn't that woman realize how we must feel? They weren't screaming, Bonnie, they weren't! Just the one. Only the one."

And we knew that those who'd stayed, who hadn't been rescued or hadn't escaped, had done it for their own reasons—reasons understood by their souls if not by themselves.

Some of them told Penelope that they'd done it because they were "family." Again and again over the preceding months and years, one or the other of them had said to us, proudly, happily, "We're a family, aren't we?" All those guys, from such diverse, often unhappy backgrounds, living and loving in harmony. People were always saying, "How come your animals never fight?" It meant so much to the animals, and to us, to be a family. Family, to Spring Farm animals, is beyond genetics. To them family means a cushion, a gathering, a wonderful confluence of souls who want and need to meld and to find little pockets, places into which they can comfortably, happily, and safely fit as they work out their own life lessons. It means other souls and bodies moving around them who are not threatening or dangerous, who understand the needs of others and give them their space, while also cuddling or comforting when that is wanted.

Keisha the dog, and the cats in our apartment, were especially close family. As dolphins refuse to abandon trapped family members and save themselves by jumping out of the nets of fishing trawlers, perhaps some of them did hear us calling when we smashed the bathroom windows and implored them to come to us. Perhaps some made the conscious decision to stay.

In the days that followed, as we and volunteers were able to get into the ruins and sift through the ashes, it was a comfort to find the bodies of some of the animals, what remained of them, in areas where we'd expect to find them, indicating that they'd been asleep in favorite places and been overcome by smoke as they slept.

The one who knew for sure what was hitting her was Zoe. We found her body down near the plate-glass window at the south end, as far from the smoke and flames as she could get. Dawn beat herself about this for weeks. She'd been just about to run around to that end of the barn and smash the window—something had told her to do it—when the firemen had arrived and diverted us to other tasks.

Finally, she asked me to talk with Zoe. She was so emotionally distraught that she couldn't trust what she, herself, was getting.

I got a scolding Zoe, unhappy that Dawn was punishing herself.

"It's *my* fault. I was the silly one. I woke up and heard you calling, Bonnie, and I tried to come to you. But then I got scared and I went back to the Good Girl Spot instead. And when it got hotter, I just kept going. You shouldn't feel bad, I was out of my head anyway, and I'm perfectly okay now."

It didn't surprise us that, her mind clouded by the smoke, hearing me call but unsure, she'd run away from me, back to the Good Girl, where everything was safe and Zoe was good.

We actually found very few bodies that could be recognized as bodies, for most of the animals had slept at the far north end of the barn. Melted copper indicated that the fire had reached at least two thousand degrees in that section. The animals sleeping there had been cremated. Furniture, plumbing, fixtures, even a refrigerator by the door had vanished, leaving only ashes, indistinguishable lumps of debris, and a medallion that said "Frigidaire." We did find many bone fragments in the spot where the bed on which Keisha and most of the cats would have been sleeping had fallen through the floor. So again we were reassured. They had all just gone to sleep there. Forever.

To a certain extent, we had to put the dead to rest—or we would have gone crazy. And there were still some fifty other animals to worry about.

The logistics of starting all over again were mind-boggling. It was difficult for people to realize at the time, and it's still difficult for us to remember, the enormity of what had been lost in the fire. So our barn burned. Rotten luck. Even with no insurance, it was just a barn.

But what was lost in just about thirty minutes that Halloween night was both of our homes, offices, conference and lecture halls, tool and carpentry shops, library, thrift shop, small-animal facility and small animals, and all storage, personal and professional. The incredible amount and variety of what was lost are important to realize in symbolic relationship to the handful of items that were salvaged.

I'd been a dancer, model, actress, author, and wife. All press clippings, reviews, scripts, films, photos, diaries, and memorabilia from thirty-eight years of professional life, plus scrapbooks, mementos, and photos from my fifty-five-year personal life, were lost. Manuscripts of two finished novels that I'd not yet submitted to publishers, ten years of daily dream records, indexed and cross-referenced, with attendant material for a book on dreams, my library of more than seven thousand books, including many rare and valuable volumes—all gone. Family genealogy had been a hobby. Lost were years of research that traced back ten to twelve generations in many lines and much further in many others. Lost was a collection of family photographs, quilts, dishes, military commissions, samplers, diaries, journals, papers, daguerreotypes, portraits, and artifacts from the American Revolution through the Civil War and to the present, plus pre–Revolutionary War family furniture and silver. My wardrobe included a large collection of costumes and vintage garments, as well as valuable designer clothing from my New York and Hollywood days, a collection of antique purses, and a few pieces of decent jewelry. Furnishings included many Tiffany-type lamps, antique oak furniture, antique beds, and fine art, including a valuable Ch'ing vase, paintings, prints, and art glass. Also lost were many hundreds of copies of my three published books and promotional materials for same.

Not having had my "glamorous" past and twenty-five-year head start, Dawn's losses were less numerous and esoteric but no less devastating. She lost all school mementos and records, personal and family photos and genealogical material, a collection of poetry she'd written, drawings she'd done, jewelry and family furniture and keepsakes. Among her lost clothing was the gown she'd worn two weeks before as bridesmaid at her sister Nicki's wedding. She lost everything that Deeteza and Sugar had dictated to her, including the unfinished manuscript of Deeteza's book, another manuscript being coauthored by Sugar and Deeteza, and a collection of Sugar's herbal remedies.

Together, we and Spring Farm lost a large collection of homeopathics and Bach Flowers with supporting libraries, a video collection of several hundred tapes, which included all of our clinics and workshops, the birth of half a dozen foals, the progress histories of many of the hard-case horses that we'd tended—Buckwheat and Chubby included—day-to-day footage of Spring Farm animals and doings, personal and family events, and publicity footage. Then there was a collection of some five hundred audiotapes, mostly Spring Farm material, interviews, spoken manuscripts, and notes, including audio notes of channeled material for a book. There was a library of written, audio, and visual material on TT.E.A.M. and hypnosis, records of every animal who'd ever been at Spring Farm, a card catalog of the seven thousand library books, our mailing list with thousands of names, all photographs and negatives of our animals, all computer data, past, present, personal, and professional, and all files and records of whatever nature.

Then there were the office furnishings, appliances, and equipment—computers, the copy machine, audio, TV, and other electronic equipment, kitchen equipment, tools, and carpentry stuff . . . it's endless.

Sitting at empty card tables in Mother's cold, unfinished attic, we set about putting Humpty-Dumpty together again.

"Buckwheat!!!"

"Don't worry, little ladies. We'll fix it for ya. Yoooh-ooooh! Move out!"

And the Ghost Brigade now had twenty-four new recruits.

≈ 17 ≈

Out of the Ashes

It must have been the Ghost Brigade that alerted them. In the next weeks and months, again and again, the U.S. Cavalry arrived just in the nick of time.

And donations began to pour in.

We had no clothes? Soon Mother's dining room was piled high with donated clothing, new—some collected by Nicki at a local shopping mall, some sent by my friend Jerry Kenion—and used, from the closets of friends and supporters. It was years before we had to buy another thing.

The veterinarian Sue Ann Lesser; our attorney, Elizabeth Hughes; and Dennis and Jackie donated computers, printers, and allied computer equipment. Friend Peggy Sneath and others brought us office supplies. Our card tables groaned; we had our phone; my nephew, Rick Kiger, ran a heavy-duty electrical line to the attic and installed outlets; and we were back in business.

Supporters Paul and Dawn Sears supplied hundreds of feet of outdoor extension cords, drop lights, flashlights, batteries, and lightbulbs, so that we could run lines from the garage for light in the stable. Others scoured homes and garages and brought us tools, nails, screws, yardsticks, tape measures, indoor extension cords, scissors, needles and thread, safety pins, whisk brooms—all kinds of things that you don't miss until they're not there.

Others brought animal supplies. Farmers donated hay for the horses; some brought sacks of feed.

The donations finally spilled out of Mother's dining room into the living room, then into the front bedroom.

Thanks to the local media and media as far away as Syracuse, word of the fire reached friends and supporters and the general public as well. Monetary donations began filling our mailbox, and people came knocking at the door. Some of the offerings brought tears to our eyes: people on fixed incomes sent us a dollar, or two, saying they'd try to send more later. Schoolchildren took up collections. And there were larger donations, even one for a thousand dollars from a lady we didn't even know.

The outpouring kept pouring.

And Dawn and I were humbled—by the generosity of people but also because people really liked what we were doing at Spring Farm CARES. This support was a vote of confidence, spontaneous, straight from the heart. No longer did we have to wonder, "What will the neighbors think?" No longer need we worry that people thought us a couple of kooks. Maybe some of them did think that. But they either accepted it or actually *liked* it! Neighbors had come running to help us save our animals the night of the fire, and now the community was putting us back on our feet, actually encouraging us two kooks. We were filled with gratitude and enthusiasm. We wouldn't let people down.

We'd get kookier than ever.

Alan Lloyd kept stirring the ashes. Three days after the fire, we were able to get the horses back to their stalls. Chubby seemed almost disappointed, but Sugar was delighted.

"You can have the great outdoors. I like my nice warm stall."

Dawn and I began to divide the work. I took over the office and began reconstructing our mailing list. The media put out the word that we needed friends to call or write with their addresses. Those who responded were asked to spread the word. Meanwhile, in the normal course of business, people who hadn't known about the fire called, were informed, and were asked to pass it on. It's amazing how quickly the network grew. By December, we'd gained back about three thousand old names, while many new people asked to be added to the list, and I was able to put out a newsletter.

Some people sent photographs that they'd taken at Spring Farm. How we treasured them. The loss of photographs and ephemera is one of the most heartbreaking things about a fire. Appliances and furniture can be replaced; photographs and personal mementos, never.

Financial records were also an imperative. Along with requests for addresses, I solicited copies of people's records regarding us, especially records from 1993, so that I'd be able to submit a reasonably correct tax return. While I was asking, I also solicited copies of our newsletters, flyers for clinics, any paperwork that could help us piece together a record of our history.

Actually, it would be more than a year before I was able to cobble together enough information for a tax return. For several years after that, in a domino effect, our returns were always late. The IRS was very decent about it.

Interestingly, though, when I contacted the IRS to ask for copies of back returns, corporate and private, and for our original 501c3 application, the IRS could find none of them. It was comforting to know that the filing system of the IRS was as hopeless as my own.

While I was wrangling with all of this, Dawn and our volunteers Gail Battinelli, Ray Romero, Andy, and Laura and Barry Watkins were out in the ruins day after day, carefully sifting, searching for the bodies of our animals and for any little treasures. The weather turned nasty, with cold rain and sleet most days, all day. But the intrepid searchers searched on. The collection of treasures that emerged from the ashes, each loaded with symbolic significance, is fascinating indeed.

They started at the south end, where the fire had burned the "coolest." Though it seemed that the fire was out, digging was hazardous. Fire still smoldered in some of the piles, flaring up when exposed to air.

The very first thing that Dawn encountered was a copy of my second novel, *The Confetti Man.* It was open to the page where one of the characters describes a fire that destroyed his home and his vast genealogical collection.

My eighteenth-century Tibetan bronze Buddha was found next. His base had melted, but he was otherwise intact, just a different color. He'd occupied a Victorian table there at the south end of the barn, radiating peace and serenity. Now he could continue to shed his grace on Spring Farm.

The next item had fallen through from Dawn's granary office. It was broken into a hundred pieces, but miraculously, the most important part had survived intact. It had been a lamp with the figure of a small girl kneeling beside a unicorn pony, the girl's arms around the pony's neck.

One day, Dawn had come home from Sangertown Mall in a tizzy.

"Bonnie, there's something at the mall that Bubbles wants me to buy. She wants it to be a gift to me from her." And she described the lamp.

"Well, go back and get it."

"We can't afford it! It's forty-nine dollars and ninety-nine cents."

"Dawn, if Bubbles wants you to get it, then get it."

It's my usual inclination to do what the animals ask of us. Within reason. Their connection to the Soul of the Universe is firmer than ours. We've never gone wrong following their advice.

So Dawn got the lamp and kept it on her desk. She'd taken it up to her new office only days before the fire. Everything in that office seemed to have vaporized or been rendered unrecognizable when the desk crashed through the floor. All except the head of the little girl and the head of the unicorn, its horn intact, with the arms of the little girl still around the unicorn's neck. It remains one of Dawn's most cherished possessions.

The next item to appear intact, and as white as though just washed, was a ceramic head of the Virgin Mary. She'd been a night-light, an item donated for a garage sale. Now, of course, as a precious relic, she'd never be sold.

Yet when next we looked for her, she was gone. And Dawn knew exactly where she'd left her. We're pretty sure we know who confiscated her. He must have needed her more than we did. Perhaps she survived the fire just to go home with him.

A bunch of iron items were found. Shoemakers' trees that my mother's father, Will Newcomb, had used to make shoes for his children. Iron pieces that had been part of the structure of the barn. And artifacts that had been dug up around the farm over the years, mementos of Spring Farm circa 1840–1940. Generally, iron items survived well.

Then, in perfect condition, a ceramic vase that I'd gotten while visiting Rome on that last trip with my parents. Its motif was grape clusters on latticework.

The morning after the fire, Dawn and I had gone out and walked up onto the barn bridge, to look down onto what was left of our barn. Standing starkly in the ruins were the iron columns that had supported the center beams beneath the haymow floor. They made the smoking debris look like Roman ruins. Roman-history-author Daddy would have appreciated that.

As we looked down at those pillars, I said, "You know, when we came here in 1945, we had a grape arbor, of Concord grapes. Whenever any of our animals died, we buried them around that arbor. It fell into ruin and finally disappeared. But I can see a new arbor, constructed on those pillars, and grapevines growing here in the middle of our barn. I think we should have a garden in here, with the grape arbor at its core. To mark the grave site of the friends who died here last night."

That surviving vase, with its grape motif, seconded my motion.

The bulk of the other items to survive intact, or in nearly presentable form, all came from one drawer in a metal chest of drawers that had been in my walk-in closet in the second floor apartment. That drawer had contained a potpourri of small personal treasures—family jewelry, none of it valuable except to sentiment, daguerreotypes of ancestors, bits and pieces of this and that. That bedroom closet had been above the hottest part of the fire, the section where almost nothing that could be recognized as part of anything had survived. That metal chest of drawers collapsed through the floor with a bunch of other stuff that continued to burn merrily. During the next three days, it was rolled over and over by Alan's backhoe. Yet when a volunteer got to it and gingerly pried open what was left of the top drawer, small miracles greeted him.

Most were charred, unusable, yes, but recognizable as to what they'd been, and intact. I'll forever keep the little glass plates that now show only a rainbow of chemicals but that once showed the faces of grandparents who were old a hundred and fifty years ago. Plus the skeletons of pins and brooches precious to generations of great-grandmothers.

Among the charred skeletons, however, was a true miracle. Dawn brought it to me, up in the attic, with wonder on her face.

It was Grampa Jones's favorite ashtray. It's a delicate thing, porcelain with a froufrou of porcelain seashells scalloped around its edges. Resting in its bowl is a little porcelain pipe.

Except for one porcelain seashell that had broken off and was quickly found, the ashtray was in mint condition. Like the Virgin Mary, it even looked newly washed.

Another item found in perfect shape in that drawer was Grampa Jones's silver Masonic pin. Andy brought that it to me later. He'd snatched it away from the volunteer who'd found it.

"He's Catholic," said Andy. "The Catholics are funny about the Masons."

Which anyone who read *Holy Blood, Holy Grail* will understand. And it would take a whole book to explain why the recovery of that pin, in regard to my Grandfather Jones, was of stunning import to me.

But I mention it here primarily in order to highlight a preponderance of "Catholic" connections among the objects found.

Also rescued from that drawer was a tiny iron horse, given to me by my friend Grace Bacon, the mother of another friend, a nun called Sister Grace.

Then two wild cards: a Lake Placid medal and a medal commemorating the first landing on the moon. I couldn't remember even having had them, and I've never been able to figure their significance, though I'm sure that deeper investigation would reveal it.

The last treasure to emerge from the drawer was a charred tangle, seemingly melted together. I was sure the items would break as I carefully coaxed them apart. But they separated intact.

The first: my uncle Noble's dog tags from World War II. All mementos of him and Aunt Pearl had gone in the fire, so the survival of those dog tags was welcome. But beyond that, I couldn't help but think of something my father had told me.

Uncle Noble was thirty-seven when drafted, just months short of whatever the "old man" age limit was at that point. He served as a combat engineer with the Black Panthers, one of those lucky "cats" sent in ahead of everyone else to throw up bridges and make roads for those who followed. He landed in Italy and built stuff all the way to Rome. Then he landed in Normandy on D-Day and built stuff all the way to Berlin. He told my father that, caught in the middle of a field in France during an especially heavy bombardment, he got down on his atheist knees and prayed: "Get me out of this. Get me home to my beautiful little wife, and I swear I'll never ask for anything again."

He got out. He came home to Aunt Pearl and never did ask for another thing. It took a crowbar to pry him away from his house, and he supported Aunt Pearl in something close to luxury by being the most sought-after carpenter in Clinton. There were no children. But how those two delighted in each other.

His biography is important here only because of the item found entwined with his dog tags.

It was a rosary.

I don't know who or what Uncle Noble prayed to that day in France. I do know that he was great friends with the local Catholic priest, whose rectory was forever in need of a carpenter and who was always trying to cure Uncle Noble of cursing and to convert him. Fat chance.

And why bother? Few people ever led a life more "Christian" or filled with thanks for a prayer answered.

The rosary had been given to me by Jackie. Neither Dawn nor I is Catholic, nor do we adhere to the tenents of any organized religion. But we have a vast respect for "The Lady," the "sacred female," the Universal or Earth Mother partially embodied in the Catholic "Virgin." Though raised Catholic, Jackie was also not "religious." Along with Dawn and me, she revered Mother Earth and the "sacred female" of the Universe.

Yet one day she walked in and handed me that rosary.

"I've had this since I was a kid. Somehow I felt that you should have it now."

I kept that rosary in a leather pouch in my desk drawer. How it got upstairs and into the miracle drawer, so that it ended up twined around those dog tags, I don't know.

Mother Mary's rosary, entwined with the dog tags of a carpenter. They're both here beside me as I write.

The finding of the night light and the rosary was not the last time "The Lady" would make herself known there in the ruins of our barn. And it's fascinating that out of all the stuff that was in that barn, so many of the salvaged items had a religious, mostly Catholic, or an esoteric and spiritual connection.

The last perfectly preserved item to be retrieved from the ashes had been given to me by—oh darn, Burt Chalfin, a Catholic ex-boyfriend. It's a large silver medal. On one side is a bas-relief of a bull. Much of Grampa Jones's fame in Holstein circles was derived from two of his bulls, Spring Farm King and Spring Farm King Cornucopia. Large, beautifully framed photographic portraits of King and Corny had been hanging in the haymow. The first time Mother cried after the fire was when she realized that those portraits were gone.

So on one side of the medal is a bull.

On the other side is an inscription: "The Best Is Yet to Be."

Whatever the symbology of the items salvaged from the fire, that really said it all.

One of the first questions that everyone asked was "What caused the fire?" Dawn worried that she might have forgotten to turn off one of the burners of the electric stove and that that had somehow been to blame. I told her no. The stove had sat right up against the window, and, when first we saw it, the fire had definitely been some feet away from the window. Additionally, when we opened the front door, we could see that the refrigerator was burning. We were left with the assumption that some fault in the refrigerator had started the conflagration.

Then we found the electrical entrance, which had been situated right inside the front door. It was fried! Burned almost beyond recognition and seemingly blasted apart.

Had we been hit by a power surge?

At which point, almost a week after the fire, someone told me that I should get an electrical inspector out to take a look. I found one listed in the Yellow Pages.

He asked a lot of questions. When I mentioned that several cars had hit light poles that night, he said, "Bingo. There's your power surge."

Electric companies will try to tell you that power surges don't happen. One wonders, then, why stores sell surge protectors for electronic equipment. Actually, electric meters should be equipped with surge protectors.

I told the inspector when the electric clock in the stable had stopped. Before he came to the farm the next day, he investigated the various accidents that had occurred on Halloween and pinned down *the* accident, *the* car, that had hit *the* light pole at exactly the right moment in the right place and sent *the* power surge zinging into our barn, frying the electrical entrance and setting the refrigerator on fire.

I met the inspector in the driveway as he drove in. He was smiling.

"I found it. I found the accident that did it to you."

Then his smile faded. He was looking out at the ruins, where Dawn and others were working.

"Who are those people? What are they doing!"

"They're trying to salvage things."

"Nooo!" He threw his pad onto the ground. "Nothing should have been touched! Nothing!"

"But . . . the fire chief said . . ."

"That place should have been taped off!"

"But we didn't have any insurance."

"That doesn't *matter!* What matters is what started the fire. Have those people gone anywhere near where your kitchen was?"

"Yes. Besides, a backhoe stirred things around there for days to make it stop burning."

He retrieved his pad and shook his head.

"Well, then, there's nothing I can do for you."

"Why?"

"Think of it as a crime scene. Absolutely nothing can be touched until experts secure the evidence. That's what I would have done. I could have documented the fact that it was a power surge. Insurance or no, you had a suit against the power company and maybe the motorist who hit the pole. I could have gotten you reimbursement for everything that you lost and then some."

I crawled into bed that day and didn't get out for nearly twenty-four hours.

I was sick. Sick at heart, sick to my stomach, sick in my soul.

How could I have been so stupid? Why hadn't I questioned the fire chief further, why had I let Alan stir the ashes with his backhoe, why had I let Dawn and the volunteers go into the ruins? All those good, well-meaning people, they'd only been trying to help us. But I was supposed to be the executive director of Spring Farm CARES, and I should be fired! Here it had been in our power to recoup all the financial losses, and I'd been too stupid to know it.

"Bonnie," said Dawn, "how were *you* supposed to know? If anyone should have known, it's people from the fire department. It's not as though you have a fire every day, and it's nothing they teach in school, there's no Correct-Procedure-After-a-Fire 101."

"I should have asked more questions."

"Well, then, so should I have. But we were in shock. And the only thing we thought about at first was getting the animals back into shelter. We had to stop the ruins from smoking."

"I know, but if I'd had my head about me I could have called that inspector the very next day."

"It's water under the bridge! We didn't even suspect a power surge till yesterday. And there's nothing we can do about it now."

She was right. Nothing.

I finally got out of bed, but the ache in my gut wouldn't go away. It took all the strength of spirit I possessed to keep from spiraling downward.

Then one day it suddenly came to me: a terrible weight lifted from off of my shoulders.

"A lawsuit wouldn't have been right," I told Dawn. "Lawsuits are ugly, full of hate and anger, and that's not what Spring Farm CARES is about. Lawsuits say that someone else is responsible for what happens to you. But we know that we create our own reality. We created the fire. We and all the animals and powers that we don't even know about. The barn was supposed to go. I don't know why yet. But we'll figure it out. And money gotten from a lawsuit would have been tainted. It would have destroyed the very thing that makes us special. We're going to rebuild. But it will all be done with donations."

Our new building would be a very special building, a very special place, built by the love of humans and animals living and dead, and by powers seen and unseen, known and unknown.

That night I sat down and wrote "Ode to Merlin":

> Dear old barn.
> I never knew that you had a name.
> I had to wait for you to burn to know it.
> I had to sit tearfully going through
> some of the mementos of Grandfather
> so fortunately stored in the attic of the house.
> These were postcards from long ago, sent to Grampa.
> The person who sent them kept calling him "Merlin."
>
> What an august name.
> And how appropriate.
> I see now that you, old barn, and Grampa
> are the same.
> You are Merlin.
> The magic teacher to my Arthur.

What golden childhood memories I have of you
as I worked each day with the animals
and helped with the milking each night
feeling warm, and needed by my parents
like a princess in the castle of yourself.

How I swung on ropes supported by the beams
of your haymow.
What a daredevil and stunt artist I became
and how steadily you supported me
in so many ways
through all of my swinging, daredevil life.

And I told people
that one day I would make you my home.
I did.
I came back from the big, bold world
to the quiet place where you were.
Trustingly, I curled myself up within you.

How I loved to sit in your haymow
of a summer's night
with dim light thrown onto your vaulting roof.
A cathedral could not have been more holy.

Then one night you burned.
Like the magician that you are
you disappeared into a puff of smoke.

But you gave me the wisdom
to see the signs that you left
to show me the way.

Merlin never dies. Merlin is.
Magic is where you make it.
Better every day.

Thank you, old barn. Grandfather. Merlin.
I'll build new magic.
And you will be there.

We first heard about the angels and butterflies on the afternoon after the fire, when Dawn went out to explain to the horses why they'd have to stay in the pasture for a few days. The horses started telling her of their own experiences the night before. Several said that they'd seen Buckwheat and Kazinka. Topaz and Amber had seen Toby as well.

Some of them said they'd seen angels hovering over the burning barn.

"And Dawn, did you see the butterflies?" asked Scherry. "There were hundreds of them. They glowed and danced over the fire, then they came out to the pasture and danced above us for hours."

"We saw them up here, too," said Story, one of five horses who lived in the hill paddocks, which horses had had loge seats for the event. "Butterflies. Beautiful butterflies."

"Those were sparks," Dawn rationalized. "And glowing embers floating out into the pasture."

Deeteza set her straight.

"They weren't sparks, and they weren't glowing embers. They were angels. And they weren't just flying around. They were protecting us."

Dawn thought back to the way we'd rushed to the pasture at the first hint of daylight, expecting to find terrible injuries and even tragedies, only to find that everything was fine. Even peaceful. A flight of angels was as good an explanation for that "miracle" as anything.

And a gift that Mother had received from Mindi Hutchinson the day before the fire began to make sense. People often sent gifts to Mother. She was such an integral part of all our goings-on, cooking for workshops, making cookies for the participants. Mindi had attended one of Dawn's animal communication workshops a couple of weeks before the fire.

Mindi had sent Mother a golden butterfly.

When we later questioned her about her choice of gift, Mindi could only say that when she'd seen it, she'd just known it was right.

How we wish that we possessed the clear eyes of the animals. How we wish that we could have seen the butterflies and angels hovering over the barn that night.

Though Dawn did, eventually, see the butterflies.

She'd read numerous books over the years that speculated on the reality of "interdimensional beings"—angels, fairies, elves, leprechauns, unicorns, and many other entities who somehow travel through time and space, appearing in and disappearing from various dimensions and realities—speculations not really so "far out" in light of the theories of the New Physics. Some of what Dawn had read even suggested that butterflies and dragonflies can be interdimensional. She found this last a bit hard to swallow; easier to believe in angels than in interdimensional butterflies and dragonflies.

Then one afternoon in early December she was working out in the ruins, patiently sifting ashes. We had no hope of finding anything else in mint condition, but we were so desperate for keepsakes that any melted, twisted item was cause for rejoicing if we could at least recognize what it had been. Dawn especially hoped to surprise me by finding a piece of jewelry to which I had great sentimental attachment, the only nice piece that I hadn't sold off to help keep Spring Farm afloat. It was an antique pin I'd purchased in Cairo in 1960, Cleopatra's asp—a little snake, twenty-two carat gold, about four inches long, with ruby eyes and a large rose-cut diamond in the head. If there was anything left of it, it would be somewhere in the ashes under where my closet had been—in the worst of the fire, yet a place that had yielded amazing finds. So she kept doggedly on, dumping shovelloads of ash into the sieve and carefully searching through them.

Finally it got late. And very cold. Snow had begun to fall, and she was tired. Sifting through that ash was hard work, even for those not burdened by the memory of what it had all once been. She put the shovel down and walked to the gap in the cement foundation that had been the front door.

Then she felt something saying, "Don't go."

She thought someone was standing beside her.

She turned and looked. Nothing there.

Again she started to leave. Again something said to turn back.

Something wanted her to put just one more shovelful of ash through the sieve.

As she approached the pile where she'd been working, five Monarch butterflies began fluttering around her head. One of them landed on her shoulder. How odd.

The butterflies then danced over to the pile of ash and fluttered around her shovel. She picked it up and took a shovelful from the place where the butterflies were hovering. As she turned it over and dumped the ash into the sieve, she heard a distinct "clink."

Eagerly she fumbled for the prize.

It was the snake brooch. With the butterflies swirling around her hands, she brushed it off.

It was in perfect condition. Perfect. Nothing was melted, nothing was broken. Gold, rubies, and diamond gleamed as though the piece had just been shined. She turned and started out of the ruins, eager to surprise me. At the front door she glanced back.

The butterflies were gone.

Her eyes swept the ruins. Vanished. Odd. But she was so excited about showing me the brooch that it didn't sink in.

. . . until she got into the back room of the house and was stripping off her soot-covered clothing.

"What are Monarch butterflies doing here in December?" she exclaimed. "And in the snow!"

Still she wasn't ready to believe in interdimensional beings. The Universe would have to rustle up an interdimensional dragonfly to convince her.

In the meantime, Christmas was coming.

Our Christmas lights had always been important, not only to us but, we'd discovered over the years, to many others. Each year, in the downstairs of the barn, we'd strung multitudinous lights along all the ceiling beams and jousts, and in each window of the thirty-five-by-seventy-foot room. Grampa had built his barn with a lot of good-size windows. Ten faced the road, the south and north ends each had four, plus there was the plate-glass window with French doors on the south. From the road, through the diffusing windows, the traveler saw a fairyland of twinkling colored lights, a magical, radiant glow from inside the building. On cold, snowy nights, the effect on people who saw that barn made for Christmas spirit—the reverential sort. Something in the subconscious remembered that Jesus was supposed to have been born in a stable.

Scores of people told us how much they looked forward to our lights. One man even stopped to tell us that, driving by one night, he'd seen the lights, driven another forty miles home, and brought his wife back to see them.

Realizing how important they were to people, we left them on twenty-four hours a day, so that even during dark, dreary days in December and early January, our barn radiated peace and joy to those passing by.

Both for travelers and for ourselves, we couldn't let "the barn" be dark that Christmas.

We invested in a whole bunch of lights. In brutal wind, cold, and snow, we strung colored lights around the charred cement foundations of the barn, all over the barn bridge that now led to nowhere, and draped them on piles of twisted wreckage. On the burned skeletons of trees and bushes around the ruins, we draped white lights. All this we hooked up to extension cords from the garage and house.

Once more, a fairyland appeared to Christmas travelers.

As one person told us with tears in her eyes, "When I saw those lights, I knew that Spring Farm was going on, better than ever."

Exactly. The best is yet to be.

18

The Best Is Yet to Be

The Winter from Hell, 1993–94. Central New York Staters gritted their teeth as they said it.

It never let up, not for an hour, blanketing us with ever-deepening snow, shriveling us with endless cold. The days were so overcast that one could hardly tell day from night. Through it all, the animals in the stable dwelt in darkness, except for the hours when we were out there, dragging our drop lights around to clean and feed them.

We'd have loved to have a new electrical system put in, but it took weeks to get cooperation from Niagara Mohawk and then to begin to understand our options. When we found that underground lines from the road to a new transformer, thence to the arena and stable and later to our future building, would be both the best and the cheapest, we still sat around for a week in shock.

It would cost $3,500. We didn't have $3,500.

By then it was academic. Winter was upon us, no digging possible until spring.

In the end, it was June before the stable had electricity again.

The Winter from Hell was also The Winter of Blow-Drying Water Pipes. Though we kept the water pipes banked with kerosene heaters, the heaters' puny warmth was helpless against the freeze. During one particularly bad week, the plumber replaced burst pipes four times.

Meanwhile, the Universe continued to supply us with animal friends, some new, some old.

One morning in December we got a call from a llama breeder who'd just had a baby llama born with a shriveled back leg. Tripod, she'd named him. She couldn't bear to put him down. Would we take him once weaned? She'd also give us a second baby llama, named Travis—because, this thoughtful breeder explained, llamas are herd animals who suffer if kept alone. Though Travis was perfectly healthy, she'd send him along as companion for Tripod.

Kazinka had goofed on the twin part of it. Yet against the odds, in a few months Spring Farm would have a pair of young llamas.

Were they really Buckwheat and Kazinka reborn? It was an odd "coincidence" if not.

Our next prize was a wild-caught African Gray parrot, whom we renamed Merlin. The people who brought him to us had rescued him from an abusive alcoholic, from whom he'd picked up some scandalous language. We were warned to guard our tongues, lest he remember his extensive smutty vocabulary and send Mother and our guests fleeing his presence in horror.

Luckily he remembered only "Hello," "How are you?" and "Where are you?"

I tried to teach him some really important phrases, such as, "Louie, I think this is the beginning of a beautiful friendship" and "Frankly, Scarlett, I don't give a damn."

The only time he ever gave any of it a try was the day he looked Dawn straight in the eye and said, "Louie . . . how are you?"

He readily learned the opening notes of the *Star Wars* theme and made it a game to whistle the first five notes, then wait for us to whistle the last two, or vice versa. And he loved improvisation. Dawn or I would make up a tune and he'd whistle it back to us, or he'd whistle a new tune and we'd whistle it back to him. He also assisted when we whistled for the dogs.

His real talent, though, was sound effects. When we got him, his only sound effect was that sinking, kazoolike sound used when someone bombs out on *Wheel of Fortune.* But he quickly picked up household sounds. Often, when both my mother and Andy were absent from the house, the front door would open and we'd hear sneakered feet entering the kitchen and the refrigerator and cabinets being opened. We'd come running downstairs and find no one there. We thought it was a new ghost until we caught Merlin "red-tongued" one day.

He was an articulate, affectionate, intelligent being with a sly sense of humor. And he was a lifetime commitment. At eight years old, he was still just a kid who might even outlive us.

In February, we received another duck, a domestic Mallard. We were pleased to get her, as Emerald and Tyrone were running Pearl ragged—literally.

The new duck said her name was Phoebe. She became known as the Egg Smasher. She never laid any eggs herself but made sure to smash Pearl's.

"It's not the baby time of the year yet," she explained crisply when we asked her why. "So I just smash 'em."

One morning not long after her arrival, Phoebe got *herself* smashed, stomped on by a horse named Belle. A volunteer came running with Phoebe in his arms. I ran for the arnica, our first first aid for injuries to anyone and anything at Spring Farm; then Dawn rushed Phoebe to the nearest animal hospital.

Her left leg was turned right around, heading backward. An X-ray showed that the knee of that leg was pulverized. Having no experience with birds, the vet recommended euthanasia. Dawn declined, gathered up her duck, and departed.

Once alone with Phoebe, she moaned, "Oh, Phoebe. What are we going to do?"

Phoebe looked her in the eye and said crisply, "Fix it. Just *fix* it!"

So we packed Dawn and Phoebe off on a ninety-mile drive to the North Country Animal Health Center in Watertown, where, we were told, they did exotic animals.

But not ducks. They were taken aback. After all, what's a duck worth? Most people would meat it. No one had ever asked for knee surgery on a duck, after driving all that distance to boot.

Their X-rays were no more promising than the first vet's. Maybe they could snap the leg back into place and get it facing forward again, but that knee was mincemeat. They couldn't tell whether there was any ligament left at all.

Dawn called me for a decision.

"How far do we go?"

I gave the Spring Farm CARES answer, which was all Dawn needed to hear. She directed North Country to do everything surgically possible to rebuild Phoebe's leg.

Then she headed home, not knowing for sure what they would do. They wanted more X-rays; then they needed to confer. She was still on the road when Dr. Klindt called and talked to me.

"We can't tell from the X-rays what we'll find when we get in there," she said. "And I don't even know what the inside of a Mallard's knee looks like."

"Well, maybe that's why this happened. To show you what the inside of a Mallard's knee looks like."

She didn't see the humor; she was too busy explaining to the crazy lady on the other end of the line why spending hundreds of dollars for a knee operation on a duck would probably be a waste of time and money. While I was trying to explain to the vet on the other end of the line about the "Spring Farm difference."

To us, no animal's well-being is more important than that of any other. Since we don't sell animals or use them for anything other than for education, they're *all* "worth it," all equally our friends. Just as we'd go all out to save the leg of a horse, we'd go all out for a duck. Plus which, extraordinary care of animals, and the knowledge to be gained from that care, is part of our reason for being.

"Is there any chance at all that the surgery could be successful?" I asked.

Dr. Klindt had to allow that there was an outside chance.

I hesitated. How to tell her that our animals are our friends and teachers? That we talk with them. And they answer. We break these things to veterinarians very, very gently.

"We want you to go ahead with the surgery," I told her. "Please don't think me arrogant, but . . . Spring Farm CARES is a place where miracles happen. We have a special relationship with our animals. Phoebe will make it. All this has happened for a reason."

How does a vet get around that mouthful?

"We'll let you know when we can schedule the surgery."

Confidence and faith aside, how Dawn and I sweated through the hours when we knew that Phoebe was under the knife.

"Fix it. Just *fix* it!" she'd said. Well, we were fixing it.

Come—on—Phoebe!

When Dr. Klindt called, we heard a tired, but deservedly proud and hopeful, lady. They'd gotten the bones back into position and the leg facing in the right direction. They'd put staples into the pulverized muscles to give them something around which to regroup. Then they'd made a ligament for her out of suturing material, fastened to pins inserted into the bones, because Phoebe's own ligament was nowhere to be found.

On the second day after surgery, Dawn brought Phoebe home.

Have you ever tried to keep a duck in a cage in your office? It's an experience, especially when that duck is Phoebe.

She had to be kept superclean. Infection could destroy everyone's best efforts. We changed her bedding four times daily. Oy, the laundry. We were also supposed to administer two antibiotic pills twice daily.

Have you ever tried to pill a duck? Dawn said Dr. Klindt had made it look easy. On Phoebe's first night home we tried it, one of us holding, the other trying to administer. We'd been warned to be sure that the pills went over, not under, the tongue, lest they go down the wrong hole and into her lungs.

Phoebe wouldn't cooperate. She was frazzled from long road trips, fed up with medical procedures and . . . well, she'd just had it. Aside from being uncooperative, she was downright aggressive. A videotape of the two of us trying to get pills into this really irritated duck would have taken a prize on some home video show.

We weren't successful. Nor was the next morning's attempt successful. So we just stopped trying to give her pills. We reasoned that the stress we were giving her outweighed the benefits.

Not only that, but, in that no-nonsense way of hers, Phoebe told us, "I don't want or need those pills. Do something else. Fix it. Just *fix* it!"

We turned to homeopathy and TTouch. Into each full bowl of water that we gave her we put arnica and hypericum. When her wounds had closed, we changed the combination to hypericum and ruta. Then, a couple of times a day, Dawn took Phoebe out of her cage and onto her lap. I knelt alongside and did the tiny, light Raccoon circles of TTouch, all around the area of the stitches. Phoebe loved it.

We'd been warned, even by the homeopathic vet Joyce Harmon, with whom we conferred, that we should be prepared for massive, messy outbreaks of infection. Phoebe never had so much as a pimple. She healed rapidly and beautifully. Within two weeks, the "knee," the site of the operation, was sprouting happy new pinfeathers, and Phoebe was beginning to place weight on the foot.

Dawn begged me not to tell the world that we never gave Phoebe her antibiotics. Whenever she took Phoebe back for check-ups and was asked if we were giving the pills, she'd respond, "Umhumugh." Which was taken for yes. Not exactly a lie, just "Umhumugh."

And so, Dr. Klindt, the truth about Phoebe's postoperative treatment is—cleanliness, homeopathy, TTouch, telepathic communication, love, and laughter. I have a feeling you'll understand. And someday you must teach us your amazing technique for pilling ducks.

Oh, and Phoebe also had the services of Sue Ann Lesser, as her spine was really out of whack from her encounter with the thousand-pound Belle.

We realized early on that Phoebe couldn't be returned to the flock. She got so she limped along very well, but she'd never be able to handle the boys' brutal amorous advances. In the case of predators, she'd be doubly a sitting duck.

Phoebe shared our opinion. She'd become really involved in office life. She began to comment on our calls, to remind us when we had forgotten something, and she loved to entertain callers with mellifluous quacks.

"If a duck answers," we told people, "hang up."

She also loved to be sung to.

"Have her sing me a duck song," she'd tell Dawn.

So I'd sing, "When the red red robin comes bob bob bobbin' along," "Be kind to your web-footed friend, for that duck might be somebody's mother," or some other watery, birdy song. Whatever it was had to be sung to a waddle beat. Phoebe would go into raptures, swaying and "ducking" in tempo.

She had a good and varied life there in the office, resting in her cage or waddling around the floor at will, taking frequent swims in Mother's bathtub once she'd healed. She developed a close relationship with our two guinea pigs, Mustard and Grey Poupon, who'd arrived on the scene when Mustard called out to Dawn as she was walking through the mall one day, insisting that Dawn take her home, and insisting that her friend Grey Poupon be brought along as well. Phoebe loved them and spent hours cuddled beside their cage. Pink Flower she tolerated, and Georgie and Clarisse whenever they came to visit. For their part, they ignored her and were perplexed by her hisses when they got too close.

In April, Dawn took Phoebe to North Country for her final checkup. After leaving the vet's office, she stopped at a Wendy's for lunch. Phoebe traveled in a smallish, top-opening carrier with peek holes and one screened lookout. Dawn had stopped carrying food for her when they traveled, as Phoebe always refused to eat. This time, however, as Dawn sat eating, Phoebe asked her to open the carrier. She craned her neck up and looked at Dawn's food.

"What's that?"

"My lunch."

"Well, thanks a lot. You didn't bring any for me."

"You never eat while we're traveling."

"What are those things you're eating?"

"French fries."

"Give me one."

"Okay, but you won't like it."

But Phoebe did like it. She began gobbling French fries.

A family left the restaurant and came to their car, right next to Dawn's.

"Daddy," said the little boy, "there's a duck in that car."

"Sure, son. Get in."

"No, really, honey," said the mother. "There's a duck in the car."

The little girl looked in and cried out, "Oh, gross! It's eating French fries!"

We tried Phoebe on McDonald's fries after that. She wouldn't touch them. Only Wendy's. We wrote to Dave Thomas. His office sent Phoebe a gift certificate for French fries.

Readers will be pleased to know that as this book goes to press, Phoebe is more than twelve years old, well and happy, sharing a room with Merlin the parrot, Milky the chicken, and three cats.

The next arrival was Snowie the goat. She'd outlived her usefulness at a goat-breeding farm, having developed a painful and grotesquely deformed udder. Additionally, the farm owners had switched to the breeding of miniature goats. To keep Snowie from mating with their miniature ram, they'd penned her up alone, at the far end of their barn. But that was a lonely existence, so to Spring Farm she came.

On the morning of April 18, we were shocked to find two more goats in Snowie's enclosure: her newborn twins, Tippicanoe and Tyler Too. Snowie's former owner insisted that there was just no way. Yet there they were. Love, and a miniature ram, had found a way.

Snowball couldn't feed them. Her udder, now additionally swollen with milk, was causing her agony. We found an Agway that sold goat milk replacer and nursing bottles for kids and relieved her of her duties.

Some weeks later, we gave her the best gift she'd ever had: a mastectomy.

That same day of April the eighteenth had yet another "impossible" surprise in store. Shortly after eleven at night, Dawn was on her way to the stable to check on the kids when she saw a stray cat running toward the upper paddocks. She shone her flashlight at it. It stopped, turned, and looked right into the light.

Dawn let out a cry.

"Archie?"

The cat started to come to her. But by then the barn cats had come to meet Dawn. The stray took off. Dawn followed.

"Archie? Kitty kitty kitty?"

Unfortunately, "Kitty kitty kitty" kept the stable cats running right along with her. The stray kept going.

Finally, he halted just long enough for her to scoop him up.

What was she doing? This couldn't be Archie, she must be nuts grabbing a stray tom, he might rake her to pieces.

The first that I knew of the matter was when I heard Dawn shouting at the back door of the house. I ran out, thinking that something awful had happened. (It would be years before alarms stopped going off in our nervous systems at the slightest "unpeaceful" sound, sight, or smell.)

Dawn was standing there wild-eyed. The girl was in shock. She was clutching a cat who was also in shock.

"Be careful. He's very scared. Tell me this isn't Archie. Tell me it's *not!*"

"It's Archie," I said flatly, a calm coming over me.

"It *can't* be. Archie's *dead.*"

My mind was already in logistics mode. We had to put him somewhere until we could figure out how to integrate him into the already overcrowded small-animal population of the house. I headed for Mother's car, the same haven in which we'd stashed survivors the night of the fire.

"Let's put him in here for the moment."

"It's not Archie."

"It's Archie."

Even after we got him into the safety of the car and piled in to pet and cuddle him, Dawn kept insisting that it couldn't be Archie.

But how could we not know Archibald Peabody III? Each morning for three years, one or the other of us had awakened, up in that now-gone bedroom on the second floor of the barn, to find him stretched out on her chest, staring, emotionless, unblinking, down into her face.

In my case, of all the cats who'd died in that bedroom apartment, Archie had haunted me the most. It seemed almost a violation of trust on the part of the Universe for such a dignified and unique being to have perished in that manner.

If I'd paid closer attention to that thought, perhaps Archie wouldn't have had to endure the Winter from Hell as an outcast.

Yet it was as if we'd entered the Twilight Zone and someone dead six months had suddenly walked in and said, "Hi, honey, I'm home."

He *had* jumped out the bathroom window that night.

"We thought you were dead," we told him.

"I thought—you weren't there," he answered.

Where had he been for months? Aside from being filthy, he was in good shape. During the winter we'd kept a big bowl of dry cat food out in the stable at all times, for our cats but also for any strays who might wander in. Dawn had often commented on how fast the dry food was disappearing. In November and December, we'd dared to hope that just maybe cats escaped from the fire were eating it. Gradually that hope had faded. Obviously, though, Archie had been creeping into the stable to eat.

Where had he been living? Elementary, my dear Watson: under the front porch of Mother's house, just where he'd lived for two years before we'd caught him the first time. Again and again throughout the winter, we'd seen cat footprints coming and going from under that front porch, usually headed toward the barn across the road, where we have our hay, general storage, and lots of mice. We'd assumed it was a stray and left food under the porch.

Between the food under the porch, the food in the stable, and mice in the barn—and able to shelter either under the porch or in the hay of the haymow—Archie had done okay.

How had the three of us managed to move around the farm for six months without seeing one another?

The answer, we think, lies in the statement "I thought you were dead."

One sees only what one believes is, or can be, there.

We weren't looking for Archie, and Archie . . .

. . . Archie had been in shock, abruptly tossed back into the lonely hell that he'd lived in before we caught him, mechanically making the moves he needed to make to stay alive. Like Sugar, who'd thought at first, when driven out into the snow that night, that it had all been a dream—the warm place, the good food, the people who loved her—Archie must have thought his three years with us had been only a dream.

He'd been in shock, and he was still in shock. After a lot of discussion, we brought him up to the office. And for several days, he alternately hid like a hunted creature or carried on like a bewildered creature. Whenever he came out of hiding, he took up a position on Dawn's desk, staring out the window at the ruins of the fire, alternately crying and scratching at the window.

"My friends. Where are my friends?" he kept asking Dawn.

It seemed that now that he was remembering us and being with us, memory of all the others was returning as well.

To make matters worse, Pink Flower, a usually docile cat, kept attacking him. In fear, Archie the pacifist was spraying, something that he hadn't done since the day we'd first met him.

We were distraught. If he was so unhappy being inside with us, we might have to get him neutered and let him return to living outside.

But then we decided that he needed a bath. We took him to the grooming parlor of our friend Carol Sparks.

The cat that came home to us was the old Archie. The change was stunning. Yet there was something new about the old Archie. He suddenly wouldn't leave our laps, soliciting our touch as the old Archie seldom had. He purred and purred, his white parts all clean again, his fur soft, lustrous, and touchable.

"I didn't feel worthy to be a house cat while I was so dirty," he told us.

And he said that he'd still been able to smell the smoke of the fire on himself, even after all those months.

We knew how that could be. A dozen times a day, from something or other, we'd get a whiff of that fire and be right back in it again. That's probably why Pinkie had been attacking him. She still hissed at him, but now he ignored her majestically.

We think also that Pink Flower's nose was out of joint. She'd been special, a celebrity, the only cat to escape the fire. Then Archie had gone and spoiled it all by returning from the dead.

Mother's house had absorbed all the animals that it could. Downstairs there were the two dogs, Spangles and Cookie, Merlin, and the cats Pookie, Elvis, George, and Clarisse. Upstairs with us were Mustard and Grey Poupon, Phoebe, Pink Flower, and now Archie.

Then, returning from shopping one day in a rainstorm, I spotted Patrick El Doggo, an elderly, unneutered, very cold and unhappy shepherd mix running down the middle of the road toward me.

The only place to take him was up to our attic office. We tried him out gingerly at first, to see how he'd behave with cats, guinea pigs, and a duck. He paid them no attention at all. We ran ads and circulated a poster, but no one ever claimed him.

Except Andy, who took a shine to him and began to keep him in his own quarters during the day.

That was the last of the new animals. For a while.

During that Winter from Hell the Universe arranged for another interdimensional creature to visit Dawn. It happened one night in February as she sat at my father's desk in Mother's dining room, conducting a phone consultation. Mother was visiting a friend in Florida, so all was quiet in the downstairs of the house.

Suddenly Clarisse ran into the dining room, leaping madly, clapping her paws together, trying to catch something. Was she after a fly? There were no flies in the house in February. Amused, Dawn watched the kitten's antics for many minutes even while concentrating on her client. Something that was invisible to Dawn was flying around the room, and Clarisse was determined to catch it.

Suddenly the kitten leaped onto a table, stood on her hind legs, reached into the air with both front paws, and grabbed her invisible prey. She settled back down onto the table with paws closed tightly.

By now Dawn was off the phone, and she walked over to Clarisse.

"Go away! Don't open my paws! I'll lose it!" cried Clarisse.

Dawn was convinced that the kitten was hallucinating. Then Clarisse moved her paws slightly. Out flew a dragonfly. It took off around the room, with Clarisse again in hot pursuit.

Now Dawn was convinced that *she* was the one who was hallucinating.

Georgie Belinda came running and joined the chase. Either they were *all* hallucinating or there was, in fact, a dragonfly flying around the dining room.

Dawn ran to the foot of the stairs and called me to hurry and come down. When we got back to the dining room, however, the kittens were just sitting, staring at a wall.

"Where is it?" Dawn asked them.

"Oh," said Clarisse, "it's gone back now. But it was really neat."

And the two kittens left the room.

Guess who finally started to believe in interdimensional beings.

Throughout that winter, the difficulties regarding electricity, and the growing animal population in the house—from whatever dimension—turned out to be the least of our problems.

It began to look as though we were going to lose the farm.

In December 1993 I'd deeded the property, after the fire my last remaining possession, to Spring Farm CARES. It was *wonderful*. It's hard to describe how light not owning a thing in the world made me feel. I'd been considering transferring the property since the inception of Spring Farm CARES but hadn't been able to make the emotional break. The fire freed me, demonstrating that personal possession is meaningless.

My gift to Spring Farm CARES was in three parcels: two parcels of woods, meadows, and tillable fields on the west of Route 12 comprising about 185 acres—which today is our nature sanctuary—the third parcel being the 50 acres on the east side, with house, stable, and other buildings.

On this third parcel, there was a homeowner's mortgage of $75,000. In lieu of rental, SFC had been making the monthly mortgage payment since its inception in January 1991. We anticipated no problem with the bank. We had our attorney call to inform it of the transfer and to arrange a rollover of my mortgage into a mortgage for SFC.

To our shock, our bank, NBT, refused.

Those with whom we spoke in the head office informed us that unless SFC deeded the property back into my name, they would foreclose. They wouldn't give SFC a new mortgage, they wouldn't allow SFC to assume my mortgage, and, without my name on the deed, they wouldn't allow SFC to continue making payments on that mortgage.

Deeding the property back was out of the question. For one thing, property owned by a 501c3 can only be sold at fair market value—in this case, after the loss of the barn, about $400,000—or given to another 501c3. We would have lost our 501c3 status by simply deeding it back.

But, most important, my gift to Spring Farm CARES had been in earnest and final. I had no children to leave the property to; Peggy's kids all had their own homes, their own lives, and none of my sentimentality about the place. In deeding it to the charity, I was doing all that I could do to make sure that Spring Farm would endure long into the twenty-first century—the fourth century that it would touch—as a proud and useful entity.

No, it would not be deeded back. Spring Farm was not a Ping-Pong ball.

The plot thickened. As it turned out, though I'd had no insurance on the property, unbeknown to me, the bank *did* have insurance. I was told I would be charged for that insurance in the final tally. Yet those I spoke with were most secretive about it, and, for a couple of months, refused to say how much insurance had been collected. The insurance belonged to the bank, they said, even though I would be charged for the premiums, and, they said, I had no right to know the amount.

As it turned out, someone at NBT had goofed and underinsured the property. Their coverage was just $33,500, not even half of the mortgage. That $33,500 would be applied against the mortgage, but to avoid losing the place, we'd have to come up with another $41,500, plus the insurance charges and other costs that they were sure to tack on. We'd need about $45,000 to pay off the mortgage and avoid foreclosure.

"I wouldn't worry about it," said our attorney, Elizabeth Hughes, an honest and decent person who still believes in fair play, common sense, and angels. "Foreclosing after Bonnie has given everything she owns to the charity, and after a fire that rallied the whole community to your side, would rank among the top ten public relations bloopers in history."

Banks, however—the corporations themselves and their boards of directors and chief officers, not the normal, honest people who work in the branches—don't give a spit into the wind about public relations. Fair play, when speaking of banks, is a contradiction in terms; banks think that angels are a baseball team, and, in our situation, those at NBT's corporate headquarters didn't care to use common sense.

They gave us the date of May 4. If we hadn't paid off the mortgage by then, we were told that they'd begin foreclosure.

Something didn't smell right. They were being *too* hard-nosed, *too* goal-oriented.

They knew how badly we were hurting after the fire. They knew how we'd been struggling even before the fire, just making it from day to day.

And that is probably the answer. They knew. Not only did they not care, some persons or someone meant to take advantage of it.

At first, when they had insisted that the property be put back into my name, we felt that there was collusion between the bank and the town tax assessor, to keep the property on the tax rolls. Spring Farm CARES would be filing for property tax exemption and was legally entitled to it. We still believe that this was the case.

We also still believe that when it was realized that under no circumstances would the property be put back into my name—well, some persons or someone decided to force foreclosure and acquire the place for a song.

Luckily, as old radio melodramas would have phrased it, "Though the forces of darkness would seek to destroy Spring Farm CARES, a band of angels would foil them."

Of course, we didn't know that; we were scared out of our wits.

How were we to come up with $45,000 by May 4? My mother had already loaned most of her savings to keep SFC afloat. And I refused to bother her with this. The fire, and our occupation of her home, had already bewildered and distressed her quite enough.

I checked with Peg, but she and Bob were having their own problems with investments gone sour. We called some friends and donors who had, in the past, contributed substantial sums. It seemed, though, that everyone was encountering financial difficulties.

"Don't worry about the date of May 4," Elizabeth told us. "Foreclosure's a long process. You can pay off what's due right up to the courthouse steps on the day of the sale. You've got time. Put the word out. The money will come in."

Put the word out to whom, to where? We'd already talked with everyone we could think of who might have been able to help.

We began talking about putting one of the two parcels on the other side of the road on the market. But one of them, though contiguous with the other, was landlocked. I'd sold off all its frontage to keep things going. No one would buy landlocked property.

Which left only the second parcel, of some 105 acres, directly across from us. There wasn't time to go through a subdivision process, so the entire parcel would have to be sold. Under the gun. We'd have to virtually give it away, then face a housing project across the road. It would break my heart. But at least we had that ace in the hole.

"Put the word out," Elizabeth had advised.

Later we realized that she'd been right. We'd just been putting the word out in the wrong places, appealing to middlemen, instead of to headquarters, where miracles are manufactured.

And we'd let ourselves slip into the negative. So frightened were we by the bank's threats that we forgot that we create our own reality. We'd remembered that fact after the fire—and that understanding had brought us through. Now we'd forgotten it again, and we were floundering, close to drowning in our own helplessness.

To add to our woes, George Kigercat began bugging Dawn.

"Get a pad and pencil. I need to dictate the plans for your new barn."

The reader will recall that Dawn is spatially challenged. In addition to not knowing east from west, she's unable to visualize how a thing will look when completed—a building, a room, even how a new sofa will look in a room. She tried for days to translate onto paper the ideas and visions that George was "telepathing" to her from the other side. At last she gave up.

"I just can't do it, George."

"Ohhhhh . . ." Long, disgusted sigh. "Okay. I guess I'll have to get Bonnie to do it."

I woke up next morning with the plan in my head. He'd given it to me in a dream. I went to my card table and drew the floor plan and elevations in detail, to scale.

What George was proposing was a forty-by-seventy-foot central hall, pole barn construction, totally surrounded by lean-tos in which he had me sketch rooms for animals, supplies, et cetera.

It was a devilishly simple design. The more we studied it, the more we realized how wonderfully functional it would be, much better and more economical than any of the ideas we'd come up with. And it would fit perfectly onto the pad of our outdoor arena.

I showed the plan to our carpenter, Doug Hughes.

"Is this feasible?"

"I don't see why not," he said.

George was planning a twenty-five-by-seventy-foot cellar under the western lean-to section. I asked Doug for an estimate on what that foundation, with windows and a floor over it, would cost. He came back with the figure of $20,000.

Lord, $45,000 for the bank, then $20,000 just to build a cellar: $65,000. We'd submitted a grant proposal of $15,000 to Lifebridge Foundation to begin a new facility. We recrossed our fingers.

On April 28, 1994, six days short of the dreaded May 4, two books arrived in the mail, gifts from Penelope Smith.

They were the "Abraham" books, *A New Beginning I* and *A New Beginning II*.

"I just have the feeling that you two need to read these," said Penelope's note.

Dawn started leafing through one of the books and was soon thoroughly stuck into it. I couldn't resist peeking into the other one.

We read for three days straight, switching volumes as each of us finished.

The books were a refresher course in the teachings of Seth, reminding us of what we'd forgotten. They were a shot in the arm, with instructions for the conscious creation of one's reality stated so clearly that a baby could follow the steps.

Following Abraham's instructions, I committed my intentions for May 4 to writing.

On that date, I stated, I'd be able to call the bank and inform them of our plans to totally satisfy the mortgage, because wonderful people and/or organizations—and I named a few possible candidates—would have come to our aid with the needed funds. From that point on, I wrote in my intentions, donations would arrive in a steady flow, enabling us to build George Kigercat's barn.

Dawn put her intentions into writing as well.

Expectantly, then, fully "intending" the rescue of Spring Farm CARES to be effected, we waited.

May 3 came and went. We kept our chins and expectations up.

On the morning of May 4, as we sat at our card tables, the phone rang. I answered. The caller was one of Dawn's clients, who'd sent some nice donations over the years. Indeed, that caller was one of the persons I'd listed in my intentions. That individual informed me that a donation had been wired to our bank account.

It was starting. It was going to happen!

I signaled wildly to Dawn and, covering the receiver, whispered the client's name. In speaking together about that client, we'd dared hope for a contribution of as much as $5,000 toward the U.S. Cavalry's May 4 rescue of Spring Farm.

"Thank you!" I said. "Whatever you sent, thank you! We need it so much right now."

"Why?" asked the donor.

I explained about the foreclosure proceedings to begin that very day.

"And how much is it that you need?"

"We need forty-five thousand dollars to pay it off."

Silence for a moment. Then the donor said, "Well, you have that amount and then some."

"What?"

I was going spastic, gesticulating to Dawn. Dawn was on her feet, hanging on my every word and hysterical gesture.

"I wired you sixty-five thousand dollars."

"Sixty-five thousand dollars?"

Dawn collapsed back into her chair.

"And I wish to remain anonymous. Please, no public announce-ments as to the source of this gift."

For about an hour, Dawn and I just sat, looking at each other, giving way to gales of laughter, and giggling like a couple of schoolkids.

"What's going on?" asked Mother, appearing in the door of the office.

"Someone just gave us sixty-five thousand dollars," I said, and we went into another gale of laughter.

Mother laughed, too.

"You're kidding."

It took a while to convince her. She went back downstairs shak-ing her head.

"Sixty-five thousand dollars," she kept saying.

It was a gift for her as well. She'd worried so, loaning her savings while secretly fearing that it was for naught, that Spring Farm CARES would fail. But now, "Sixty-five thousand dollars."

Maybe, she was given sudden reason to hope, we'd make it after all.

I called the bank. The wire had indeed been received. The cash would be credited to our account at the close of business. I called NBT headquarters and informed the people there that the bank would have its money the following day.

They said they were starting foreclosure anyway.

Finally, they agreed to wait till the next day.

"But we'd better have it then, or we *will* begin foreclosure."

I told Dawn what they'd said. It sent us into more gales of laughter.

We paid it in full the following day, May 5, my father's birthday. Also the date on which Sugar had come to us. Someone at the head office told me the total amount due, and I authorized a cash transfer from SFC checking to the bank.

A month later, I contacted the bank, wondering why we'd received no final paperwork. I was told that the bank was not going to accept the payment that had been made.

"What? Why?"

"We won't accept payment from Spring Farm CARES. We'll only accept payment from Bonnie Reynolds."

"That's the most ridiculous thing I've ever heard! You accepted the cash transfer. It's right here on our statement."

"The person who accepted that transfer should not have done so."

"But the person *did* do so. The mortgage is paid."

"No, it's not. We'll have to reverse that transfer."

Elizabeth's words echoed mine.

"What? That's the most ridiculous thing I've ever heard! *Anybody* could pay that mortgage for you. Cash is cash."

She called the head office. After a couple of go-arounds they backed off on their demand to accept payment only from me.

But then they said they couldn't accept cash.

"Oh come *on!*" Elizabeth told them. "Give me a *break!*"

That matter finally settled, they then found something else to charge us with—a charge for a monthly payment due almost three years before, which they claimed had never been paid. With our records burned, we had no way of disputing their claim. All in all, it took months before we received the official paperwork that declared the mortgage paid.

If we'd ever had any doubts that there was something suspicious about the whole thing, those final attempts to reject payment put those doubts to rest.

But the miracle donation of May 4 also laid to rest any doubts that we might ever have had about the angels' plans for the future of Spring Farm CARES.

It was icing on the cake, when I awoke on the morning of May 5, to find Archie, for the first time since his return, spread out

Sphinx-like on my chest, looking down into my face, an expressionless basilisk as in days of yore.

But this time the basilisk was purring.

Life was good.

A new beginning indeed.

And the best *was* yet to come.

Far from the End

Acknowledgments

If we acknowledged every person or entity to whom or to which Spring Farm CARES owes its gratitude, we'd have another book. So for the most part, we must speak in generalities.

We can, though, be specific about our agent, Fran Collin, who "discovered us," went to bat for us, and made this book possible. We love you, Fran.

And to Simon & Schuster and Pocket Books, and to our editor, Mitchell Ivers— thank you for believing in us.

Our thanks to Gail Andrews, who is to blame for the whole thing.

We can also be specific in thanking the three ladies to whom this book is dedicated.

Bonnie's mother, Willa Dean Newcomb Jones, opened her bank account, toiled alongside us in the early days, and never stopped cheering for us. Were it not for Deanie, we would not have had the courage to begin, or survived even the first year.

Without Dawn's stepmother, Jacqueline Hayman, who repeatedly, and at personal risk, went way out on a limb to protect us in business matters, we would never have survived the second year.

Without the gracious attention and encouragement of Bertl Unkel, mother of the partner who joined us in 1995, Margot Unkel, we might not have been able to survive at all.

To you three dear ladies, up there in the Heaven to which we know you have flown—our eternal gratitude.

We then want to thank all the private donors, supporters and volunteers of whatever kind, foundations, local businesses, professional people, local media, students, friends, family members, neighbors, and clients who, since our incorporation in 1991, have helped us to keep chugging along—however large or small your contributions have been. We do not forget the days when the donation of just a dollar was cause for rejoicing and made the difference between being able to buy a needed bag of food for our animals or not. Nor do we forget the days when your material or professional aid, your words of encouragement, or your hands pitching in to help get a job done made the difference between being able to go on or giving up.

Our thanks to the special veterinarians who you have learned about in this book.

Our thanks to our board members, past and present, who make board meetings a pleasure and not a chore.

Our thanks to the readers of our newsletter, *All That Is*, whose unwavering eagerness to receive the next issue constantly reassured us that we were doing something very right.

Our thanks to our employees, past and present, without whom Spring Farm CARES could not get from one day to the next.

Thanks also to the workmen who build Spring Farm's buildings and keep them functioning, Doug Hughes and Jim Reddington in particular.

Our thanks to our teachers—our animals—past and present. We understand the gift conferred upon us and the honor paid to us when you share your lives and your thoughts with us. We give thanks for your unconditional love and pray to be worthy of your examples.